Modern
Melbourne

Cultural Studies of Natures, Landscapes and Environments

Series Editors: Donna Houston, Emily Potter and John Charles Ryan; Founding Editors: Rod Giblett, Warwick Mules and Emily Potter

Coming out of cultural studies, this series examines nature as the largely forgotten other of culture. It also considers landscapes and the environment, as well as the political, economic, semiotic, philosophical and psychological dimensions of all three terms. Firmly placed in the tradition of cultural studies of nature and landscape begun by Raymond Williams and continued by Alexander Wilson and others, it will publish interdisciplinary work that draws on established approaches within cultural studies, as well as develop new ones. It will make a unique and vital contribution not only to academic inquiry but also to new ways of thinking, being and living with the earth. The series will be of interest to a wide range of theorists and practitioners who are seeking directions out of, and solutions to, our current environmental and cultural malaise.

Published previously:

Rod Giblett, *People and Places of Nature and Culture*; *Black Swan Lake: Life of a Wetland* (2013); and *Canadian Wetlands: Places and People* (2014)

Warwick Mules, *With Nature: Nature Philosophy as Poetics through Schelling, Heidegger, Benjamin and Nancy* (2014)

Emily Potter, *Writing Belonging at the Millennium: Notes from the Field on Settler-Colonial Place* (2019)

Modern Melbourne

City and Site of
Nature and Culture

Rod Giblett

Bristol, UK / Chicago, USA

First published in the UK in 2020 by
Intellect, The Mill, Parnall Road, Fishponds, Bristol, BS16 3JG, UK

First published in the USA in 2020 by
Intellect, The University of Chicago Press, 1427 E. 60th Street,
Chicago, IL 60637, USA

A catalogue record for this book is available from
the British Library.

Series: Cultural Studies of Natures, Landscapes and Environments
Series ISSN: 2043-7757
Cover designer: Aleksandra Szumlas
Copyeditor: Emma Rhys
Production manager: Emma Berrill
Inside cover image: Dean Stewart
Typesetting: Contentra Technologies

Print ISBN 978-1-78938-195-5
ePDF ISBN 978-1-78938-197-9
ePub ISBN 978-1-78938-196-2

Printed and bound by 4Edge.

To find out about all our publications, please visit
www.intellectbooks.com.
There, you can subscribe to our e-newsletter,
browse or download our current catalogue,
and buy any titles that are in print.

This is a peer-reviewed publication.

Dedicated to Mother Marsha Melbourne, Lutetia du Sud

Contents

Acknowledgements

Various people have helped with the research for and writing of *Modern Melbourne*. For Chapters Two and Five, I am grateful to Robin Ryan for pointing out that, unknown to me at the time in 2014, Melbourne is a wetland city, and I am grateful to her for lending me her copy of Gary Presland's *The Land of the Kulin* (1985). I am also grateful to John Charles Ryan for his helpful comments and suggestions on an earlier version of these chapters, and to Janet Bolitho, Nandi Chinna and Andrew Lemon and two reviewers for the *Victorian Historical Journal* and its then editor, Marilyn Bowler, for their helpful advice and suggestions regarding many useful sources for Chapters Two, Three and Four. I am also grateful to Nandi for passing on to me an extract by Ellen Clacy about the Yarra River and its swamps. When I presented a shortened version of this material as the annual 'Melbourne Day' lecture in September 2015 at the Royal Historical Society of Victoria, a few people present, especially Andrew Lemon, made helpful comments and suggestions for which I am grateful, as I am for the invitation to deliver the lecture. Shorter and earlier versions of Chapters Two, Four and Five were first published as 'Lost and found wetlands of Melbourne', *Victorian Historical Journal*, 2016, 87:1, pp. 134–55. I am grateful to the Royal Historical Society of Victoria for their permission to reproduce this material.

For Chapter Three, I am grateful to Janet Bolitho, former councillor and mayor of the City of Port Phillip, for first sparking my interest in Fishermen's Bend and Westgate Park; for giving me a guided tour of the Park in April 2015; and for her website Port Places, which contains a wealth of information that has been an invaluable resource for the writing of this chapter. Go to: http://www.portplaces. com. Janet also writes for the Port Melbourne Historical and Preservation Society website; see for example: http://www.pmhps.org.au/2013/11/a-sodden-expanse-fishermans-bend/; http://www.pmhps.org.au/2013/11/fishermans-bend-the-past-and-the-future/; and http://www.pmhps.org.au/2013/07/fishermans-bend-do-the-maps/. I presented a shortened version of Chapter Three to a meeting of the Port Melbourne Historical and Preservation Society in February 2016. I am grateful for the invitation and opportunity to do so.

For Chapter Four, I am grateful to Marilyn Bowler, David Blyth and Karl Just for fanning my interest in Bolin Bolin Billabong and for supplying useful information about it, most especially to David for giving me a guided tour of the Billabong in July 2015.

For Chapter Five, I am grateful to Chris Coughran for drawing my attention to Lloyd Williams's chapter on 'the stream that became a street' in *History Trails in Melbourne* (1957), and for passing on a copy of the book to me.

For Chapter Seven, I am grateful for the opportunity to have presented an earlier and shorter version of this chapter as a paper to the *Environmental Humanities* symposium held on the Gold Coast Campus of Southern Cross University (SCU) on 1 July 2016, and I am grateful to SCU for funding my airfare to attend. I am also grateful to Tim Entwisle, current director of the Melbourne Gardens, for making helpful comments on an earlier version of this paper; to Warwick Mules for suggesting the multimedia diorama; and to Grayson Cooke of SCU for encouraging me to think about the paper more in terms of environmental art.

For Chapter Eight, I am grateful again to Robin Ryan for drawing my attention to Tony Birch's *Ghost River* (2015) and Maya Ward's *The Comfort of Water: A River Pilgrimage* (2011), and to Ursula Heise for drawing my attention to George Turner's *The Sea and Summer* (2013).

Finally, I am grateful to three anonymous reviewers for their extensive, detailed and helpful comments and suggestions. They have helped to sharpen the argument, improve cohesion, remove repetition, reduce obsessions, correct factual errors and make for a much better book. I am grateful to Emma Berrill of Intellect Books for seeing the book through a long process to publication. I am also grateful to Dean Stewart for permission to reproduce his map inside the front cover.

Australian Capital of Modernity

Melbourne has repeatedly been voted the most liveable city in the world (Anon. 2016). Part of its recent liveability has its foundations in the mid- to late nineteenth century and the early to late twentieth century when it was the Australian cultural capital. It was also the political capital of Australia for 26 years in the early twentieth century, after Australia became a nation in 1901 and while the city of Canberra and the Federal Parliament were being built. From its swampy beginnings as a squatter settlement in the marshy delta of the Yarra and Maribyrnong Rivers in Port Phillip Bay, south-eastern Australia, in 1835 (discussed in more detail in Chapter Two), Melbourne achieved its status as the Australian capital of the mid-nineteenth century in three ways: (1) through the naming and sanctioning of the settlement as Melbourne in 1837; (2) through the incorporation of Melbourne as a town with municipal governance in 1842; and (3) through the proclamation of Melbourne as a city in 1846. All these events were packed into the short time span of just over a decade during the first half of the nineteenth century.

During the second half of the long nineteenth century there were more exciting developments, with the separation of the Port Phillip District from New South Wales in November 1850; the official proclamation of the colony of Victoria in July 1851; and the beginning of the Victorian gold rush in August 1851. The gold rush in Victoria ushered in what Geoffrey Serle (1963) calls the 'golden age' of Victoria from 1851 to 1861, during which Melbourne, according to Graeme Davison, 'held the world record for urban growth' (1986: 120), quadrupling its population. The Victorian gold rush has been described recently by Ben Wilson as 'one of the greatest upheavals of the [nineteenth] century' (2016: 30), and one of the leading instances of what he calls the 'heyday' of Britain and its empire, and 'the birth of the modern world' in the 1850s (as proclaimed by the title and subtitle of his book) – or at least of high modernity, as the modern world has its origins posited as much earlier than that, including, according to Robert Marks (2015), the fifteenth century. Wilson also relates how the nouveau riche, the 'swaggering, bearded diggers', were dubbed 'the hairystocracy', for they 'seemed to rule Melbourne' (2016: 38), as he puts it in a chapter named after, and devoted to, 'the hairystocracy' (Wilson 2016: 30–52). The latter-day hairy hipsters of the inner suburbs and inner north of Melbourne are following in their footsteps (and Ned Kelly's), as far as facial hair is concerned, but without the wealth of the diggers (and without facing Ned's fate of death by hanging).[1] For Miles Lewis, the Kelly family and gang epitomize (rather disparagingly) 'the recalcitrant bog Irish settlers' (1995: 63). Melbourne was a bog settlement from its beginnings in 'swampy marshes', as Lewis (1995: 2) acknowledges (and as we will see in the following three chapters).

According to Bill Bryson, Melbourne during the gold rush was 'probably the richest city in the world per head of population' (2001: 81). 'The hairystocracy' were the most demonstrative exhibitionists of their newfound wealth, and, as Serle notes, became 'the new class of conspicuous consumers' (1971: 29), the precursors of the cashed-up 'FIFOs' ('fly in, fly out') who work in the mines today.[2] The gold rushes, Wilson concludes, 'bequeathed [to] Melbourne some of the finest public buildings of the Victorian period, including the State Library, the University [of Melbourne] and [the State] Parliament House, among others' (2016: 49). They ushered in a period of prosperity and created, according to Arnold (1983: 7), 'the inner suburban slums' (a typical feature of modern cities; see Giblett 2009: 36–54).

In keeping with the boom-and-bust cycles of capitalism, the 'golden age' of Victoria in the 1850s (as Serle [1963] calls it) was followed by what he later calls 'a period of prolonged and painful adjustment' (Serle 1971: 1). The 'post-gold-rush decades' of 1861–82 culminated in the era of 'the rush to be rich' from 1882 to 1889 (Serle 1971: 1). The 1880s included the short-lived period of 'Marvellous Melbourne' (1887–88) and the 'Fools' Paradise' of the contemporaneous 'land boom' period (Serle 1971: 1). They were followed by the depression of the late 1880s and 1890s. In his book, *The Land Boomers* ([1966] 1976), Michael Cannon sees 'the lush 1880s' as followed by what he calls 'the hungry 1890s'.

Australian capital

Melbourne was also indisputably the cultural capital of Australia in the late nineteenth century, as illustrated by its being the setting of 'the world's first crime best seller', which became the best-selling detective fiction of the nineteenth century (Grimwade 2009: 184): Fergus Hume's *The Mystery of a Hansom Cab*, first published in 1886. Detective fiction was invented in the nineteenth century and, with its modern mass urban settings, it was the quintessential genre of the century. Late-nineteenth-century Melbourne was an ideal setting, and Hume's *Hansom Cab* is, for John Arnold, 'the first popular Melbourne novel' (1983: 7–8). More specifically, for Serle, it is 'redolent of Melbourne of the period', that is, of 'Marvellous Melbourne' (1971: 291).

For Davison, it 'fully deployed' 'the slum reporters' conventional repertoire of imagery [...] in the most famous fictional reconstruction of Melbourne life' (1978: 238). This conventional repertoire of reportage imagery, however, is tinged with biblical, epic and literary allusions and allegories, just as the slum reporting and novels of London and Paris in the same period were tinged with such overtones (see Giblett 2016: 35–81). As with the slum reporters and novelists of London and Paris, these allusions and allegories in Hume's *Hansom Cab* manifest the symptoms of the cultural, class and urban repressed (as we will see in Chapter Six).

The Federation of the six colonial states into the nation of Australia was proclaimed in the Royal Exhibition Building (a fitting location for such an event) in Melbourne on the first day of 1901. The opening ceremony of the first Federal Parliament took place in early May 1901 in the Exhibition Building, the only space large enough in the new nation to host such an event. This event was not only 'one of Melbourne's most defining historic moments', as Maree Coote (2012: 70) puts it, but it was also one of Australia's most defining historic moments, as it brought the nation into being. While the site for the national capital was being chosen, and subsequently while Canberra was being developed, the Federal Parliament of Australia sat in the State Parliament Building in Melbourne (and the State Parliament sat in the Exhibition Building in a game of governmental musical chairs).

Melbourne was certainly the Australian capital of the second half of the nineteenth century, while, for Walter Benjamin, Paris was the universal capital of the entire nineteenth century (1999a: 3–26). Both Benjamin's *Arcades Project* ([1982] 1999a) and Coote's *The Melbourne Book: A History of Now* (2013) are encyclopedic collections of thematically arranged sections of archival and contemporary materials, snippets of information, valuable references and illuminating discussions with accompanying illustrations. Both provide labyrinthine passageways into their respective multifarious cities that are worth jumping into at any point and seeing where they lead, even if you get lost. There are some noteworthy differences, however, between the two books. For instance, Benjamin mentions the marshy origins of Paris, while Coote does not mention those of Melbourne. The greatest difference is that, unlike Coote's history of 'the now' in her *Melbourne Book*, Benjamin's *Arcades Project* is a profound philosophical meditation on modernity and the modern city, introducing such concepts as the dialectical image that links the past, present and future in the messianic now, a politically charged moment of transformation (as we will see in Chapter Six). Following in Benjamin's footsteps, *Modern Melbourne* applies his work to modern Melbourne, including its arcades. *Modern Melbourne* also discusses the history of Melbourne and Paris as marshy metropolises in terms of the dialectical image.

For David Harvey (2006), Paris is 'the capital of modernity', according to his book of the same title. For more than a century (comprising the second half of the nineteenth century and most, if not all, of the twentieth), Melbourne was the Australian capital in more ways than one, including the capital of modernity. For Davison, post-World War II Melbourne was 'a leader, or hero, of Australian modernity' (2016: 178). Thus from 1945 to some indeterminate moment in the not too distant past, even the recent past, Melbourne was a leader, or hero, of Australian modernity.

The 'modern Melbourne' of the title of the present book is shorthand for the Melbourne of nineteenth- and twentieth-century high modernity. A primary feature of nineteenth- and twentieth-century high modernity was the rapid development and growth of mass cities, such as London, Paris and New York (see Giblett 2016). Melbourne participated in this phenomenon, although unlike these cities it was founded in the nineteenth century, along with other New World cities including Chicago, Perth and Washington. Similarly to these cities (see Giblett 2016), Melbourne was founded among wetlands that were drained and filled. Like other wetland cities, such as New York and Toronto (see Giblett 2014: 133–52 and 2016: 197–213), Melbourne began as a colonial settlement and port. The development of Melbourne was part and parcel of the process of colonization which involved exploration and the establishment of settlements in 'far-flung' places.

Melbourne is a modern marsh metropolis and swamp city, what I call an 'aqua-terrapolis' for short (see Giblett 2016:15–32). It is a modern city not only because it was founded in modern times, but also because it was founded among marshes (as discussed in more detail in Chapters Two to Eight). Founding or developing a city among marshes represents the triumph of the city over the marsh. Founding or developing a modern city among marshes represents the added triumph (and injury) of modernity over pre-modern marshland. All the iconic cities of modernity, including Paris, London, Berlin, St Petersburg, New York, Chicago and Washington, were founded and developed among wetlands.[3] Melbourne is thus a member of this illustrious or dubious group of cities as it followed suit in its foundation and development. For a city to be built directly on wetlands (such as Venice and St Petersburg), or developed after initial settlement (such as New York and Melbourne), the wetlands had to be drained, filled or canalized to create dry land on which solid structures can be built and supported. In addition, for some cities (such as New York and Melbourne) the wetlands were landscaped into aestheticized lakes.

Melbourne and Paris are similar not only because of their marshy origins and modern status, but also because both cities have been figured as women. Paris, for Benjamin and other writers, is variously a goddess and a whore, whereas Melbourne is figured as a grand new dame, the Dame Nellie Melba of cities, the Mother Marsha Melba of a wetland city (hence the dedication of *Modern Melbourne* to her/it). Dame Nellie Melba was the pseudonym of soprano singer Helen Porter Mitchell, who named herself 'Melba' after her native Melbourne. She first appeared in Europe in 1887 and, as Jürgen Osterhammel puts it in his monumental 'global history of the nineteenth century', she

> went on to become one of the first truly intercontinental divas, her voice reproduced after 1904 on gramophone discs; she was the icon of a new cultural self-confidence in her reputedly uncouth homeland. Nineteenth-century European opera was a global phenomenon.
>
> (Osterhammel 2014: 6)

Melba was the icon of global modernity for modern, urbane Melbourne and otherwise uncouth Australia. Melba was a modern Melbourne star of opera. She was, for Coote, 'the first Australian superstar' and 'the world's first famous Australian woman' (2013: 82).[4] Her father, David Mitchell, built some of the iconic Melbourne buildings of the age, such as the Exhibition Building (perhaps the Dame Nellie Melba of buildings, a grand new dame of buildings), further cementing (excuse the pun, though Mitchell did run a cement factory in Richmond for many years) the connection of the family with high modernity (Willingham 1996: 55).

The 'Melbourne' of the title of the present book has obviously changed over time and its geographical area has varied over the historical period under discussion. From its beginnings as a colonial camp, it went on to become a settlement and a village, and then a grid-plan town with the design and implementation of 'the Hoddle Grid' bounded by Spencer, Flinders, Spring and Lonsdale Streets. This area is now the central business district. Later it became a mass city and included outlying suburban areas. The context in which I am discussing Melbourne should indicate which Melbourne I am referring to from among a variety of different senses of 'Melbourne'. The development and extent of these 'Melbournes' are traced in what I call 'temporal geography', as discussed in Chapter Five (see also Giblett 2016: 9–10).

Melbourne, for John McLaren, is 'a modern city', in part because 'it is a product of industrial capitalism' (2013: ix), though it began as a maritime port and marshy mercantile city, then later became an industrial city. Many iconic industrial technologies of modernity, such as railways, trams, electrical telegraphy, telephony and lighting, as well as cinematic film and hydraulic lifts, were first introduced to Australia in Melbourne, or had their early Australian uptake in Melbourne (discussed in Chapter Nine).

The first full-length narrative feature film in the world was recognized by the UNESCO Memory of the World Register in 2007 as *The Story of the Kelly Gang*. It was directed by Charles Tait and screened in Melbourne in 1906. Cinema, with its modern urban audience, was the quintessential entertainment mass medium of the early twentieth century, and it had its birth in Melbourne in 1906. In 1959, when the Cold War was at its height, Melbourne was also the backdrop for filming the end of the world. During the filming of the nuclear apocalyptic film, *On the Beach* produced and directed by Stanley Kramer, Ava Gardner reportedly said that Melbourne was 'a great place to film the end of the world' (cited in Lewis 1995: 127). This sound grab, too good to pass up, was wrongly attributed to her by the frustrated cadet journalist Neil Jillett (1982: 11), who later cleared up the confusion, or fessed up to the fictional concoction.[5] Melbourne is thus positioned and figured at the end of world, both spatially in the sense of being at the bottom of the world (or least of continental Australia) and temporally in the sense of being at the end, or finish, of the world. Melbourne is also the spatial setting for George Turner's prescient 1987 science fiction novel, *The Sea and Summer*, set temporally in the mid-twenty-first century and centuries later when anthropogenic global heating ('the greenhouse effect') has melted the Antarctic ice caps, drowning low-lying areas of Melbourne (discussed in Chapter Eight).

Besides screening the first feature film in the world, Melbourne as a modern metropolis had some other world media births and deaths. The newspaper was the quintessential print advertising and news medium of modernity. It had its colourful birth in Melbourne when *The Argus* was the first newspaper in the world to publish daily news pictures in full colour in 1952 (Lewis 1995: 111). It ceased publication five years later with the advent of black and white television in 1956 for the Olympic Games in a bizarre twist of fate.

The history of Melbourne begins with the European discovery of its site in 1803 by maritime explorers and with the founding of the settlement in 1835 made possible by ships and shipping. For Robyn Annear (2014: xii), the period from 1835 to 1851 is not only 'early Melbourne' (it certainly is not the 'modern Melbourne' of 'car-parks, concrete and cafes' [xiii], though there is much more to modernity than that), but it is also an earlier place called 'Bearbrass', 'a mis-rendering of *Birrarung*' (xi), the local Wurundjeri name for the landmark river that winds through the city now called the Yarra. With the discovery of gold in 1851 in payable amounts, and the ensuing rush to the goldfields, Melbourne, according to Annear, emerged 'as the capital and port of the world's richest goldfields' (2014: 231). Melbourne also emerged into high modernity as Australia's first federal capital.

The history of pre-modern Melbourne begins with the Australian Aboriginal people's ownership, habitation and use of the area going back tens of thousands of years (as we will see in later chapters). The wetland and riverside site of early and modern Melbourne has a pre-modern history, like that of Paris. Both cities have an indigenous history that predates colonial conquest, by the Romans in the case of Paris, and by the British in the case of Melbourne. Both have similar landmarks and built structures, such as shopping arcades, department stores, market halls, landscaped parks and gardens, tree-lined boulevards, broad bridges and b(l)ackblocks of slums: all iconic features of modernity. Both cities also have a longstanding bar and café culture, and their residents share a great love of good food, wine, beer, coffee, music, theatre and sport.

From its very beginnings, various writers (locals and visitors alike) have vigorously advanced their views of Melbourne's stellar status. Thomas Strode wrote in 1838: 'Melbourne will become the Metropolis of the Southern Hemisphere' (cited in Annear 2014: 231). British novelist Anthony Trollope, who visited Australia and New Zealand in 1871, proclaimed that Melbourne was 'undoubtedly not only the capital of Victoria but also of Australia' (1876: vol. II, 29). Richard Twopeny reiterated Strode 45 years later when he pronounced that

> Melbourne is justly entitled to be considered the metropolis of the Southern Hemisphere [...] [W]hile the situation of Melbourne is commonplace, if not actually ugly [...], it is in the Victorian city that the trade and capital, the business and pleasure of Australia chiefly centre [...] The headquarters of nearly all the large commercial institutions which extend their operation[s] beyond the limits of any one colony are to be found there.
>
> (Twopeny [1883] 1986: 112)[6]

By the 1870s, 'Melbourne had become the greatest Australian centre of trade and finance', as Asa Briggs (1963: 294) puts it in his study of Victorian cities (in the sense of the era named after Queen Victoria), in which an entire chapter is devoted to Melbourne. Over a century later nothing much had changed. Writing in 1985 on the 150th anniversary of the British settlement of Melbourne, Rear-Admiral Brian Murray, the then Governor of Victoria, stated that Melbourne was 'the economic capital of Australia', and 'a prosperous, elegant and sophisticated city' (1985: x). For Bill Newnham, in his 'biography' of the city (as proclaimed by the book's subtitle),[7] which was also published in 1985, Melbourne was '*still* the financial centre of Australia' (Newnham 1985: 37, original emphasis). For Johann Geist also, Melbourne had the 'status of Australia's major trade and financial center' (1983: 363). Twenty years later much has changed. Melbourne is no longer the greatest Australian centre of trade and finance, as Sydney has supplanted Melbourne as the financial capital of Australia.[8]

In 1985, the Port of Melbourne was 'the largest container port in the Southern Hemisphere' (Newnham 1985: 37). Melbourne was, and still is, a port city. Without ships and shipping, the city of Melbourne, the colony of the Port Phillip District and later the State of Victoria would not have been possible (discussed in more detail in Chapter Nine). Ships were the means of transport by which the site for settlement was discovered, and the means by which the colony and city were established and developed. Before Melbourne was a city and when it was a British settlement, the area at the head of Port Phillip Bay was named the 'Port Phillip District' and was part of the colony of New South Wales.

Melbourne may not have been the official political capital of Australia until 1901, but in the mid-nineteenth century it was a world leader in radical, progressive politics, a noble tradition that it has carried forward into the twentieth and twenty-first centuries. In 1856, 'Victoria led the world in the achievement of the eight-hour day' (Serle 1971: 98), with several unions calling for, and winning, an eight-hour working day for workers in their unions (Newnham 1985: 29; Coote 2013: 224; Cunningham 2011: 28). Also in 1856, the secret ballot for elections was 'adopted for the first time in the British Commonwealth' (Newnham 1985: 29). Melbourne also led the way in equal access for women to universities. In 1880, 'the University of Melbourne [...] was the first in Australia to admit women students' (Cannon [1966] 1976: 19). In the twentieth century, also, Melbourne was a leader in radical, progressive politics. The Moratorium March of 5 May 1970 attracted 70,000 people who marched through Melbourne against the Vietnam War (Lewis 1995: 127, see photo on 128).[9] Various protest rallies and marches have been held since, including for Aboriginal and refugee rights, marriage equality and action on global heating and climate catastrophes.

Currently Melbourne is the only federal electorate in the lower house of the Australian parliament to have a Greens member. Adam Bandt was first elected to the seat in 2010 and retained it during the 2013, 2016 and 2019 elections with an increased majority on each occasion. The federal electorate of Melbourne includes the central business district and surrounding suburbs such as Parkville, Carlton, Collingwood, Richmond and Fitzroy. These suburbs are also part of what is colloquially called 'the green belt', also including Brunswick, which recently elected a Greens member to State Parliament. Many voters in 'the green belt' would not be aware of the environmental history and bioregional context of the city in which they live, a history that *Modern Melbourne* traces for them.

Modern Melbourne is an environmental and cultural history study of Melbourne from its beginnings to the recent past. The sub-discipline of environmental history studies the natural and built environments of ecology and technology, as well as the ways in which nature has shaped culture. The sub-discipline of cultural history studies the cultural environments of public and private places and bodily activities, as well as the ways in which culture has shaped nature (including the human body and perceptions of nature).

Rather than adhering to a hard and fast divide between culture and nature, *Modern Melbourne* shows culture and nature as intertwined in cultures of natures (as I have argued previously; see Giblett 2011: 15–38). *Modern Melbourne* also places the history of Melbourne within both the bioregional context of the Yarra and Maribyrnong catchments, and the international context by drawing on the work on modernity and the modern city by Benjamin ([1950] 2006, [1950] 2015, [1982] 1999a, 1999b, 2003), Michel Foucault (1970, 1977, 1980), Peter Sloterdijk ([1999] 2014, [2004] 2016, [2005] 2013, [2014] 2017) and Raymond Williams (1973, [1982] 1989, [1983] 1985, [1984] 1989), and by comparing and contrasting Melbourne to other colonial wetland modern cities, such as Toronto. It links the local to the global and vice versa via the bioregional. It invites the reader to make the link between living in their own bioregional home-habitat and living in the globalized world.

Melbourne is arguably still the cultural capital of Australia. For Lucy Sussex in her 'biography' (as she calls it [2015: 6]) of Fergus Hume's *The Mystery of a Hansom Cab*, late-nineteenth-century Melbourne was 'the wealthy commercial capital of the country' (58) and 'the busy theatrical capital of Australia' (69).[10] And it still is, certainly for musical theatre. Melbourne has developed into what Sophie Cunningham calls 'a cultural and sporting event capital' (2011: 156) (discussed in greater detail in Chapters Ten and Eleven). And for chef Adam D'Sylva, Melbourne is 'without doubt the food capital of Australia' (2017: 91).

With the designation of Melbourne in August 2008 as 'only the second UNESCO City of Literature' in the world, Melbourne's status as 'the nation's capital of books, writing and ideas' was consolidated (Grimwade 2009: xii, see also endpaper). Perhaps this designation was much to the chagrin of Sydney in that perpetual popular Australian pastime of inter-city rivalry. Debating over a barbecue with a beer in hand about the merits of one's own city involves proponents protesting too much the virtues of their home or own city and denigrating the vices of the other cities. If Melbourne is the Australian capital of the nineteenth century (as I and others suggest), then Sydney is the Australian capital of the eighteenth century (as the only sizable and substantial settlement in Australia which was proclaimed a city in 1788) and of the mid-twentieth century (particularly with the design and construction of the iconic Sydney Harbour Bridge in the 1930s and the superlative Opera House in the 1970s).

Located on the marshy banks and in the delta of the Yarra and Maribyrnong Rivers, between West and South Melbourne Swamps and other swampy areas, and in the bioregion of the Yarra catchment, nature and culture are inextricably intertwined in and by the city of Melbourne. The intertwining of nature and culture on the site and in the city makes Melbourne what it is today. *Modern Melbourne* traces the history of the relationship between nature and culture on the site of, and for, the city. *Modern Melbourne* shows the ways in which nature has shaped the city from its beginnings to the present day (as Gary Presland [2008] has shown for the early years of the settlement and the city, and as proclaimed in the subtitle of *The Place for a Village*). *Modern Melbourne* also shows the ways in which the city and its denizens have shaped nature (as Presland does not do, even when considering the ways in which landscape aesthetics have shaped perceptions of nature [including his own] and the landscaping of nature). *Modern Melbourne* argues that Melbourne is both a city and site of nature and culture, a city on, and in a site of, nature and culture.

Modern Melbourne is divided into two parts. The first part, 'City of Ghost Swamps', is devoted to discussing Melbourne's wetlands in the past and present and for the future; the second part, 'Visible City, Invisible Site', discusses Melbourne's natural and built environments and their cultural and natural heritages in their bioregional, global and historical contexts.

City of ghost swamps

Melbourne was founded among wetlands; the site for Melbourne was wetlands. They shaped the foundation and development of the city. Settlers drained and filled the wetlands on the site to build the city. Unlike many other cities, Melbourne has done little to commemorate its lost wetlands, its ghost swamps, or to celebrate its current wetlands. The following four chapters discuss Melbourne's wetland setting and settling. Chapter Two critically traces the history of Melbourne and its wetlands in the context of European landscape aesthetics, focusing primarily on West Melbourne Swamp (or Batman's Swamp) and South Melbourne Swamp, as well as other swamps such as Le Mans Swamp and Carrum Carrum Swamp. The chapter shows that these wetlands were crucial in constituting the site in and on which the city was built. They posed an initial limitation and impediment to its development and spread that were eventually overcome. The city took the place of wetlands. Where the city now is, wetlands once were. The city displaced and overtook wetlands. Even though the original wetlands are lost or landscaped, they remain a defining feature of the relationship between the colonial centre and the city of today in its geographical location. Melbourne is still haunted by its ghost swamps.

Chapter Three goes on to focus more minutely and extensively on a variety of wetlands. It begins by critically tracing the history of Fishermens Bend, at one time a wetland that became a wasteland, and of Westgate Park where a rehabilitated remnant of the Fishermens Bend wetlands can be found today. Chapter Four focuses on the remnants of another wetland which can be found today in Bolin Bolin Billabong in the Templestowe/Doncaster area. It was once one of fifty billabongs along the course of the Yarra River and is one of only a few billabongs remaining, including Banyule Billabong. The chapter also focuses on the Cheetham wetlands, with its artificial and natural lagoons that lie on the western side of Port

Phillip Bay and on the western outskirts of Melbourne. Artificial wetlands were constructed in Royal Park in the 1990s and 2005. They are a window into the lost wetlands of Melbourne and are discussed briefly in this chapter.

Melbourne's wetlands past and present are largely absent from *Nearamnew* (2001), Paul Carter's inscription in stone of the history of the city of Melbourne and the colony of Victoria, created for the commemoration of the Federation of Australia in 2001 in Federation Square and set beside the Yarra River on the corner of Flinders and Swanston Streets, an area which was a wetland at the time of settlement and for some time thereafter. Melbourne's past wetlands are also absent from Carter's chapter on the history of Melbourne in *The Road to Botany Bay: An Essay in Spatial History* (Carter 1987: 202–09). This absence is surprising as the presence of these wetlands is well-documented in many of the same sources that were used for his chapter as were used for the second chapter of *Modern Melbourne*, such as the anthology of historical documents, *The Melbourne Scene* (Grant and Serle 1957). It is also a surprising absence from a book that is 'an essay in spatial history', as proclaimed by its subtitle. Carter's spatial history does not seem to include the history of the place (or what I call 'placial' history) he is discussing. Carter abstracts place into space. Chapter Five of *Modern Melbourne* critiques this process and suggests that *Nearamnew* represents a lost opportunity to create a public work of art that celebrates and commemorates the wetlands that were the environmental context in which the city of Melbourne and the colony of Victoria were founded. The chapter concludes by making some speculative proposals for celebrating the lost and found wetlands of Melbourne.

Federation Square initially turned its back on the Yarra River and turned inward to focus on itself. The most recent account by Kim Dovey and Ronald Jones of the development of Melbourne from the 1980s announces that 'having once turned its back on the water, Melbourne has now embraced the Yarra River and Port Phillip Bay, becoming a waterfront city' (2018: 9). Wetlands do not rate a mention as part of 'the water', or as part of the past 'waterfront'. As Carter abstracts place into space, so do Dovey and Jones abstract wetlands and river into water, a resource to be exploited, including for its views and for recreation on or beside it. Melbourne is not yet a wetland city as it has not embraced its wetlands past and present (as these writers of *Urban Choreography* [Dovey and Jones 2018] demonstrate), and as it continues to turn its backside on the wetlands by ignoring, destroying or polluting them. The map of 'Central Melbourne' on the facing page (Dovey and Jones 2018: 8) shows an unnamed Yarra River as a mythologized solid blue line of clean water (when it is in fact brown-coloured muddy water) wending its way through the city. The lost wetlands of central Melbourne are invisible. Recent plans for the redevelopment of Federation Square will result in turning the face of the city towards the Yarra River and giving greater access to the Yarra River.

Whether this constitutes embracing and celebrating the lost and found wetlands of Melbourne is another question. (The answer is 'no' if *Urban Choreography* [Dovey and Jones 2018] is anything to go by.)

The four chapters in the first part of *Modern Melbourne* (and indeed the whole book) are written unashamedly and critically from the point of view of environmental conservation and from within the transdisciplinary environmental humanities, drawing on the work of Benjamin, Foucault, Sloterdijk, Williams and others. These thinkers conceptualise nature and culture in dialogue with each other across the 'two cultures' of the sciences–humanities divide which assigns nature to the sciences and culture to the humanities. Transdisciplinary thinking crosses this great divide, brings a plague on both their houses and sometimes gets shot down in the 'no-man's land' between them (see Giblett 2011: 15–38).

Thinking nature and culture together could also occur in what might be called 'the science humanities' (rather than in the more narrowly construed 'environmental humanities'), in which the natural and cultural environments are considered with, and in relation to, technology and the human body, for instance, in the intertwined cultural and environmental histories of communication and transportation technologies and of the human body (see Giblett 2008a, 2008b). The second part of *Modern Melbourne* goes on to discuss the intertwining of nature and culture in Melbourne's landscapes, such as its parks and gardens; and in its transportation and communication technologies, such as shipping, trains and trams; its cultural institutions and practices, such as exhibitions and exhibition buildings; and its bodily activities, such as sport.

Visible city, invisible site

The Royal Botanic Gardens Melbourne, the topic of Chapter Seven, are a case in point of the intertwining of nature and culture. They are the visible product of both the sciences and humanities, though there is little acknowledgement of the contribution of both as such to the history and provenance of the Gardens. The site for the Gardens also had wetlands that were then landscaped into an ornamental lake and have now been partially restored in floating, artificial wetlands. Chapter Seven traces the history of the Gardens and proposes a diorama for the Gardens that presents historical images of the Gardens' and Melbourne's wetland site.

A marker of colonialism in Australia is the clearing (or 'taming' and 'cultivating') of the 'wild', rude and ill-mannered bush and the establishment of gardens, farms and suburbs. In the case of Melbourne, as Davison puts it, 'the bushland on the city's edge was tamed and cultivated into great public gardens' (1986: 125), including the Royal Botanic Gardens Melbourne. The bushland on the city's suburban edge was tamed and cultivated into private gardens, great and small, so that Melbourne became what Davison calls 'the most private, respectable and suburbanized of Australian cities' (1986: 125).

The Yarra River is a defining feature and prominent landmark of Melbourne and the major source of drinking water. Melbourne is where it is because of the Yarra, as the river provided a source of fresh water and safe anchorage for the ships of the first settlers. The city and its suburbs are located within the catchment and biogeographical region of this river and its tributaries. Chapter Eight discusses the Yarra River and its billabongs in the context of the geography and history of Melbourne, and of its depictions by landscape painters. It also highlights the recent legislation that recognizes the Yarra River as a living entity along similar lines to recent court cases in India and New Zealand (Ainge Roy 2017; Safi 2017).

In the early nineteenth century, maritime explorers, merchants and crew transported people and products in their ships to and from what was initially and mainly a port. The first round of settlers in Melbourne were escaped convicts that came by sea from Tasmania; the second round of settlers were squatters who came by the same means and route. Melbourne, as Coote writes, is 'made of [and by] boat people' (2013: 150). However, ships and shipping were quickly forgotten as the city sprawled outwards and developed an internal transportation system of trams and trains. Today, Melbourne's public transport system makes it one of the most liveable cities in the world. Melbourne was also an early adopter of modern communication technologies such as the telegraph, telephone and television. Chapter Nine discusses Melbourne's mechanical modes of communication and transportation, beginning with ships and going on to railways, trams, cinema, radio and television. It also discusses the built structures of railway stations. The first railway line in Australia was constructed between Melbourne and Hobsons Bay in 1854. Melbourne also has the only surviving tram network in Australia, the largest tram network in the southern hemisphere and the busiest tram network in the world (Coote 2013: 108, 148).

Melbourne is arguably the sporting capital of Australia, and the Melbourne Cricket Ground (MCG) is the physical and spiritual home of sport in the city, and in the State of Victoria and across the country for Australian rules football. The MCG was also the main venue and athletics stadium for the Olympic Games in 1956. Initially founded as a cricket ground (as the name obviously indicates), it was also an Australian rules football ground from early in its history. Although Australian rules football was developed in rural Victoria near the town of Moyston, the MCG is the spiritual home for devotees of the game. Melbourne is a city where the body is put on display in the 'body culture' of sport and games. Melbourne is also the city where the richest racehorse in the world is run for the Melbourne Cup. Chapter Ten discusses Melbourne's love of, or obsession with, sport. It also discusses the homes of sport in the city, placing them in the context of environmental and architectural history, especially considering the MCG as a stadium.

Melbourne is also a city where culture is put on display, often similarly to the ways in which nature is put on display. Chapter Eleven is devoted to the iconic events and buildings of Australian modernity, such as the Exhibitions and Exhibition Buildings of the late nineteenth century that developed in the heyday following the gold rush. The current Exhibition Building is a cathedral to industrial capitalism. It was to industry what the Botanic Gardens were to flora and the MCG was to sport: a place of display.

Rather than present Melbourne as a city where the displays of nature and culture often compete with each other for time and attention, *Modern Melbourne* is devoted to tracing the intertwining of nature and culture in the history and development of the city, in the past, present and future of the city, in its lost wetlands, visible landscapes, distinguishing landmarks, prominent monuments, iconic restaurants, commemorative memorials, built structures, defining features, momentous events, telling moments, trademark activities and notoriously changeable weather. By no means is the present book an exhaustive survey of all these aspects of Melbourne over its 180-year history. Rather, it concentrates on many of the most prominent of these aspects and places them, unlike most books on Melbourne, in a global and international context from within the transdisciplinary environmental humanities. It showcases Melbourne as a metropolis with ancient and built environments, with lost natural spaces and places and present cultural landscapes. The book calls on Melbourne residents to live bio- and psycho-symbiotic livelihoods in our home-habitat of the Yarra River catchment and bioregion by loving and looking after this place and not trashing it.[11] Melburnians would then be taking up the challenge to live in what Glenn Albrecht calls the Symbiocene, the hoped-for age superseding the Anthropocene (2019: 102–06; see also Giblett 2019e: 108–11).

The Anthropocene has come out of the economic politics of mercantile capitalism, industrial capitalism, the enclosure of the commons, private property, the commodity market and the 'feral quaking zone' (Giblett 2009: 1–14). The Anthropocene also came out of its drive for, and the failed paradigm of, mastery. The anthropogenic stratigraphic layers of the Anthropocene have given rise to what Bruno Latour (2017) calls 'the new climate regime' (or, more recently, 'the new climatic regime' [Latour 2018]), in which 'there is no longer any question of "mastering" nature' (Latour 2017: 111–15). Rather, 'nature' is mastering, or monstering culture. The new, anthropogenic climate regime rules – and it is *not* OK. The Anthropocene is also what I call (the) Anthropobscene, a laying bare of the wastes and pollutants that modern industrial capitalism and its technologies wanted the -ospheres (the atmosphere, hydrosphere, biosphere, etc.) to hide.

The Symbiocene can be defined as the geological age of the laying and layering up and down of bodies of land, waters, air, beings and things in biogenic and non-biogenic strata, and the inter-corporeal relationship of loving union between them in the feral and native quaking zones (see Giblett 2009: 1–14). The Symbiocene comes out of the economic politics of the commons, compassion for all beings, mutual aid, the carnivalesque marketplace (not the capitalist market) and the native quaking zone. The Symbiocene comes out of its love for, and the paradigm of, mutuality.

The symbiotic body of the earth comes out of the traditional cultures in which earth is body and/or body is earth. It supersedes the machine body of modern western medicine, the battlefield body of illness narratives, the grotesque body of the lower strata, the monstrous body of the slimy depths, the Fascist body of the war machine, the textual body of the surface of inscription, the sporting body imprisoned in the time-machine of mechanical time recording and the cyborg of the body-machine of the civilian soldier.[12] The Symbiocene embraces these bodies in the body of the earth in which healthy bodies, minds, lands and waters can and do flourish in their bioregional and local home-place of the living earth (see Giblett 2006, 2008a, 2009: 125–37, 2013). The stratigraphic Symbiocene cuts across the biosphere, the ecosphere, the public and private spheres, the electro-magnetosphere that makes wireless telecommunication possible and the extraterrestrial sphere where the communication satellites orbit. Transportation and communication technologies function in these spheres. They are the greater ambit of the earth home (see Giblett 2008b, 2011: 39–56).

Making a connection to local place, its plants and animals and their seasonal changes, is a necessary response, and antidote, to the globalized world in which many people now live and work and which impacts on our lives in numerous ways. It is vital to think and act locally as well as globally. Connecting to local place can end up being a reclusive retreat into a smaller, narrower and safer world away from the incursions of the bigger, badder global world. But it is also a way of acknowledging and respecting the interconnectedness of all life from the local to the global and back again. Our lives are lived locally (if not also lived globally in the networks of trade and communication) and are dependent on local air, water and food mainly supplied from within and by our bioregional home-habitat. We have aerials and cables, but we also have roots – however shallow or transient they may be. We feed off nutrients in the soil and although we may uproot and change soil occasionally or frequently, we are still putting down our roots into the soil and up into the air like mangroves, drinking local water, breathing the air around us and largely eating local food. That air and soil has a history, a human and a natural history. Knowing the soil's composition enriches our lives and helps us to connect to the other beings living in the same soil. That sense of mutuality between people and place is vital to conserving a place as well as the planet.[13]

All living creatures – plants and animals, human and non-human – live in a bioregion, catchment or watershed, and an air-shed with its unique suite of plants and animals. The bioregion is the place of home, the home-place. All creatures are dependent and impact on their bioregion to a greater or lesser extent, with longer- or shorter-term damaging and/or rehabilitating effects. The relationship between creatures and their bioregion (and ultimately the earth and the biosphere) takes place on a continuum from the parasitic to the symbiotic through the inquilinistic (in which one party shares the home of another without significant disadvantage to the home-owner, such as normally the embryo in utero; see Giblett 2011: 237–58). This continuum is not only biological and biogeographical, but also psychological and spiritual (see Giblett 2011: 237–58).

NOTES

1. The literature on Ned Kelly and the Kelly gang is now voluminous. See Serle (1971: especially 11).
2. FIFOs ('fly in, fly out') are those workers in the mining industry who fly in for several long days on the job, sleeping on site in 'dongas' (transportable accommodation huts), then fly out for several days off work back home.
3. *Cities and Wetlands* (Giblett 2016) devotes a chapter to each of these iconic cities of modernity, some of which were founded and developed in modern times (St Petersburg, New York, Chicago and Washington), some of which were founded in pre-modern times and developed in modern times (Paris, London and Berlin).
4. Melba, for Kristin Otto too, was 'the first international Australian star' (2009: 1, see also 36).
5. I am grateful to an anonymous reviewer for this information and reference.
6. In the mid-1950s, James Grant and Geoffrey Serle (1957: 136, 160) reproduced most of Twopeny's statement and concurred that in the late nineteenth century, 'Melbourne was unquestionably the financial and commercial pivot, not merely of Victoria, but of the whole continent'.
7. The first edition of Newnham's *Melbourne: Biography of a City* was published in 1956, a long time before it became fashionable in the current century to write a biography of a city, such as Chicago, London and Paris.
8. I am grateful to an anonymous reviewer for pointing this out.
9. Coote says 100,000 people on 8 May 1970 (2013: 222, see also photo on 223).
10. *Blockbuster!* for Sussex is 'not the biography of a man, more the biography of a book' (2015: 6); it is 'the story of Hume and *Hansom Cab*' and not 'a conventional literary biography' (226).
11. Living bio- and psycho-symbiotic livelihoods in the bioregional home-habitats of the living earth is discussed extensively in Giblett (2011: especially 237–58).
12. Each of these bodies receives a chapter-by-chapter treatment in Giblett (2008a).
13. For my bioregional connection to the local place where I lived for 30 years, see Giblett (2006, 2013a, 2013b).

PART I

CITY OF GHOST SWAMPS

Lost Wetlandscapes

Melbourne is a UNESCO (United Nations Educational, Scientific and Cultural Organization) 'City of Literature'; it is also, or was, a city of wetlands, although UNESCO does not have such a designation. If it did, Melbourne would qualify, as would a variety of other famous cities around the world founded among marshes and swamps, such as London, Paris, Venice, Berlin, Hamburg, St Petersburg, Boston, New York, New Orleans, Washington, Chicago, Toronto, Vancouver, Mexico City, Bangkok, Dhaka, Jakarta, Kampala and Perth.[1] Like many of these cities, Melbourne dredged, drained, filled or canalized many of its wetlands located within close proximity of the early settlement. Melbourne's wetlands were, and still are where they survive, places of great significance and sources of sustenance (physical, spiritual and social) for the local Aboriginal people (see Eidelson 2014). I thus begin this chapter by acknowledging and thanking the clans of the Kulin people: the traditional owners, inhabitants and users of the wetlands and drylands of Melbourne that sustain the lives and livelihoods of the residents of Melbourne today in the bioregion of the Yarra River catchment and delta.

The founding and developing of these famous cities meant the loss of their wetlands; gaining ground meant losing wetlands. In the case of Melbourne, some of its wetlands were completely lost to drainage or filling, such as West Melbourne Swamp (or Batman's Swamp)[2]. Others were landscaped into lakes and parks, such as South Melbourne Swamp, which was transformed into Albert Park Lake. Others did not have English names, such as those adjacent to the Yarra River between Russell and Swanston Streets, which are now lost beneath the railway lines of the Jolimont Marshalling Yards and beneath Federation Square. Remnants of others remain and can be found today, such as Banyule Billabong and Bolin Bolin Billabong. Others are rehabilitated remnants that can also be found today, such as Westgate Park in Fishermen's Bend. Artificial wetlands have also been founded, such as those in Royal Park in Parkville, while other wetlands, such as the Cheetham wetlands that can be found on the western side of Port Phillip Bay, have both artificial and natural lagoons. By no means is this is all the wetlands of Melbourne – lost or found. This chapter is not an exhaustive inventory of the wetlands of Melbourne. It is more a scenic tour of the highlights, or lowlights, that skates across the surface of the tip of an iceberg.[3]

The history of the Melbourne wetlands is largely unknown to most of the residents of Melbourne today, but these wetlands were a prominent feature of the site and the city in the past. Even though they are absent today, they are still present as a defining feature of the current city, its location and its bioregion, especially in the Yarra River catchment and delta. The history of the Melbourne wetlands traced here is thus what Michel Foucault called 'a history of the present' (1977: 31), a history not only of the present moment in time but also of the present place in space, what is present in place. The journals and maps of the first explorers and early settlers note the presence of these wetlands; colonial chroniclers and municipal historians describe them; and recent history retells their story and the stories of the place and its peoples: the Aboriginal owners and the European dispossessors. All these observers across two centuries saw these wetlands in terms of the European landscape aesthetic in which they were valued, at a time when they presented a clear sheet of beautiful water or were suitable for cattle grazing; otherwise, they were denigrated as 'bad swamps'. A similar settler view of wetlands can be found in Canada in writings about wetlands, that persists into recent times (see Giblett 2014: 30–33).

Exploration and settlement

Early European maritime explorers of the vicinity of the site of present-day Melbourne located on Port Phillip Bay noted the presence of wetlands on their maps and in their journals. Matthew Flinders's map of 1802 of Port Phillip Bay and its adjacent coastline describes what would become the future site of South Melbourne as a 'swampy shore' (Shaw 1989: 201, Figure 37). A year later, Charles Grimes's map of 1803 of Port Phillip Bay not only describes this site as 'low swampy land' (or 'country'), and north of the 'Yarra' as 'swampy', but also describes seven other 'swamps' around the Bay as 'very bad', 'swampy', 'ground', 'soil' or 'swampland', including Carrum Carrum Swamp and the Cheetham wetlands (both discussed below) (Shaw 1989: 203, Figure 38; Poore and Poore 2014: 4).

This is a salutary instance of the moralization of the landscape in which swamps (or woody wetlands) are denigrated. In his field book of 1803, Grimes wrote that 'the Country appeared full of swamps' (cited in Poore and Poore 2014: 3). James Flemming, in his 1802–03 journal of Grimes's voyage, also noted the existence of many lagoons and swamps around Port Phillip Bay. However, unlike Grimes, Flemming noted that the soil of many of these swamps was 'fine black soil' ([1802–03] 1984), probably a signifier for fertility ideal for European settlers seeking to source sustenance for themselves and their domesticated animals. Many of these swamps were filled or drained, or transformed into parks.

The lost and found wetlands of Melbourne make an intermittent cameo appearance in more recent histories of the city: the place, its peoples and their practices, principally in the work of Gary Presland over the past thirty years, to which I am indebted and upon which I rely heavily, as we will see later in this chapter. These swamps have ceased to be waterbird habitats or a source of sustenance and home to the local Aboriginal people, but they are still sites of significance for them. Presland acknowledges these people when he conducts the readers of his books *The Land of the Kulin: Discovering the Lost Landscape and the First People of Port Phillip* (1985), later revised and republished as *Aboriginal Melbourne: The Lost Land of the Kulin People* (1994), on 'an imaginary tour' of 'the landscape of early Melbourne' (Presland 1994: 16–34). More precisely, and given the emphasis on lost land and lost landscape in both subtitles, the area is now the lost *wet*landscape of early Melbourne as the dry landscape remains, though its flora and fauna have largely been lost, except for remnants. The wetlandscape sustained and nurtured much of the flora and fauna, and the Aboriginal peoples (as emphasized by Presland [2014: 96–105] in his latest foray into this topic, in which he focuses specifically on the Melbourne wetlands).

Typically, early explorers, colonial naturalists and recent historians, such as Presland, do not consider the wetlands of early Melbourne to be aesthetically pleasing, though some early settlers did (as we will see later in this chapter in some specific instances). Presland sees the wetlands positively as a rich source of Aboriginal food gathering, but he also views them negatively in terms of the European landscape aesthetic, such as when he asks his readers to imagine that we are 'coming up' Port Phillip Bay along the edge of Hobsons Bay: on the left 'there are mud flats and marshy ground', while on the right

> at the top of the bay there is another wide expanse of low-lying marshy ground [...] The marsh sedges, swamp grass and ti-tree which cover this area are relieved only by a strikingly green grassy hill which rises prominently above its low surroundings. This is soon to be named Emerald Hill.
>
> (Presland 1985: 11, 1994: 16–17)

The green hill for Presland relieves the weary eyes of the traveller (imaginary or otherwise) from having to look at yellow grass and dull trees; the prominence of the hill relieves their unimpressed eyes from having to look at the surrounding supine countryside; the rising, vertical hillscape relieves the traveller from the tedium of the level, horizontal wetlandscape. He operates with the European spatial hierarchy that valorizes the high over the low.

Presland's view that wetlands are not aesthetically pleasing persists with his most recent book on early Melbourne, *The Place for a Village: How Nature Has Shaped the City of Melbourne* (2008). In his description of the 'lost [wet] landscape' of Melbourne, he describes the area around Batman's Hill as 'a low-lying area of little scenic attraction' with 'no advantage for scanning', so 'the hill presented itself well suited for the purpose' of taking in the pleasing prospect from a commanding height (Presland 2008: 2). The hill, or more precisely 'hillock' as Robyn Annear suggests as it was 'only eighteen metres or so in height' (2014: 3) (so not a very commanding height, but the best the site could offer [something else to hold against it]), is figured as an obliging servant ready to indulge the desire of the roving eye to see and master the surrounding, denigrated and ultimately enslaved wetlandscape from above, all of which have been press-ganged into the service of the European landscape aesthetic. Presland's (2008) rich account of how nature shaped the city of Melbourne is also an instance of how culture shaped, and still shapes, the nature of Melbourne. It also shows how the conventions of the European landscape aesthetic shaped, and continue to shape, perceptions, representations and valuations of the land – wet and dry. Nature shapes culture and vice versa. Nature and culture shape each other in a back and forth, to and fro dialogic process (see Giblett 2011: 15–56).

Presland's (2008: 2) devaluation of the view from Batman's Hill flies in the face of John Lancey's description of it in August 1835 as 'a pleasing prospect' (cited in Shaw 1989: 210). Lancey, for Miles Lewis, can 'best claim paternal rights to Melbourne' (1995: 17).[4] Lancey was the acting commander of John Fawkner's schooner the *Enterprize*, which sailed from Launceston and landed on the banks of the Yarra River on 30 August 1835. Rather than the founder of Melbourne, Bill Newnham calls Lancey 'the finder of the attractive site on which the city was built' and Fawkner the 'Founder of Melbourne' (1985: 5).

Lancey described the view of Batman's Swamp from Batman's Hill (for him a marsh) in terms of the European landscape aesthetic as having 'a beautiful prospect. A salt lagoon and piece of marsh will make a beautiful meadow and bounded on the south by the river. This hill is composed of a rich, black soil, thinly wooded with honeysuckle and she-oak' (Lancey cited in Lewis 1995: 17). George Henry Haydon described Batman's Hill in 1854 as 'a beautiful green hill' (cited in Arnold 1983: 13). An open meadow of grass can be both aesthetically pleasing and agriculturally productive (aesthetically pleasing because it is agriculturally productive). Typically, the first explorers and early settlers regarded grassy marshes as good meadows for grazing cattle and sheep. Subsequently the later settlers saw them as limitations to development to be eliminated by draining.[5] Typically, thinly wooded, rich black soil indicates both fecundity and ease of clearing native vegetation.

21

Lancey was largely following in the footsteps of Flemming, who, in 1803 on Grimes's surveying expedition, described Batman's Swamp as 'the lagoon [...] in a large swamp between the two rivers [of the Yarra and Maribyrnong]; fine grass, fit to mow; not a bush on it. The soil is black rich earth about six to ten inches deep', though the land 'about two miles farther' up river is 'much better' with 'soil black, ten to fifteen inches deep' ([1802–03] 1984: 41).[6] The land (and wetland) is subjected to both a pastoral observation and assessment of its suitability for mowing, presumably as feed for stock, and to an agricultural calibration and calculation of the depth of its black, presumably hence fertile, soil.

Presland's aesthetic devaluation of wetlands (1985: 11, 1994: 16–17, 2008: 2) follows in the footsteps of the nineteenth-century naturalist Horace Wheelwright, whose *Bush Wanderings of a Naturalist* published in 1861 has been described by Tim Flannery as 'a classic of Australian natural history writing' (2002: 237), perhaps with all the problems and prejudices that go with the discourse of natural history and the genre of nature writing (see Giblett 2011: 15–38). Wheelwright voiced the opinion that

> [t]here is a monotony in the scenery of this part of Australia [around Port Phillip] which is very wearying to the eye [...] the thick forests and the low swamps and plains are of such vast extent, that the wayfarer in Victoria may plod on for many a weary mile with one unvarying landscape continually before his eyes.
>
> (Wheelwright 1861: 217)

Earlier, Wheelwright describes 'dreary swamps miles in extent' (Wheelwright 1861: 66), and 'the weary shooter [...] plodding his way homeward, after evening has closed in over the dreary swamps' is confronted with 'the desolation which reigns over all' (87).

Later, Wheelwright describes how 'some of the swamps are wild and dismal enough to hold any kind of uncouth reptile' (1861: 207). He came to this conclusion when he camped 'on the edge of one of these dreary, impenetrable marshes' (207). In Wheelwright's register of 'swampspeak', 'dreary', 'weary' and 'plodding' figure prominently. In his hierarchy of natural value, the monotonous and reptilian are beneath the monstrous as he insists that 'we are hardly justified in regarding as monstrosities any peculiarities in the works of nature which we cannot understand' (54). Wheelwright seems to understand reptiles, swamps and marshes, so he does not even regard them as monstrous (though they have been regarded as such; see Giblett [1996]), but merely as uncouth and monotonous, and so beneath contempt (though not consideration, just inconsideration).

The dreariness of the marsh can be relieved in the European landscape aesthetic when placed within the broader context of a pleasing prospect viewed from a considerable eminence, such as Batman's Hill. The prospect has the military function of being a vantage point for seeing an approaching enemy from afar. Traditionally, it applied to a castle or fortified village on top of an eminence or gently rising hill. In the eighteenth century, the military function of surveillance was sublimated into aesthetic appreciation for the 'pleasing prospect' of 'the gentleman's park estate' (see Williams 1973: 121; see also Giblett 2011: 79–94, drawing on the work of Williams). The castle, fortified village and gentleman's house all had a commanding prospect of the country before and below them. In fact, the commanding position constitutes and makes possible the pleasing prospect. Raymond Williams notes how 'castles and fortified villages had long commanded "prospects" of the country below them' (1973: 121, see also 125). The same applies to the city of Melbourne set partly atop Batman's Hill.

When Europeans encountered land in Australia that looked like a gentleman's park, they assumed that it had been created by God, or 'Nature', and not by indigenous people (see Giblett 2011: 91–94). For instance, in the case of Melbourne, John Norcock, an officer aboard the HMS *Rattlesnake*, which transferred the first government officials from Sydney to Melbourne in 1836, described what he saw as follows:

> [t]he country here is enchantingly beautiful – extensive rich plains all round with gently sloping hills in the distance, all thinly wooded and having the appearance of an immense park. The grasses, flowers and herbs that cover the plains are of every variety that can be imagined, and present a lovely picture of what is evidently intended by Nature to be one of the richest pastoral countries in the world.
>
> (Norcock cited in Boyce 2011: 5)

Aboriginal people, not 'Nature', created this and other parks. The Australian gentleman's park is Aboriginal country (see Giblett 2011: 91–94).

Although Melbourne was by no means a fortified village, its founding was seen by J. J. Shillinglaw, in his untitled preface to Flemming's 1802–03 *Journal*, as a pre-emptive move against the French who may have had 'a design to establish herself [*sic*] somewhere in Australia' (Shillinglaw 1984).[7] Newnham agrees that Governor King 'wished to forestall any attempt by the French to claim this part of Australia' (1985: 5). Grant and Serle likewise concur that 'a major motive was to forestall any possible designs by France' (1957: 3). Shillinglaw (1984) concludes that the 'concurrent testimony' of a variety of mariners, such as John Murray, who first discovered and entered Port Phillip Bay in 1802, and Flinders, who arrived in the Bay two months later, 'lent weight' as to 'the suitability of the south coast as a place for settlement'.[8] Collins's expedition of 1803, with Grimes and Flemming aboard, was 'the prompt result determined by the British Government'.[9]

Although Melbourne was not established for another 33 years, these factors are the pretext, or at least the context, for its founding, like other Australian settlements and cities, such as Perth, which was founded in 1829 also as a pre-emptive move against the French, who may have had a design to establish themselves somewhere in Australia with the testimony of James Stirling to the suitability of the west coast as a place for settlement. However much these designs were the result of paranoia, or produced by the British out of a desire to provide a pretext to colonize, they were still the context for the establishment of settlements and the foundation of cities. From settlement as a process to a settlement as a product, then to a town and later a city, marks the process of colonization in Australia. Melbourne was no exception, for, as Grant and Serle put it, 'the settlement on the bank of the Yarra could not be called a town' (1957: 5). That came later with the naming of the settlement as 'Melbourne' by Governor Bourke in 1837 (Grant and Serle 1957: 5).

The city in general, for Paul Virilio, is 'founded on war, or the preparations for war' (1983: 3), not only war against colonizing rivals and a potentially hostile indigenous population, but also against a partially hostile land, especially wetlands. The city fights a war against wetlands, and Melbourne is no exception. The city and the wetland have been inimical to each other. It has largely been impossible for them to coexist in the same place. In most cases, when a city has been located in or close to a wetland, the wetland has had to be drained or filled, or dredged and canalized, to make land for the city to be founded or developed (see Giblett 2016). The war of the city against wetlands included Fascist Mussolini's war against the Pontine Marshes outside Rome, the kind of war he said he liked to fight because it was so easy to win with modern technology (see Giblett 1996: 115).

In making his pronouncement about the city and war, Virilio was merely following in the footsteps of previous writers on the city. For Jacques Ellul, 'urban civilization is warring civilization', 'the city and war have become two of the poles around which the entire economic, social and political life of our time move' (1970: 13), and 'war is an urban phenomenon, as the city is a military phenomenon' (51). The first three index entries under 'War', in Lewis Mumford's monumental *The City in History*, list war 'as chief urban activity', 'as natural state of cities' and 'as new urban institution' (1961: 656). In the case of war 'as chief urban activity', Mumford argues that 'war and domination, rather than peace and cooperation, were ingrained in the original structure of the ancient city' (1961: 44). The layout and materials of ancient and medieval cities, with their buttresses, ramparts and moats, were designed for military purposes. A modern city like Melbourne does not have these features but it does have its liminal spaces, quaking zones and protected points of ingress and egress. Conflict and domination, rather than peace and cooperation, characterize the modern city, especially in relation to wetlands, and Melbourne is no exception. Iconic modern cities were founded in premodern swamps (see Giblett 2016).

Military considerations were one of a variety of factors operating during the early British discovery and exploration of Port Phillip Bay. These considerations were also one of the reasons that it took over another thirty years for the settlement of Melbourne to be established, as the Bay was not a good harbour. The final impetus to settlement was the search for what Alan Shaw calls 'good grazing country' (1989: 212). Grant and Serle begin their collection of 150 years of writings about Melbourne by stating that 'Melbourne was born of the pastoral movement' (1957: 3). Lewis largely concurs by beginning his chapter on the 'frontier town' with the statement that 'the pastoral industry was the whole *raison d'être* for the Melbourne settlement', though on the following page he suggests that 'Melbourne was an afterthought of a settlement and a by-product of the pastoral industry rather than a colony in its right' (1995: 15–16). That came later. Settlers, sheep and cattle all need fresh water. A major consideration in siting the settlement was 'the availability of fresh water, just above the Falls' on the Yarra River. For Lewis, this did the 'most to determine the point of settlement' (1995: 31). Grant and Serle are more emphatic that 'the supply of fresh water above the Yarra Falls' determined 'the site of Melbourne' (1957: 7–8).

Although Australia was no longer threatened by competing European powers, it was still threatened by the power of an alien land. The city was a defence not only against an external enemy (potential or actual), but also against an internal one: the threatening indigenes and the alien wet land. Against these threats, cattle and sheep were the foot soldiers in the war against both, commanded by the cavalry of horseback drovers. Fawkner called Batman and his associates 'Shepherd Kings' (excerpted in Grant and Serle 1957: 4). Pastoral squatters became sheep, and cattle barons, in turn, became 'kings in grass castles', by making what Serle calls 'pseudo-aristocratic claims' (1986: 128).[10] They quickly rose up the economic class scale by virtue of their appropriation of land and labour as the basis for wealth generation and, in turn, for social and political power and privilege.

What was described by Lancey as 'beautiful grass' (cited in Shaw 1989: 210), and recently by James Boyce as 'benign grassland country' (2011: xiv), and by Jenny Sinclair as 'hilly grassland, marked as good grazing land on the early maps' (2015: 73), was mainly to the north of the Yarra, and not to the south and west where the malign wetland country of what Boyce also calls 'the oft-forgotten swamps' of 'the lower Yarra' (2011: 3) was located, and of what Sinclair calls 'the low lying southern suburbs' of 'former marshes' (2015: 73). The region around the Yarra River, for Boyce, was 'dominated by swamps and grasslands – the two ecosystems that were most comprehensively transformed by conquest' (2011: 4).

Melbourne, for Boyce, was established 'without government sanction'[11] as a squatter outpost (2011: xiv). For Boyce, 'Melbourne's birth, not Sydney's settlement, signalled the emergence of European control over Australia' (2011: xiii) and the birth of Australia as 'in this place, at this time, "Australia" was born' (xv). Pastoralism was the impetus for the founding of the settlement of Melbourne and the opening up of the continent to conquest. 'The opening up of the grasslands, not the discovery of gold', for Boyce, 'began the "rush that never ended"' (2011: 210).[12] Thus, Boyce locates the birthplace of Australia in Victoria's benign grassland country and malign wetland country around Melbourne, not in its beneficent gold country elsewhere in Victoria.

What made Melbourne good grazing country also made it good land for urban development. The physical attractions of the site for Melbourne meant that K. J. Fairbairn, an urban geographer, could conclude that the site 'has not seriously hampered its [Melbourne's] expansion. Certainly, local topographic differences have directed some of its development and these add variety to an otherwise continuous mass of urban sprawl' (Fairbairn 1973: 3). Fairbairn does not specify what these local topographic differences are, nor does he indicate that in the case of wetlands many of them have been lost or incorporated into parks where they do add variety to an otherwise continuous mass of urban sprawl. They could also have acted as mitigation against the urban 'heat island' by absorbing heat and transpiring it into the atmosphere. Melbourne is the worst city in Australia for producing a heat island effect. Perhaps it is no wonder given that it has destroyed so many of its wetlands and so much of its bushland.

Fairbairn goes on to wax lyrical about some selected local topographic differences:

> The site can be divided broadly into two parts. To the east of the city centre the land surface consists of gently undulating hills of low relief interspersed with numerous valleys. The western and northern suburbs spread over a very gently undulating basalt surface into which the streams have cut some steep valleys.
>
> (Fairbairn 1973: 3)

Fairbairn makes no mention of the wetlands that were and still are features of the area, albeit landscaped as vestiges in parks.

Fairbairn is merely following in the footsteps of Garryowen (the nom de plume for the colonial journalist Edmund Finn) in the mid-nineteenth century who, in his *Chronicles of Early Melbourne* (1835–52), also pressed into service the descriptor 'undulating' from the lexicon of European landscape aesthetics, with its overtones of pleasing pastoral prospects in the gentleman's park estate:

> The site and surrounding of the embryonic city, when in a state of nature,
> formed a picture of wild and wayward beauty [...] The Eastern Hill was a gum
> and wattle tree forest, and the Western Hill was so clothed with she-oaks as to
> give the appearance of a primeval park where timber-cutting and tree-thinning
> were unknown – whilst away northward as far as the eye could see was a
> country umbrageous and undulating, garbed in a vesture of soft green grass.
>
> (Garryowen [1835–52] 1967: 6)

The 'primeval park' was the product of Aboriginal land care that made it suitable
for hunting. Tree-thinning in the form of timber-clearing was unknown, but not
in the form of fire, either anthropogenic or meteorological. The timber clothing
was later to be unceremoniously stripped off the body of the earth, rendering it
naked and the land laid bare for suburban sprawl.

When Europeans came to Australia, they found parts of it that conformed to
their ideas (and ideals) of the gentleman's park, so they could conveniently overlook the fact that it was already Aboriginal country. This similarity did not lead
to any fellow feeling or solidarity with the Aboriginal people, nor did the fact
that European and Aboriginal cultures were agricultural and hunter cultures lead
to such solidarity (or at least, European culture was an agricultural and hunter
culture before hunting became an aristocratic privilege and recreational pursuit,
and the hunting preserve became alienated and sublimated into the gentleman's
park estate). On top of the fortuitous irony that in places the land looked like a
gentleman's park, it was doubly and cruelly ironic that this land was also the product of a hunter culture like the settler's own. The land was already conforming
to the British model. The 'gentleman's park' (whether in England or Australia),
with its pleasing prospects devoid of understorey, was originally designed (and
produced) to make the hunter's prey visible (see Giblett 2011: 91–94).

Unlike Fairbairn, however, Garryowen had acknowledged previously the presence of the wetlands, both those adjoining the Yarra and those further afield:

> The River Yarra['s ...] low sides were [...] skirted with marshes covered with
> a luxuriance of reeds, wild grass, and herbage [...] whilst trending away
> north-westward spread out a large expanse of marsh of deep black soil, and
> without a solitary tree, its centre a deep lacune [sic] where swans, geese, ducks,
> quail, and other wild-fowl swarmed.
>
> (Garryowen [1835–52] 1967: 6)

This 'lacune' is West Melbourne Swamp (or Batman's Swamp), as Garryowen
describes elsewhere how 'the grassy flat that surrounded it [Batman's Hill] on all
but the Yarra side [...] stretched away into the swamp, then swarming with native

wild fowl' (excerpted by Grant and Serle 1957: 30).[13] This 'lacune' became one of a variety of lacunae, or gaps and omissions, in the geography of the city to be filled with rubbish or sewage and later drained, as well as a gap in the history of the city.

For Garryowen (excerpted in Grant and Serle 1957: 30) the waterbirds swarmed, so they are an abomination in biblical terms according to the Levitical interdiction that 'every swarming thing that swarms upon the earth is an abomination' (Leviticus 11:41). Perhaps they could then be killed with divine sanction, certainly with impunity. Swarming creatures, Mary Douglas has commented, are

> [b]oth those that teem in the waters and those that swarm on the ground. Whether we call it teeming, trailing, creeping or swarming, it is an interminable form of movement [...] 'swarming' which is not a mode of propulsion proper to any particular element, cuts across the basic classification. Swarming things are neither fish, nor flesh, nor fowl. Eels and worms inhabit water, though not as fish; reptiles go on dry land, though not as quadrupeds; some insects fly, though not as birds. There is no order in them [...] As fish belong in the sea so worms belong in the realm of the grave with death and chaos.
>
> (Douglas 1966: 56)

Swarming creatures cut across the basic classification of the four western elements of earth, air, fire and water, and belong to none in particular and some in general. However, eels from several Melbourne wetlands provided sustenance for the Aboriginal people (as we will see later in this chapter).

Wetlands are made up of, and mix, the elements of earth and water. They are often in transition from one to the other. In hot and steamy climates, they also mix the elements of air and fire. They cut across all four western elements of earth, air, fire and water. They are out of place in all the major western categories of matter: solid; gas; heat/light; and liquid. They are slimy, in between the solid and the liquid, and miasmatic, in between the liquid and the gaseous. Wetlands can also be darkness in the place of light. They are dirt in Douglas's sense of 'matter out of place' (Douglas 1966: 35; see also Giblett 1996: 156–60). The typical western response to the dirtiness of wetlands has been to try and put the matter back in its proper place wherever possible, and where it is impossible to denigrate wetlands' deviation from the norm. Drainage, for instance, is putting the earth and water of wetlands back in their respective, and respectable, places. In the process, wetlands are put in their subjugated place and drylands are substituted in wetlands' proper place.

Along similar lines to Garryowen ([1835–52] 1967), the Yarra was so swampy that Ellen Clacy, en route to her 'Lady's visit to the gold diggings' in 1852–53, queried if it was a river at all and remarked that she could only 'discover a tract of marsh or swamp, which I fancy must have resembled the fens of Lincolnshire, as they were some years ago, before draining was introduced into that country' (Clacy 1988: 117). The drained fens were a phantom that the Yarra and other Melbourne wetlands were doomed to become.

South Melbourne Swamp/Albert Park Lake

On his 1803 map of Port Phillip Bay, Grimes described an area at the head of the Bay and to the south of central Melbourne as 'low swampy country' (cited in Poore and Poore 2014: 3–4).[14] W. H. Ferguson reminisced in the 1860s that 'the glory of Albert Park was the lagoon, a marshy place with brackish water' (cited in Daley 1940: 358). This marshy place, or swampy country, or land, was depicted in a British Admiralty map of 1864 (British Admiralty 1864).

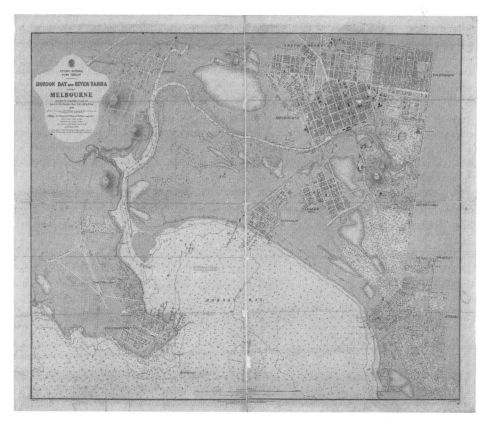

FIGURE 1: Henry L. Cox (Henry Laird) and Thomas Bourchier and P. H. McHugh and Great Britain Hydrographic Department 1866, *Victoria-Australia, Port Phillip: Hobson Bay and River Yarra Leading to Melbourne*, 1866 ed., published by the Admiralty, London.

Albert Park Lake was 'still only marshy swampland' in Henry de Gruchy's 'Isometrical Plan of Melbourne and Suburbs' of 1866 according to Coote (2012: 62–63). It was eventually landscaped to become a park with a lake in an all too familiar story.

The lost wetlands of Melbourne, including the West and South Melbourne Swamps, make an intermittent cameo appearance not only in maps but also in municipal histories of the city, its site and surrounds, such as Charles Daley's *The History of South Melbourne*, first published in 1940 (Daley 1940: 3–4, 8–9, 19, 30, 33, 36–37, 108, 111, 202, 204). Daley's history eventually segues into an account of the wetlands' 'reclamation' (109) by 'filling in, levelling, raising [and] draining' (137), thereby 'overcoming swampy conditions' (167, see also 210, 324). Without noticing or noting the contradiction, Daley concludes his history on a brighter note by assembling '[s]ome early reminiscences of South Melbourne', including James Barrett's: 'Port Melbourne lagoon in the [eighteen] sixties was a beautiful sheet of water, clear as crystal' (cited in Daley 1940: 352). Barrett subscribes to the European landscape aesthetic in which the open water of wetlands is beautiful (see Giblett 1996). The closed water of both the woody wetlands of swamps and the grassy wetlands of marshes is generally ugly and repulsive, following the conventions of the European landscape aesthetic.

The convenient location of the Melbourne wetlands on the outskirts of the city was ideal for waste dumping, but the resulting appearance and smell of the wetlands further diminished their value in the eyes and noses of Melburnians. The smell of the Melbourne wetlands was offensive to the European nose, though in the case of the Melbourne wetlands the offensive smell was due to the dumping of human waste. For one contemporary in the 1880s, the Port Melbourne lagoon was 'abominably malodorous', one of a number of 'foul swamps on the outskirts of the city' used for waste dumping (Cannon [1966] 1976: 18). The foulness of the swamps and their abominably bad smell were not of their own making, but they helped malodorous Melbourne to earn the dubious title of 'Marvellous Smellbourne' in the 1880s, to counter the overblown 'Marvellous Melbourne' of the same period (as we will see in Chapter Eight).

Presland recounts the history of South Melbourne Swamp and how

> [t]he low-lying country around the hill [Emerald Hill] forms a shallow [but large] swamp. This feature will become known as the South Melbourne Swamp and, during the Depression of the 1930s, will be formed into Albert Park Lake [...] The marsh will be drained and built over as the area develops until virtually the only reminder of its original state is the Albert Park Lake.
> (Presland 1985: 11, 1994: 17, see also map 1985: 17 and map 1994: 26)

Albert Park and its Lake are more famous today for being the site and circuit around which Formula One racing takes place than for once having been a swamp.

The marsh forms a swamp, though why these two terms are used synonymously is not clear as a marsh is grassy and a swamp is woody. The hill is named after a jewel, Emerald Hill, while the swamp was rather prosaically called a 'feature' (see Presland 1985: 11, 1994: 17) and was named after a compass point in relation to the city ('South Melbourne Swamp'), only to be renamed after royalty (Queen Victoria's consort, Prince Albert) and rehabilitated as a lake ('Albert Park Lake').

Writing about Albert Park Lake, Sophie Cunningham, in her recent contribution about Melbourne to a series of books about Australian cities, describes how during 'some months the marshlands dotted through it are dry. Dozens of water birds gather here, the most magnificent being the native black swan [with their] snow-white flight feathers contrasting [with] their coal black bodies' (Cunningham 2011: 126–27). These swans are the black and white, yin and yang birds of the black waters of the wetlands.

Although the nineteenth-century naturalist Wheelwright (1861: 66, 87) had negative things to say about the aesthetics (or lack thereof) and desolate effect of the swamps and marshes (as we have seen), he had positive things to say about them as habitat for waterbirds (without seeing the contradiction), including black swans. Wheelwright writes: 'the black swan is a graceful, elegant bird [...] They have a very musical call-note' (1861: 68), which he later describes as 'the soft musical hoop of the black swan' (76). Wheelwright's (1861) and Cunningham's (2011) views of the black swan contrast with Nicholas Taleb's recent view: '([it] I am told, [is] quite [an] ugly) black bird' (2007: xvii). I defy Taleb to look at a black swan, either in flight or paddling, or to look at depictions of black swans, such as those of Elizabeth Gould, and then to continue to agree with those who told him that the black swan is 'quite ugly'.[15]

Cunningham goes on to relate of Albert Park Lake that '[t]his sometimes beautiful, strangely shallow lake is a remnant of South Melbourne Swamp, an enormous salt lagoon that formed a part of the delta where the Yarra met the sea' (2011: 127). The Yarra River did not have a 'mouth' but a delta of multiple outlets to Port Phillip Bay. The unrelieved low-lying marshy ground forming a shallow swamp of the future Albert Park contrasts, for Presland, with 'rolling pastures as far as we can see' (1985: 11, 1994: 17). This 'undulating country covered with native grasses' for Presland is 'not unlike English Downs' (1985: 11, 1994: 17). Such pastoral-looking landscape was the product of Aboriginal fire practices.

West Melbourne Swamp/Batman's Swamp

South Melbourne Swamp was not the only wetland to be accorded the indignity of being named after a mere compass point in relation to the city, which renders the city as the centre and marginalizes the swamp as peripheral. West Melbourne Swamp was originally named Batman's Swamp. This name has got nothing to do with the comic book character and superhero but everything to do with John Batman, who is popularly regarded as the founder of Melbourne. Annear cannot resist a sly dig in his direction by describing the wickerwork perambulator in which the syphilis-infected Batman was transported around early Melbourne (or around 'Bearbrass', as Annear [2014: xii, 34] prefers to call it) as his 'Batmobile' (2014: 4).

For Lewis, John Batman 'chose something close to the present site – but further west and mainly on the south bank of the river' (1995: 17), whereas the present site is on the north bank. Batman's map indicates his preferred site at what Newnham calls 'the mouth of the river near [old] Fisherman's Bend' (1985: 7). Flemming noted in 1803 that 'the ground is swamp on one side [of "a large river"] and high on the other' (side of the river, the current site of Melbourne's Central Business District [CBD]) ([1802–03] 1984: 39).[16] Batman's map also indicates the junction of the Maribyrnong and Yarra Rivers as 'extensive marsh reserved for a public common' and it includes a 'lagoon' (see Lewis 1995: 17, 143). This marsh was later to be called Batman's or West Melbourne Swamp. Batman presumably indicated the marsh and designated it as a public common because of 'its unsuitability for permanent occupation', as Lewis (1995: 25) comments. Yet Batman's preferred site on the south bank was also unsuitable for permanent occupation because it was also 'swampy', so Lewis argues that 'this indicated the northern bank as the place for settlement' (1995: 25), east of Batman's Swamp.

In 1835, John Batman described Batman's Swamp in his journal as

> a large marsh, about one mile and a half wide by three or four miles long, of the richest description of soil – not a tree. When we got on the marsh the quails began to fly, and I think at one time I can safely say I saw 1,000 quails flying at one time – quite a cloud. I never saw anything like it before [...] At the upper end of this marsh is a large lagoon. I should think, from the distance I saw, that it was upwards of a mile across, and full of swans, ducks, geese, etc.
>
> (Batman cited in Billot 1979: 101)

Clouds of birds were a commonplace figuring of their numbers for nineteenth-century explorers and early settlers, for whom these clouds blocked out the sun, blackened the sky and turned day into night. These 'clouds' are indicative of the profusion of life that pre-contact wetlands nurtured. Similarly, nearly half a century later in 1884, Rolf Boldrewood related how 'countless swans and ducks are disporting themselves in unscared freedom upon the great West Melbourne marsh' (Arnold 1983: 19).

The size of the lagoon of West Melbourne Swamp (or Batman's Swamp) can easily be seen in the background of John Noone's photograph taken in 1869 of William Street looking north-west from Lonsdale Street.

FIGURE 2: John Noone and Victoria Department of Crown Lands and Survey 1869 (shows William Street looking north west from Lonsdale Street): from the tower of Dr Fitzgerald's residence Lonsdale Street West, Crown Lands and Survey (Melbourne).

To borrow from Walter Benjamin's discussion of Eugéne Atget's photographs of the streets of Paris as 'the scene of a crime' ([1982] 1999b: 527), the photographed streets of Melbourne are not only the scene of a crime, the stage on which a crime has taken place, but they are also a crime scene in themselves, the scene of a crime against wetlands, the killing of wetlands, what I call aquaterracide, and the forgetting of the stage of the swamp world. Noone's photograph of the streets of Melbourne with Batman's Swamp in the background is the scene where a crime is about to take place. In pondering Atget's photographs, Benjamin wonders if 'every square inch of our cities [is] a crime scene' ([1982] 1999b: 527). In viewing Atget's photographs of the streets of Paris and Noone's of the streets of Melbourne, every square inch of our former swamp cities and marsh metropolises, our aquaterrapolises, is a crime scene.

Benjamin concludes that Atget's photographs of the streets of Paris 'pump [or suck] the aura out of reality like water out of a sinking ship' (1999b: 518). 'Aura' is Benjamin's term for the unique appearance of an object imbued with a strange weave of time and space, which he found in early photographs with long exposure times and slow shutter speeds, but not in Aget's photographs. Benjamin differentiates 'aura' from 'trace' on the basis that aura is present presence, whereas a trace is past presence and present absence (see Giblett 2008b: 59–63; Giblett and Tolonen 2012: 32–36). Noone's photographs of the streets of Melbourne drain the aura of the reality of Melbourne as a city, just like the city that drained the marshes in and upon which it was built. These photographs drain the aura out of the reality of the matrifocal 'Great Mother' of the marshes, which preceded and refuses the patriarchal city (see Giblett 1996: 34–36, 145–50).

Along similar lines to Barrett's description of South Melbourne Swamp in the 1860s as 'a beautiful sheet of water, clear as crystal' (cited in Daley 1940: 352), George Gordon McCrae in 1912 recollected that Saltwater Lake, or Batman's or North or West Melbourne Swamp (as it was variously called by McCrae and others), was in the 1840s 'a beautiful blue lake [...] a real lake, intensely blue, nearly oval, and full of the clearest salt water; but this by no means deep' (McCrae 1912: 117).[17] Batman's or North or West Melbourne Swamp was even depicted in blue on early maps, such as Christie's map of 1853 (Christie 1853).

For both McCrae and Barrett, an open body of clear water is beautiful. By contrast, McCrae goes on to relate how in the 1910s 'you may search for it in vain to-day among the mud, scrap-iron, broken bottle, and all sorts of red-rusty railway debris – the evidences of an exigent and remorseless modern civilization' (1912: 117) that typically and habitually transforms wetland into wasteland. Flannery (2002: 136) surprisingly omits this passage and the following one from his anthology, *The Birth of Melbourne*. This is especially surprising given his critical comments regarding the transformation of Melbourne into the hypermodern 'Los Angeles of the south' (to which I return later in this chapter). McCrae goes on to trace mournfully the transition of the wetlands from beautiful blue lake through swamp and 'the stickiest mud that I can remember anywhere' to 'all dry land now' (1912: 118), the sad and sorry story of the demise of many wetlands in and on the outskirts of many modern cities.

A century after McCrae, and citing him in an epigraph, Sinclair, in her account of 'Where Dynon Road runs now: The Ghost of Batman's Swamp', shows that nothing much has changed in one hundred years, just the addition of detritus from more recent technology:

> There were junkyards piled high with broken stuff, festooned with purple-flowering creepers; there were patches of dried mud infested with old bottles glinting like jewels; maintenance tracks heaped with ute-loads of household rubbish: fridges, pink plastic toys and snarls of ruined fabric.
>
> (Sinclair 2010: 68, see also 2015: 60)

She concludes that 'the land itself was dead – a wasteland' (Sinclair 2010: 70, 2015: 60). Wetland to wasteland marks the sad and sorry story of the demise of many wetlands in modern cities, including Fishermen's Bend (to which I return in the following chapter). Sinclair (2010: 71, 2015: 61) finds history and geography intertwined in West Melbourne Swamp (or Batman's Swamp), though its history, and of other Melbourne wetlands, is now largely forgotten, and their geography is now largely lost.

Along similar lines to McCrae, Presland also describes how West Melbourne Swamp (or Batman's Swamp) was 'another extensive swamp' (1985: 12, 1994: 20). He goes on to relate how it came 'to be noted in the early years of settlement of Melbourne for its abundance of water plants and its birdlife' (Presland 1985: 12, 1994: 20), not surprisingly for a wetland. When Sinclair 'squints and shades the upper part of my vision [...] this could be a calm lagoon on an early misty morning, teeming with life' (2010: 71, 2015: 61), as it was for McCrae a century earlier without squinting or shading his eyes.

Sinclair describes how in 1860 'the fate of the swamp was sealed' (2010: 70) when a Royal Commission inquired into how 'to get big, modern ships to dock in Melbourne. Dredging the Yarra was considered, but a new channel was cheaper' (Sinclair 2015: 60). So that option was taken and it resulted in the construction of Coode Canal and Coode Island (as we will see later in this chapter). Like McCrae, Lewis relates how

> for many years up until the 1880s West Melbourne Swamp was used as a dumping ground for rubbish collected in Melbourne, [increasing] to a depth of two meters, and with it was dumped raw sewage sludge form street chan-nels and sewage catchpits, making the area very offensive. It had become 'a nuisance, injurious to health, and a disgrace to the city' in view of the Low Lands Commission in 1873. The Commission recommended that the land be drained in accordance with a plan proposed by [... the] Chief Engineer of Water Supply, and it is apparently this which was followed.
>
> (Lewis 1995: 66)

Yet the city had caused the swamp to become a disgrace to the city; the city had created the nuisance, injurious to health, and the offence to the eyes and nose of the city and its citizens, to the senses of sight and smell. The swamp had ceased to be a swamp and had become a rubbish dump and was then subjected to the discipline-and-drain discourse of the 'low lands' commission.

A similar fate was to befall another Melbourne swamp courtesy of another governmental body. For the committee of the Melbourne Corporation reporting on the health of the city in 1848:

The large swamp on the eastern side of the city, known as Lake Lonsdale, is moreover admitted to be most injurious to the health of the citizens, from the noxious vapours it emits in warm weather; and those residents that complain loudly of the injurious effects of the nuisance upon the health of the families [...] The diseases which prevail at particular seasons in Melbourne may be attributed to the crowding, the want of water, the absence of sewerage, the non-removal of decayed animal and vegetable refuse, and the poisonous liquid and gaseous matter generated within the city.

(excerpted in Grant and Serle 1957: 60)[18]

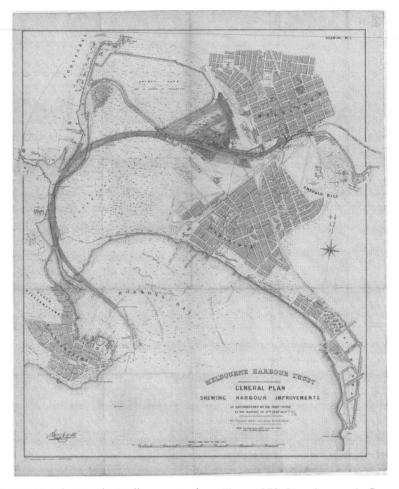

FIGURE 3: Sir John Coode, Melbourne Harbour Trust 1879, Drawing no. 1, *General Plan Shewing Harbour Improvements: As Recommended by Sir John Coode in His Report of 17th February 1879*, London: Thomas Kell, Lith. 40 King St Covent Garden.

And generated by the city, and not by the swamp as such. As the report goes on to point out, the diseases should not be attributed to the swamp but to the city, but they had already been attributed to the swamp in a presumption of guilt. These two views are presented in close succession without any awareness of the contradiction between them. Swamps are guilty until proven innocent. Swamps are made guilty of crimes they did not commit. The city committed the crimes, but it is not convicted of them. The swamp is made to bear the blame as a scapegoat, or more precisely a 'scapewetland'. From wetlandscape to scapewetland marks the sad and sorry state of wetlands in and on the outskirts of cities. Melbourne is no exception.

This view justified the drainage and reclamation of the Melbourne swamps. The Melbourne Harbour Trust *General Plan Shewing [sic] Harbour Improvements* of 1879 shows 'Swampy Land now in course of reclamation' (see Carroll 1972: 59).

On his imaginary historical tour of the wetlandscape of early Melbourne, Presland describes how Batman's Swamp 'covers an area of almost two hundred hectares' (1985: 14, 1994: 20). Recently, Presland has recalculated this figure and doubled the size of Batman's Swamp at settler contact to 'greater than 1000 acres (404.7 hectares)' (2008: 91). Presland earlier says that West Melbourne Swamp (or Batman's Swamp) 'will gradually be reclaimed for industrial use as railway yards. Parts of the original swamp will be visible into the 1930s' (1985: 14, 1994: 20). 'Reclaimed' is the stock-in-trade term and euphemism for triumphalist wetland drainage and filling as if the water wrongfully claimed the land and the drainers rightfully claimed it back (see Giblett 1996, 2014: 52).

In his history of the development of the Port of Melbourne over a century, Sanay Yarnasan also noted in one of five sections of his thesis devoted to 'Drainage and reclamation' – a persistent theme – that the period of 1907–11 'saw steady progress in the reclamation' of 'a useless swamp in West Melbourne' (or Batman's Swamp) (1974: 68) which was 'turned into valuable land suitable for the erection of cargo sheds and warehouses, and over which was placed roads and railways' (75, see also 66). Useless swamp versus valuable land, useless wetlands versus valuable drylands: wetlands are useless and valueless in this view until they are made useful and given value by 'reclamation'.

Yet wetlands are useful and valuable as providers of 'ecosystem services'. Wetlands are vital for life on earth, including human and non-human life. The leading intergovernmental agency on wetlands states that 'they are among the world's most productive environments; cradles of biological diversity that provide the water and productivity upon which countless species of plants and animals depend for survival' (Ramsar Convention Bureau n.d.). Australia is no exception because, as Maya Ward puts it, 'wetlands are one of the most highly productive wildlife habitats in Australia' (2011: 109). The intergovernmental agency on wetlands goes on to state that

[w]etlands are indispensable for the countless benefits or 'ecosystem services' that they provide humanity, ranging from freshwater supply, food and building materials, and biodiversity, to flood control, groundwater recharge, and climate change mitigation. Yet study after study demonstrates that wetland area[s] and [their] quality continue to decline in most regions of the world. As a result, the ecosystem services that wetlands provide to people are compromised.

(Ramsar Convention Bureau n.d.)

Yet more than the mere providers of 'ecosystem services', wetlands are habitats for plants and animals, and homes for people. They are also principally under threat on the outskirts of cities, where they are drained and filled to create sites for more homes for more people. The relationship between cities and wetlands is fraught to say the least, and Melbourne is no exception.

The filling and draining (or 'reclamation') of Batman's Swamp was proposed by Alexander Kennedy Smith (1859: 9–18) in 1859. Flannery relates how in the 1860s 'Batman's Hill was gouged flat and the refuse used to fill the Blue Lake' (2002: 13), or West Melbourne Swamp (or Batman's Swamp). Or as Grant and Serle put it, 'the disappearance of Melbourne's favourite pleasure garden, Batman's Hill', occurred when it was 'levelled down and used to fill in the "Blue Lake"' (1957: 77).[19] This is an early instance of civil engineering 'cut and fill' that cut down, or cut off, one

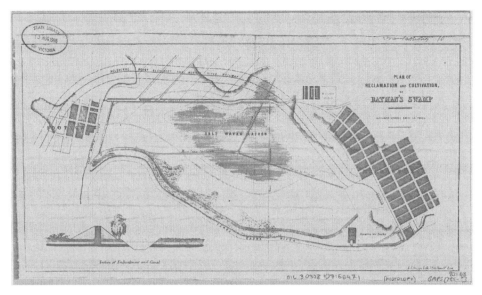

FIGURE 4: Alexander Kennedy Smith n.d., *Plan of Reclamation and Cultivation of Batman's Swamp.*

geographical feature rising above the surface in order to fill another subsurface geographical feature, and in the process destroyed both features and wiped the names of 'Batman's Hill' and 'Batman's Swamp' off the map and off the surface of the earth, except for the 'Batman's Hill Hotel' on the corner of Collins and Spencer Streets.

Even in its absence, 'the former Batman's Swamp' is, for Lewis, one of the features that defines the relationship of Melbourne to its location:

> Melbourne's 'Golden Mile,' the central one by one half mile grid which is the core of the Central Business District, or CBD, is one of the great colonial centres of the 19th century, distinguished by its Victorian architecture, characterised by its regularity of layout and defined by its relationship to the Yarra River [...] and the former Batman's Swamp.
>
> (Lewis 1995: 12)

Batman's Swamp is added on almost as an afterthought. Typically, even archetypically, the colonial centres of Melbourne, Perth, New York, Toronto, Washington DC and other cities were defined by their relationship to their wetlands by establishing the centre adjacent to the wetlands and then by draining them.

To borrow from Benjamin, writing about 'the hetaeric stage' of 'the swamp world',

> the fact that this stage [of Melbourne's history] is now forgotten [by the vast majority of Melbourne's residents] does not mean that it does not extend into the present. On the contrary: it is present by virtue of its very oblivion.
>
> (Benjamin [1982] 1999b: 809)

Benjamin's statement could have been the epigraph for my book *Cities and Wetlands* (Giblett 2016), as it reads the traces of the absent wetlands of cities in history, literature, geography, cartography and photography, as I do in this book with Melbourne (and so it could have been the epigraph for this book too). The majority of Melbourne's residents today are oblivious to Melbourne's lost wetlands, but these wetlands are still present (in the present) by virtue of their very oblivion.

The lost and found wetlands of Melbourne are, in short, ghost swamps. They are either dead swamps that still live on with a spectral life, such as South Melbourne Swamp and Batman's Swamp; or living swamps that have a tenuous existence, such as Bolin Bolin Billabong, or that are threatened with extinction, such as Banyule Billabong (as we will see in Chapter Four), all of which are a vestige of the billabongs and swamps that have been destroyed or landscaped. Ghost swamps are like ghost species which have been 'out-evolved' by their environment and are probably headed for extinction. They are also like ghost rivers, such as the ancient bed of the

Yarra River underneath or beside the present river, and the sinuous course of the lower Yarra at settlement before it was straightened (as we will see in Chapter Eight).

The ghost swamps and billabongs of Melbourne and the hetaeric stage of the swamp world which are present by virtue of their very oblivion have, using Benjamin's word, left a trace. In fact, for anything from the past to be forgotten and to extend into the present by virtue of its very oblivion is a precise definition of a trace. The trace is current absence and past presence, and presence in the present by virtue of absence. Absent wetlands also leave other traces in technology and climatology. All machines and vehicles powered by steam and internal combustion engines are traces of the stage when the world was a swamp, as its fossilized remains fuel these machines and vehicles in the era of carboniferous capitalism and in the age of climate catastrophes.

Lewis goes on to relate that 'the early removal of Batman's Hill and the draining of [West Melbourne Swamp or] Batman's Swamp largely eliminated that topographical limit to the town to the west' (1995: 12). Wetlands run the gauntlet of being features that define the relationship of the colonial centre to its location and that pose a topographic limit to the centre. Wetlands are then drained to eliminate that limit, but in their absence they remain a defining feature of the relationship of the colonial centre to its location – provided of course that one knows that the wetland was present in the first place. The wetland, indeed, was present *as* the first place *of* the first people.

Other swamps

On his imaginary mystery tour of early Melbourne's wetlandscape in South Yarra, Presland imagines that 'there are swampy lagoons' and 'much of the area between the [Yarra] river and the future location of Dandenong Road is swampy and prone to flooding, and in winter there is often water on the ground' (Presland 1985: 20, 1994: 29). This area qualifies as ephemeral, seasonal or temporary wetland. By contrast, Presland goes on to relate, 'in the vicinity of the future suburb of Caulfield there are [...] a number of permanent swamps' (1985: 20, 1994: 29). These include Le Mans Swamp, which, Presland writes,

> in later years [...] will be reclaimed and become Koornang and Lord Reserves. This is a particularly favoured spot of the Aborigines. The vegetation in the area consists of ti-tree, marsh grasses, sedges and tubers such as *Typha*, which is a favourite vegetable food. There are places where Aborigines catch birds and collect eggs. Most importantly, however, they provide eels and fish.
>
> (Presland 1985: 20, see also map 21, 1994: 30, see also map 31)

Just like Batman's Swamp, Le Mans Swamp was a source of sustenance and nurturance, including the abominable swarming creature of the eel.

The municipal history of Caulfield calls this swamp 'Leman Swamp' and relates the history of how, 'in a somewhat shrunken state, [it] became the Sugar Works Swamp and later the Koornang and Lord Reserves' (Murray and Wells 1980: 3). Similarly, Paddy's Swamp and Black Swamp in Caulfield were 'gazetted as permanent public reserves in 1879' (3). Paddy's Swamp is now Caulfield Park (3, 10). From the time of white settlement, these swamps posed the problem of 'control of the swamps' (5–6) and 'the seemingly eternal question of control over the swamps' (7). The ultimate solution, after a brief flirtation with peat extraction from Leman Swamp and Paddy's Swamp (194), was 'converting the swamps to public parks' (6). The swamps had to be converted from the eternal 'now-time' of swamps to the Christian chronology of the past, present and future memorialised in public parks.[20] Colonization is just as much about colonization of time as it is of space; and not just of the past, but also of the future.

Presland relates that 'further south from the Caulfield area [...] there is another very large swamp, so large that it will pose problems for the earliest European settlers and their grazing cattle' (1985: 22, 1994: 30). Hard-hooved ruminants are not suited for grazing in soft-bottomed wetlands. Presland goes on to describe how

> [t]his will be known as Carrum Swamp [...] Although the area of this swamp is huge and water lies on the surface of the ground all year round, it will often be referred to by settlers as the Little Swamp to distinguish it from an even larger one, the Great Swamp of Koo-wee-rup [...] at the top of Westernport Bay [that] will effectively cut off movement by Europeans into Gippsland to the east.
>
> (1985: 21–22, 1994: 31)[21]

Yet Flemming, in his journal of Grimes' voyage of 1803, described Carrum Carrum Swamp as 'a large swamp, with three lagoons in it, all dry. The land appears to be covered with water in wet seasons' ([1802–03] 1984: 3).[22] This is a typical feature of many wetlands around the world, but one that perplexed European explorers familiar with lakes that did not dry up in dry seasons.

The Carrum wetlands, for Presland, were 'a major hydrological feature of the metropolitan area [...] This series of swamps and marshes extended for about fifteen kilometres in length and its widest point, in the north, was eight kilometres across' (2008: 100–01). Like the other Melbourne swamps (south, west, wherever), 'beginning in the 1860s, the Carrum Swamp will be gradually reclaimed by draining and other public works. Some of the area will be used for market gardening' – a typical use for wetlands in close proximity to cities, such as South Perth and Northbridge in Perth[23] – 'in an area that was once a rich source of food and materials for Aborigines' (Presland 1985: 22 and 1994: 32).

41

The Melbourne swamps were not only a source of sustenance and home to the Kulin, the local Aboriginal people, in the past, but they were also a site of entertainment for settlers as one of the swamps was the place for the first race meeting. Another swamp is now the venue for the running of the Melbourne Cup horse race. West Melbourne Swamp (or Batman's Swamp) was the site of Melbourne's first race meeting. In 1838, Garryowen described how 'the grassy flat' that surrounded Batman's Hill

> on all but the Yarra side, and stretched way into the swamp, [...] was if formed by Nature's hand for a racecourse, unless when inundated by floods. Here, where the Spencer Street [Southern Cross] Railway Station now stands, was marked out with a few stakes, saplings, and broad palings, Melbourne's first racing ground.
>
> (Garryowen excerpted in Grant and Serle 1957: 30; also cited in Lewis 1995: 29)

The flatness of the swamp made it suitable for the first race ground, and for the second one.

Googling 'Melbourne swamps' yielded one result from 2002 that 'in 1840 [...] a racecourse was laid out along the swampy banks of the Saltwater River [now Maribyrnong River], four miles (6.5km) from the town centre' (Anon. 2002). The Saltwater Flat location, as it was also named in keeping with the general flatness of swamps, developed into the Flemington Racecourse, the home for one of the richest horse races in the world in terms of prize money. The swampy banks are no longer the home for one of the richest peoples in the world in the richest of places, the swamp. The swampy homes for Melbourne's first race meeting and now for the Melbourne Cup give new meaning to the idea of a wet and heavy track.

Given the rich history of the Melbourne wetlands, Cunningham draws the conclusion that 'to make sense of Melbourne, look to its erratic, brackish wetlands; its muddy, beautiful rivers; its sometimes smelly old lagoons and lakes; and the sudden shock of those moments after heavy rain when the city's cup runneth over' (2011: 127). The biblical allusion to Psalm 23:5 is to a cup of wine running over as an image for having more than enough. In the case of Melbourne, its cup runneth over with water after heavy rains. This is when the Melbourne Cup becomes a sick joke, when Melbourne *is* a cup, and when the city's repressed wetlands return with a vengeance. To make sense of Melbourne, of its history and development, look to the draining and filling of its wetlands, as Presland does when he argues that 'no feature of the original landscapes of the Melbourne area has been so deliberately altered as the wetland and drainage patterns' (2008: 62). Perhaps no feature of the original landscapes of the Melbourne area has been so deliberately forgotten as its wetlands, if the general lack of commemoration and interpretation in and around Melbourne, as well as Fishermen's Bend and Westgate Park, are anything to go by (the topic of the following chapter).

NOTES

1. Many of these cities are discussed on a chapter-by-chapter basis in Giblett (2016).
2. For the history of the drainage of many of Melbourne's wetlands, see La Nauze (2011: 2–3, 70–73). I am grateful to Robert La Nauze for drawing my attention to this book.
3. Many wetlands (past/absent and present) adjacent to the middle reaches of the Yarra River in Melbourne are discussed in Lacey (2004).
4. This book claims to be the first history of Melbourne (Lewis 1995: 8), but it largely ignores the history of the site prior to the foundation of the settlement, especially that of the geological formation, the Aboriginal owners and the European explorers, although it does not ignore the wetlands (as we will see later in this chapter). For Lewis (1995: 12), Melbourne began in 1835, though it had many beginnings before and after that. Shaw (1989: 213) largely concurs with Lewis regarding Lancey.
5. A similar situation and transition also occurred in Canada (see Giblett 2016: 11, 33, 52).
6. Shillinglaw (1984) adds a footnote here that 'the lagoon [...] in a large swamp' is 'Batman's or West Melbourne Swamp'. Flannery (2002: 38) also excerpts this entry from Flemming's *Journal* without specifying which swamp it was. Also excerpted in *The Melbourne Scene* (Grant and Serle 1957: 18), with 'Batman's or West Melbourne Swamp' in square brackets.
7. See also Bach (1976: 31). I can't help wondering facetiously whether the title of this book (*A Maritime History of Australia*) should be its second subtitle and that its title and subtitle could have been 'Girt by Sea: Girdled by Ships and Shipping', with a nod to the Australian national anthem, which acknowledges the importance of the sea to the colonies and nation of Australia geographically, if not historically, and certainly not to the importance of the sea for its Aboriginal people.
8. See also Newnham (1985: 5).
9. For John Murray as 'the first British seaman' to enter Port Phillip Bay in February 1802 see also Newnham (1985: 5); Grant and Serle (1957: 3); Shaw (1989: 200); and Yarnasan (1974: 18).
10. *Kings in Grass Castles* is the title of Mary Durack's ([1959] 1966) triumphalist family history of cattle droving to the Kimberley region of Western Australia and the founding of a cattle kingdom there in the late nineteenth century; see Giblett (2011:199–216).
11. Boyce is repeating the words of Grant and Serle (1957: 3): 'without governmental sanction'.
12. Boyce is alluding to (and countering) Blainey (1963).
13. 'Swarm' is also a favourite descriptor for Wheelwright (1861: 66, 208, 209). Newnham (1985: 1) follows in their footsteps by describing how in 1835 waterbirds 'swarmed on swamps where now large ships lie at anchor in docks'.
14. Shaw (1989: 203, Figure 38) has 'low swampy land' on his version of Grimes' map.

15. See Giblett (2013a: 69–88) for the black swan's natural and cultural history. Elizabeth Gould's depiction of black swans is reproduced on the cover of Giblett (2013a).

16. Shillinglaw (1984) footnotes 'a large river' as 'the Yarra Yarra River'. Flannery (2002: 37) also excerpts this passage from Flemming's *Journal* without specifying the precise area, though the reference to 'a large river' is unmistakably to the Yarra River. Also excerpted in Grant and Serle (1957: 17) with 'Yarra' in square brackets.

17. See also Flannery (2002: 8, 135), Grant and Serle (1957: 52–53) and Lewis (1995: 30), where the latter also calls these wetlands Lake Lonsdale, mistakenly I believe as the latter was on the east side of the city.

18. Lewis thus seems mistaken to equate Lake Lonsdale with the Saltwater Lake, or Batman's or North or West Melbourne Swamp. See Lewis (1995: 30).

19. Lewis describes the cutting down of Batman's Hill from 1863 to 1865, but not its use for filling Batman's Swamp. See Lewis (1995: 71). Lewis also cites an elegy (or obituary) from the *Illustrated Australian News* that 'waxed lyrical' about the cutting down and loss of the bucolic Batman's Hill (but also without mentioning the filling in or up and loss of Batman's Swamp). See Lewis (1995: 73).

20. Now-time (a translation of the German '*Jetztzeit*') is a concept developed by Walter Benjamin coming out of traditional Judeo-Christian theology and combined with Marxist eschatology to indicate a messianic irruption in the present that blasts open the continuum of history. Benjamin first developed the concept of now-time in the fourteenth thesis of his essay 'On the concept of history' (Benjamin 2003: 389–400, especially 395).

21. The Great Swamp was eventually drained in the Koo-wee-rup drainage scheme, the background for Liam Davison's great novel, *Soundings* (Davison 1993). Liam Davison is one of the unforgotten victims of the Malaysian Airlines flight MH17 shot down over Ukraine in 2016.

22. Shillinglaw (1984) footnotes 'a large swamp' with 'Carrum Carrum'. Flannery (2002: 39) also excerpts this entry from Flemming's *Journal* without specifying which swamp it was. Also excerpted in Grant and Serle (1957: 17) without 'Carrum Carrum' in square brackets.

23. For the Perth wetlands, see Giblett (1996: 55–76, 2013a: 105–22).

Wasteland and Wetland

If any place in Melbourne shows the contradictions between cities and wetlands today, it is Fishermen's Bend with its Westgate Bridge and Park. Lying on the edge of the central city of Melbourne, this once wetland, then wasteland, then industrial site, now partly reconstructed wetland in Westgate Park, is what Val Plumwood calls 'a shadow place' (2008: 8). She defines shadow places as 'all those places that produce or are affected by the commodities you consume, places consumers don't know about, don't want to know about, and in a commodity regime don't ever need to know about or take responsibility for' (Plumwood 2008: 8). What she seems to have mainly in mind are the sweatshops in various Asian countries where our clothing and sneakers are produced. Industrial shadow places can also be found much closer to home in the wastelands of commodity production such as Fishermen's Bend, which is famous as the industrial site for manufacturing Holden and other cars. Underneath the shadow place of the defunct industrial site of Fishermen's Bend that consumers don't know about, don't want to know about and don't want responsibility for is another place, the wetlands of Fishermen's Bend, an overshadowed place that was there at contact between the colonizing settlers and Aboriginal owners that has since been lost. It is also a place that most citizen consumers in an ongoing colonial regime don't ever need to know about or take responsibility for. This, and other lost wetlands of Melbourne, is a ghost swamp in an overshadowed place.

The industrial sites of Fishermen's Bend are a former wetland on one side of the Yarra River with a wasteland, never again to be wetland, on the other. The Westgate Bridge and Freeway slashes a scar across the sky above the Park to the south, filling the air with traffic noise that competes with the calls and songs of the bush birds and water birds (see Freeman and Pukk 2015: 248, with accompanying photograph). The city skyline of skyscrapers jutting above the Park to the north reminds me of Central Park in New York City squeezed between the office towers of Manhattan, another urban park on the site of former forests and wetlands (see Barlow 1971a, 1971b; Sanderson 2009). The sublimated world of the city above, its skyscrapers and freeways, looks down on the park founded on the slimy world of the swamp below its surface. Yet rather than the New York, or Gotham, or Paris, or Los Angeles of the south as various writers have suggested (as we will see later in this chapter and several others in *Modern Melbourne*), I regard Melbourne as the Toronto of the south because both are port cities set beside river delta wetlands with similar histories and maps of their colonial founding, of losing their wetlands and of their urban and industrial development (see Giblett 2014: 133–52 and 2016: 197–213). Both cities are provincial or state capitals and they also have trams.

Over the past 30 years, the Friends of Westgate Park have lovingly landscaped, wetlandscaped and regenerated bushland and wetland vegetation in the area. By reconstructing wetlands in this Park, the place was being consciously or inadvertently returned to its previous, pre-contact state. The British Admiralty map of 1864 shows the wetlands of Fishermen's Bend, as well as those of West Melbourne and South Melbourne Swamps, as we have already seen (see Figure 1 in Chapter Two; British Admiralty 1864). This map shows wetlands near the 'mouth' of the river roughly in the same location as present-day Westgate Park. Westgate Park is a liminal place and time with a toehold on the threshold of the city where it is caught in suspension between a chequered past, tenuous present and uncertain future. It is also in suspension between the time of the hypermodern speed of the traffic on the Westgate Bridge and Freeway, and the premodern slowness of the rhythms of the life of Westgate Park harking back to the pre-contact wetlands and drylands of the area.

In the second part of this chapter, I trace this history and call for improved interpretation of the place, for greater appreciation of its features and for more resources to be dedicated to its conservation and regeneration, though it can never be rehabilitated to its pre-contact state. As a rehabilitated wetland and as a remnant wetland in what was once a much bigger wetland, Westgate Park could be the site for a memorial of the lost wetlands of Melbourne, such as West Melbourne and South Melbourne Swamps.

Melbourne does have what is now called the Port Phillip Monument positioned at the original junction of the Yarra and Maribyrnong Rivers, where, as Bill Newnham puts it, 'the Yarra was later cut off by the Coode Canal, giving the Yarra a more direct outlet to Port Phillip Bay' (1985: 264). According to the City of Melbourne on the eMelbourne website, 'this sandstone monument was erected in 1941 to commemorate the first landing of Europeans in the Melbourne area' (n.d.). It was also erected to commemorate the original junction of the Yarra and Maribyrnong Rivers. The inscription on the monument says that 'this memorial has been erected to mark the original junction of the Yarra and Maribyrnong Rivers, which was near this spot' (Newnham 1985: 264). It was not erected to mourn the loss and commemorate the life of the marshes in the delta at the junction of the two rivers. The year of erection in 1941 seems to have no great significance. Claude Smith, whom Newnham calls 'a keen local historian and

Footscray councillor' (1985: 264), proposed the monument in 1937, two years after the centenary of the settlement of Melbourne. It took another four years for the monument to eventuate. How long will it take to erect a memorial to the lost wetlands of Melbourne?

The recent heritage study of Fishermen's Bend for Places Victoria relates how 'Fishermans [sic] Bend once provided an extensive wetland habitat for flora and fauna that was an important resource for Aborigines, who may have occupied the area for thousands of years prior to European settlement' (Vines 2013: 3). Like many wetlands located close to European settlements, Fishermen's Bend was good grazing land and good for game. Many of the features that made the wetland so productive for indigenous dwellers, such as well-watered and nutritious low-scale vegetation, ideal as waterfowl habitat and for grazing and hunting, also made it attractive and useful to European settlers. These features may also have made the area an important fish hatchery. The bend in the river certainly was a good fishing spot as, in the words of Newnham, it was 'the favourite haunt of anglers' who supplied fish to Melbourne (1985: 142). Thus Fishermen's (possessive plural) Bend acquired its English name for its being a site for supplying sustenance to the city without ever having been given an English name for being a wetland.

The value of Fishermen's Bend was recognized well into the twentieth century. One resident of Sandridge, writing a letter to the editor of *The Age* in 1935, recalled how

> Fishermans Bend was a fine place, almost in its primitive state, a great resort for sportsmen, rabbits, wild duck and other game being plentiful. Thick tea tree scrub grew on the south side of the Yarra from the present timber dock almost to the mouth [...] The Bend was a fine grazing ground; hundreds of cows and horses were grazed there paying so much a head to the local council, which employed a herdsman.
>
> (F. N. 1935: 8)

The fact that indigenous and settler cultures both took game from this highly productive place did not lead to any solidarity or fellow-feeling between the two hunting and cultivating cultures – quite the contrary, it led to conflict over the same ground and game, especially as introduced species, such as rabbits, and pasturing hard-hooved animals, such as cows and horses, were detrimental to the native vegetation and so to native game.

The Sandridge letter writer uses the conventional nomenclature of the mouth of a river. This is a misnomer as water and solid matter flow out at this point, and not in. It is also a mistaken view of the anatomy of the human body, and of the body of the earth, because this place or point should be called by the name for the other end of the body. Sea-going and ocean-faring explorers always say that they entered the mouth of a river because it would not be gentlemanly and would be an act of buggery to say that they entered the rectum of the river, let alone to use other more vernacular and vulgar terms for this act and organ. The mouth of a river is, in fact, at the opposite end of the earthly alimentary canal or digestive tract of a river, in the conventional nomenclature of the head of the catchment or the headwaters of a river. The conventional nomenclature of 'the mouth of the river' inverts the rectum and the mouth so as to hide the fact that the exploratory journey up the river is a journey up the rear and inner passage entering through the rectum, rather than a journey down the upper and inner passage entering through the mouth. The connotation of oral sex in entering the mouth of the river was probably more socially acceptable than the connotation of buggery in entering the rectum of the river. Ironically, the Yarra River later became a drain for liquid and solid wastes and was reduced to merely excretory functions like a digestive tract (as we will see in Chapter Eight). Regarding the city as a body is a commonplace of writing about the city (as I discuss in the final chapter).

More recent nomenclature of the head of the catchment is at odds with the traditional terminology of the mouth of the river because they are at opposite ends of the river but both are at the same end of the human body. These metaphors of 'the head of the catchment' or 'the headwaters' of the river and 'the mouth of the river' continue to be used without considering the politics of language, the body and the earth in which they are engaged and in which they engage their users. Meaning is made through metaphor; 'tropes are the dreams of speech,' as claimed by Vladimir Nabokov; and 'dreams are the royal road to the unconscious of speech,' as stated by Sigmund Freud (both cited in Giblett 2011: 209). These tropes lead to the unconscious in speech and manifest the repressed in culture of an oral, excremental, sexual and environmental nature that coalesces in the grotesque lower strata, whether it be that of the body or the earth (see Giblett 1996: 127, 2011: 179).

European settlement had a devastating impact on Aboriginal Fishermen's Bend as it was turned into a kind of artificial waste wetland, or wet wasteland. The Places Victoria heritage study goes on to relate how

> [a]s the area was originally low lying swamp and sand ridges and on the fringes of settlement, it was considered a 'wasteland' and became a convenient dumping ground for the undesirable activities that were shunned from the commercial and residential parts of Melbourne.
>
> (Vines 2013: 3)

Fishermen's Bend has had a sad and sorry history located on the edge of the city of Melbourne, particularly in the mid-nineteenth and early twentieth centuries. Nancy U'Ren and Noel Turnbull, in their history of Port Melbourne, relate how by 1858, 'due to the sand mining and manure pits, Fishermen's Bend was an unlovely piece of sandy, marshy low ground' (1983: 43). Fishermen's Bend may have been unlovely in terms of the European landscape aesthetic precisely because it was mined and well-manured miry marsh low ground, but it was not necessarily unloved in terms of the European naturalist appreciation for native plants and animals (as we will see shortly in this chapter), nor had it been initially for game and grazing (as we have seen). This contradiction also marks the fate of the wetland on the margins of the city – initially pastorally pleasing and good for game, subsequently aesthetically displeasing but naturalistically pleasing. Here a parallel can also be drawn with Toronto (Giblett 2014: 133–52, 2016: 197–213).

Some writers, even recently, have been less than enthusiastic and even downright disparaging about the physical and aesthetic qualities of the area, and have expressed their displeasure in pejorative terms. Sanay Yarnasan describes how 'the Yarra Delta which occupies the large area around the Port of Melbourne is a flat surfaced, low lying land' (1974: 13). In other words, it is a horizontal surface and blank sheet suitable for development for port facilities. Similarly, Allan Meiers, in *Fisher Folk of Fishermans Bend*, relates how 'the area was a low-lying wilderness pockmarked by swamps and covered in any slightly elevated area with scrub' (2006: 9). 'Pockmarked' implies that some foul disease had disfigured the surface, or face, of the area, to which the only civilized response was to avert one's gaze in horror. 'Wilderness' and 'scrub' are loaded and pejorative terms in the lower register of the lexicon of the European landscape aesthetic and its settler diasporas. 'Low-lying' is contrasted disapprovingly with high standing in the spatial and value-laden hierarchy of preferred landscape locations.

Fishermen's Bend also suffered the indignity of a spatial dislocation and a slight name change. It was originally not where it is now. In the glossary for *Fisher Folk of Fishermans Bend*, Meiers relates how 'Fishermans Bend [was] a term used by Sandridge Council to designate all the land bounded by the seashore at Hobsons Bay, the northernmost bend of the Yarra River and Boundary St, which divides South Melbourne and Port Melbourne' (Meiers 2006: iv). In this entry, Meiers goes on to relate how 'Fishermen's Bend [was] an alternative spelling of Fisherman's Bend used interchangeably since settlement, but especially in the later 20th century', culminating in 1998 with the gazettal of 'the industrial portion north of the Westgate Freeway' as 'Fishermans Bend' (Meiers 2006: iv).

Fishermen's Bend is now a shadow or phantom place, an amputated site as it 'no longer exists' (Lewis 1995: 78) in, and as, the place it once was, because the construction of Coode Canal in the 1880s cut off the bend in the Yarra River which gave the place part of its name and rerouted the flow of water across the 'marshy peninsula' that had been embraced by Fishermen's Bend (Anon. 1887: 5). 'Coode's deep-cut canal', as Geoffrey Serle (1971: 275) calls it, cut deep into, cut across and cut off the wetlands of Fishermen's Bend. In his master's thesis at Melbourne University on the history of the development of the Port of Melbourne (as distinct from the suburb of Port Melbourne), Yarnasan makes a useful distinction between the old and the new Fishermen's Bend, with the old Fishermen's Bend being between the old course of the Yarra River and Coode Canal, and the new Fishermen's Bend south of Coode Canal. Coode Canal eventually became the new course of the Yarra River as the old course was filled, and so it was 'reclaimed', often with material gained from dredging the Yarra River. Yarnasan relates that 'the material excavated [for the construction of Coode Canal (see also Newnham 1985: 144–45; Otto 2005: 81–84)] was used mostly for reclaiming low-lying lands on the river banks and near Sandridge' (1974: 57–58). 'Reclaiming low-lying lands' is a euphemism for destroying wetlands. As dredging was a constant requirement for maintaining the operations of the Port of Melbourne, after World War I, 'the material dredged' – which was 'soft and easy to deal with' (Yarnasan 1974: 91), was used for 'filling up [...] the swampy land at Coode Island and old Fishermen's Bend' (92). Wetlands, in this view, are soft land, not hard land, 'easy to deal with', not like hard land. They are also empty low lands to be filled up by other, dry lands as if they are deficient or lacking and need to be 'reclaimed' from wetness to dryness and filled to the same level as the surrounding drylands.

A 'General Plan' of the proposed canal as recommended by Sir John Coode was produced in 1879 by the Melbourne Harbour Trust '[s]hewing [sic] [h]arbour [i]mprovements' (see Carroll 1972: 59 and Figure 3). The wetland area above, named 'Sandridge Flats', is now what is known as Fishermen's Bend, a place that has not only been amputated but that has also shifted location and been obliterated in the process. The suburb, named 'Sandridge', now Port Melbourne, was built over at least some wetland areas as previous maps (such as Christie's map of 1853) show, and because Horace Wheelwright could say in 1860 that 'the swamps and lagoons near Sandridge are all drained or built on' (1861: 67). The place named Fishermen's Bend no longer exists and is buried beneath docklands. By a further transformation, Fishermen's Bend became Fishermans Bend. Even Microsoft Word objects to the loss of the possessive plural apostrophe! The online Register of Geographic Names for Victoria has it registered definitively as 'Fishermans Bend' (Victoria State Government n.d.), though its maps continue to show 'Fishermens Bend'. The Register currently has no historical information about Fishermens Bend, though in previous iterations it evidently did as Janet Bolitho wrote in 2013 that it had 'some interesting historical information about the fishermen who lived there in the early days' (Bolitho 2013b).

After the river was rerouted via Coode Canal, Fishermen's Bend became Coode Island, as the Places Victoria heritage study relates how

> the old course of the Yarra remained as a shallow channel for many decades, creating an area of about 240 acres surrounded by water. The Island was then effectively isolated from major human impact from the 1880s to 1950s. As such it became a sanctuary for wildlife. The original vegetation as described on early survey plans was dominated by tea tree scrub, salt marsh, swamp and sandy waste with a small stand of trees, possibly swamp paperbark, which was destroyed when the canal cut through it. The swamps harboured a variety of species of plant, animal and insect life.
>
> (Vines 2013: 36)

A map of 1914 shows Coode Canal and describes Coode Island just about in its entirety as 'Swamp' (Anon. 1914).

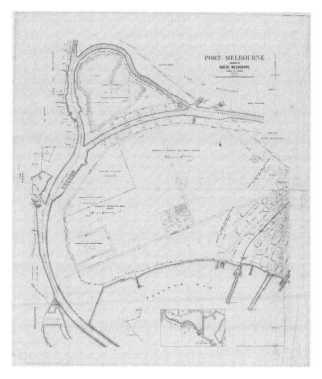

FIGURE 5: Victoria Dept. of Crown Lands and Survey 1914, Port Melbourne, Parish of South Melbourne, County of Bourke, Dept. of Crown Lands and Survey, Melbourne.

By 1914, the wetlands near the 'mouth' of the river shown on the 1864 map (see Figure 1), the site of present-day Westgate Park, had disappeared only to make a reappearance about 120 years later in the Park. The wetlands of Fishermen's Bend indicated elsewhere on the 1864 and 1879 maps had disappeared from the 1914 map, never to make a reappearance. Coode Island remained a wetland for some time.

A one-time long-term resident of the Island remembered what Coode Island was like when he was growing up. Bill Lemarquand was born on the Island in 1901 and remembered, when he was 93 years old, how

> [t]he sky was ablaze with skylarks. Every few yards there were nests on the ground. Springtime was full of their music. Sometimes there were dolphins in the river [...] The most beautiful thing I have ever seen was pigface growing on the island in spring. It was a huge pink carpet. There was a swamp in the middle before they drained it. I will never forget that pigface.
>
> (Lemarquand cited in Lahey 1994: 7)

While Coode Island was a paradise for birds because it was cut off by water from the mainland, Fishermen's Bend remained a waste wetland.

Like Coode Island, Ashbridge's Bay Marsh in Toronto was also a paradise for birds (see Fairfield 1998). Some residents of Toronto expressed similar appreciation for Ashbridge's Bay Marsh, beside which the city was built. Some residents of Melbourne, such as Michael Veitch, have recently expressed appreciation for the birdlife of Westgate Park. In a series for the Saturday edition of *The Age* devoted to 'My Secret Melbourne', in which a number of celebrities (major and minor) were interviewed (and which sadly seems to have disappeared in 2016), Veitch was asked by a journalist, 'what is your favourite escape from the city?' (2012: 10). He answered:

> Westgate Park is the great undiscovered treasure of Melbourne. It's the park under the Westgate Bridge and it's beautiful. My hobby is bird-watching and I first saw a white-fronted chat there. I discovered the park when we were filming an episode of *Fast Forward* years ago and it's a little lost spot. I've just come back to Melbourne after living in Tasmania for three years and I'm seeing the city with refreshed eyes.
>
> (Veitch 2012: 10)

Veitch is like Fred Bodsworth, a famous journalist and noted birdwatcher in Toronto, who wrote an article for the *Toronto Star* as part of a series of articles by prominent residents about their favourite places in Toronto, which for him was Ashbridge's Bay Marsh (Fairfield 1998: 13–15).

Like Melbourne and its wetlands, explorers and settlers noted Ashbridge's Bay Marsh on their maps. Like Melbourne and Fishermen's Bend, Ashbridge's Bay Marsh was subsumed into and beneath a port and an industrial site. Like many cities around the world, both Melbourne and Toronto are, or were, wetland cities, and the maps of both cities trace the transformation from swamp to city.[1] Yet rather than the Toronto of the south, Melbourne with its West Melbourne Swamp, could lay claim to being the Gotham of the south, though as the slightly larger city Sydney might object. Yet Melbourne may not want to be the Gotham of the south, if it knew that it means 'Goats' Town' in Old English (Burrows and Wallace 1999: xi).

In the late 1930s, Charles Daley related in his triumphalist history of South Melbourne that around the turn of the twentieth century

> [t]he once-despised Fishermen's Bend – a no-man's land – under the pressure of economic circumstance, has come into its own, and its sodden expanse bids fair, under the exercise of human knowledge, skill and labour, directed to its reclamation, to provide eventually scope for great projects and undertakings conducive to the advantage of the State.
>
> (Daley 1940: 325)

In other words, Fishermen's Bend for some time was a no-man's land between the competing and warring parties of industrial capitalism on one side and the sodden expanse of wetlands on the other, until the former conquered the latter in a typical war that modern industrial capitalism and its technologies liked to fight against wetlands because it was a war that was so easy to win.

This war has also been construed as a war between enlightened civilization and benighted barbarism, or between barbarisms. In the eighteenth century, the Prussian Emperor Frederick the Great proclaimed that 'whoever improves the soil, cultivates land laying waste, and drains swamp is making conquests from barbarism' (cited in Blackbourn 2008: 13). By contrast, whoever lays waste to wetlands by dumping wastes into them is making conquests from one sort of barbarism into another sort under the guise of civilization. Civilization and barbarism are closely tied, as Walter Benjamin (2003: 392) argues. Civilization is not possible without constructing and constituting barbarism as its other. Laying waste to wetlands converted them into a no-man's wasteland, like the wet wasteland of the western front in World War I (see Giblett 2009: 59–68). Such was the sad and sorry fate of Fishermen's Bend. With the development of Westgate Park, the same war continues, with the Park more an everyman and woman's wetland for recreation and regeneration in between the city, the river and the Port of Melbourne, and in suspension between the speed of hypermodernity and slowness of wetlands.

It took several decades for Fishermen's Bend to achieve the potential for industrial development that Daley envisaged:

> In this long-neglected and unoccupied area of 'Siberia', [...] great activity and interest have been aroused. On 5th November, 1936, occurred on, the north side of 'The Bend', the opening of the great and extensive factory for motor construction of the noted firm of General Motors-Holden's, whose enterprise has set the example for other leading industrial ventures and subsidiary factories.
>
> (Daley 1940: 344)

Daley does not invoke Siberia in the sense of the salt mines of Siberia, which were started by the tsars and became probably the worst destination in Stalin's 'Gulag Archipelago' of prison camps in the 1930s. Perhaps Fishermen's Bend had the same air of desolation as Siberia in the early 1930s, hence the invocation of Siberia made by contemporaries made and repeated by Daley (1940).

In her recent history of South Melbourne, Susan Priestley relates how General Motors 'moved to a virgin site at Fishermen's Bend' in 1936 (1995: 262). Perhaps the site was a virgin in the sense that it was ready for the deflowering penetration of industry. It was certainly not a virgin in the sense of being pure and unsullied because Priestley later relates that

> While in no sense a pristine wilderness, the waste land of Fishermen's Bend provided budding naturalists [...] with plenty of scope for thrilling discoveries spiced with occasional danger [...] Before it was sold off as industrial sites in 1936 the area was home to larks, water birds, monitor lizards, frogs, spiders and an infinite variety of insects.
>
> (Priestley 1995: 331)

No doubt it was also home to snakes, as is Westgate Park in the present day. Among its water birds are black swans. I saw four adults and four cygnets at Westgate Park on 14 April 2015. The Friends of Westgate Park have produced a brochure about the birds that frequent and inhabit the park, and Birds Australia conduct regular surveys.

The opening of the General Motors-Holden (GMH) plant was a momentous occasion bruited as (another) 'transformation of Fishermen's Bend', 'previously known as Siberia', into 'a hive of industry' (Anon. 1936: 4). For the managing director of GMH, 'the whole history of the factory was a romance' (Anon. 1936: 4), no doubt in the sense of being a story with a happy ending of a marriage between industrial capitalism and wasteland (though the latter was largely the creation and product of the former), and not in the sense of being the disavowal of the violence that masculinism does to feminized wetlands (see Radway 1991). The design of the GMH plant was modelled on the General Motors plant in Detroit and was described as being 'a monument to their success' (Anon. 1936: 4). The manufacturer's monumental factory overcomes the monstrous maternal marsh of the 'Great Mother' earth (in which new life is created and from which it is born) of the wetland of Fishermen's Bend in the triumph of the patriarchal paradigm over the matrifocal one.[2]

At the opening of the GMH plant, the Mayor of Port Melbourne suggested in his speech (and it was reported in the same newspaper story) that Fishermen's Bend would become the Birmingham of Australia in the next few years. This putative exemplar was taken up and echoed by the Governor of Victoria. In April of the following year, *The Argus* reported that the opening of the GMH factory at Fishermen's Bend in 1936 heralded 'the tremendous advance in secondary industries in Victoria', which 'prompted the Governor [of Victoria] to predict that Fishermen's Bend would eventually become the "Birmingham of Australia"' (Anon. 1937a: 10), even though Footscray contended with it as 'the self-styled "Birmingham of the South"' (Davison 1978: 154). No doubt the Mayor drew the parallel with Birmingham (and the Governor echoed him) because it was the city that hosted the Austin car factory, at one time 'the largest self-contained factory in the world' (Anon. n.d.). These speeches were so newsworthy that the *Border Watch* of Mount Gambier in South Australia reprinted it almost word for word on the following Tuesday. Rather than aspiring to become the Birmingham of the south in the 1930s, Melbourne in the late nineteenth century was, for Serle (1986: 130), 'in many essentials [...] very similar to Birmingham', because 'economically and culturally Victoria was [...] an offshoot of Britain'. Melbourne was a large provincial city, like Birmingham, of 'Greater Britain' across the seas. Rather than Birmingham, perhaps the Mayor and Governor should have intimated that Fishermen's Bend was the Manchester of the south because Manchester was also an industrial city built in part on wetlands (see Platt 2005).

A year after the opening of the GMH plant, *The Argus* reported that the Minister for Lands prophesied that 'the time was not far distant' when Fishermen's Bend would be 'covered with factories' (Anon. 1937b: 4). The Minister made his prophecy in announcing the sale of the second parcel of land at Fishermen's Bend after GMH for the development of the Commonwealth aircraft factory. The Minister described the area sold as having been, 'up to a year or two ago [...] almost "a no man's land"' (Anon. 1937b: 4), invoking the metaphor drawn from the trench warfare of World War I, a war fought in and over mud, much like the war fought against Fishermen's Bend by industrial technology (for mud in World War I trench warfare, see Giblett 2009: 59–68).

The first Holden rolled off the production line at the General Motors factory in Fishermen's Bend in November 1948 (Presland 2008: 62–63; Chapman and Stillman 2015: 140–41).[3] In her history of the Yarra as 'a murky river', Kristin Otto relates how 'by the mid 1960s one in every three cars on the road in Australia was a Holden; in 1974 the three-millionth Holden rolled off the line' (2005: 127). Many Australians who owned a Holden car would have known that they came from the GMH factory at Fishermen's Bend, but they would not have known anything about the wet and miry place on which the factory was built by the murky river and from which their clean, bright and shiny new commodity had come. The latter was not possible without the former. The beautiful, fetishized surfaces of the commodity are not possible without the ugly, horrific depths of the aesthetically displeasing early wetland or later wasteland where the commodity is manufactured. The sublime technology of the car powered by, and built in part from, petro-chemical products is not possible without the slime of the carboniferous wetland (for further discussion of the car along these lines, see Giblett 2008b: 92–109).

The GMH factory at Fishermen's Bend is an iconic industrial site in Australian culture and folklore; the wetlands at Fishermen's Bend should also be an iconic wetland site in Australian culture and folklore. No doubt with the closure and sale of the GMH site some sort of nostalgic memorial will be erected to this lost phase of Australian car manufacturing. Even if it isn't, the site will still live on in the memories of many Australians. Fishermen's Bend is also a fitting site for a memorial to the lost wetlands of Melbourne, a place to acknowledge and remember that Melbourne is, or was, a city of wetlands. Such a memorial would commemorate the indigenous site of Melbourne.

Fishermen's Bend is not only an iconic industrial site for the manufacture of the iconic Australian car, an icon of modernity, but also an iconic urban site for the construction of an iconic Australian freeway bridge, another icon of modernity. In 1968, work began on the construction of the Westgate Bridge, 'the largest bridge constructed in Australia' (Newnham 1985: 142) and 'one of the longest cable-stayed box girder bridges in the world' (Otto 2005: 95). The construction of the bridge not only had a huge impact at the time on the aquaterrestrial environment of Fishermen's Bend, and devastating consequences for some of its workers, but it also produced a permanent scar across the skyline and generated perpetual noise. Jenny Sinclair describes how 'its 5.6 kilometre span [Otto states 2.5 km (2005: 95)] sits over the flat lowland just south of where the Maribyrnong flows into the Yarra' (2015: 63). This statement needs to be qualified as its span sits over the flat lowland of new Fishermen's Bend just south of where the Maribyrnong River now flows into the Yarra River. It also sits over the flat lowland that sits over the wetland of old Fishermen's Bend much further south of where the Maribyrnong River once flowed into the Yarra River in the past. The result for Sinclair is that 'the Westgate Bridge partly erased the Yarra' (2015: 72), just as the rerouting of the Yarra with the Coode Canal partly erased the wetlands of Fishermen's Bend.

The construction phase cost the lives of 35 men when, as Sophie Cunningham describes in detail, 'on 15 October 1970 2000 tonnes of steel box girder grids fell 45 metres. Workers inside the hollow spans that fell were killed, and those in the construction huts below were crushed' (2011: 231). The bodies of these men were, as Peter Temple of 'Jack Irish' fame describes them, 'sunk in the foul grey crusted sludge of the Yarra's bank' (cited in Cunningham 2011: 231). 'The Westgate Bridge disaster', for Cunningham, was 'one of Melbourne's most significant tragedies' (2011: 20); Otto calls it 'Australia's worst industrial accident' (2005: 96). Work was suspended for some months, a Royal Commission followed, then some parts of the bridge were redesigned and work recommenced in 1972. It was officially opened in November 1978 and cost $202 million (Newnham 1985: 141–42). Leftover materials from the construction of the bridge were made into a hideous front entry gate to Westgate Park off Todd Road.

'The bridge', as Cunningham calls it, 'was intended as a symbol of modern Melbourne, much as the Royal Exhibition Building had been a century before. And it had failed' (2011: 233). Both the bridge and its collapse are symbols of modernity because the bridge symbolizes the monumental achievements of modern engineering while the collapse symbolizes the concomitant accidents of the modern age of disasters (Virilio 2007, 2010). An editorial in *The Age* published after the collapse called the bridge 'a monument to many dead men' (cited in Cunningham 2011: 233). Many monuments around Melbourne are to dead men who died elsewhere, whereas the Westgate Bridge is a monument to the men who worked and were killed there. Westgate Bridge is most famous, or infamous, today for being the location from which to commit a highly visible and public act of homicide or suicide, 'almost one a month' at one stage, according to official figures cited by Sinclair (2015: 73). For Otto, somewhat flippantly, 'to off oneself from the Westgate must be rather like jumping into a very large, huge, solid, muddy brown wall. A permanent outcome is not guaranteed, depending on degree of difficulty and angle of entry' (2005: 169). It is not a diving competition!

Fishermen's Bend has recently been subject to governmental planning policy and so has come under media scrutiny. On 5 July 2012, the Minister for Planning rezoned a large area of Fishermen's Bend to the capital city zone of Melbourne (City of Port Phillip 2012). Totalling 240 hectares, the Fishermans Bend Urban Renewal Area (FBURA) is bigger than the Docklands and Southbank areas of Melbourne combined. It is the largest 'urban renewal' project in Australia. Bolitho, former City of Port Phillip Mayor and Councillor, wrote a year later that 'the rezoning was made without a planning framework of any kind being in place which has led to a rash of speculative development proposals' (2013a). With

General Motors ceasing the production of cars in Australia in 2017, the end of a nearly 70-year era, the General Motors site may become the site or new Siberia of suburbia and industry. GMH is 'gearing up' to sell 'chunks of its site that was former swamp land', as reported by *The Age* on 18 April 2015 (Pallisco 2015: 12). Indeed, formerly it was wetland, but then in became wasteland before GMH took over the site and 'reclaimed' it (Otto 2005: 130).

On the same day as this report, *The Age* also reported that the Victorian government announced plans to develop Fishermen's Bend into 'an employment precinct' (cited in Preiss 2015: 11). As the then leader of the opposition pointed out, Fishermen's Bend is already 'an employment area' (cited in Preiss 2015: 11). It has been one for 80 years, and FBURA was proclaimed three years before the latest announcement. Fishermen's Bend suffers from announcement overload and is a kind of blank slate ripe for transformation, about which boosters and politicians are wont to make grandiose statements, as history attests. Ten years ago, *The Encyclopedia of Melbourne* affirmed that 'the site is best known as an industrial hub' (Brown-May and Swan 2005: 267). Once it was a wetland and wildlife habitat.

For 30 years a small section of Fishermen's Bend has also been a park. It was officially opened in November 1985 as West Gate Park. In 1996, it was rebadged as, or included in, Westgate Riverside Park that included the riverbanks, which are not part of the current Westgate Park. *The Age* reported that the then Conservation Minister announced that '[a] degraded strip of land closed off for the past 100 years will be opened to the public as a park this summer […] A triangle of land next to the Westgate Bridge has been designated as a maritime theme park' (Winkler 1996: 3).

One wonders what a maritime theme park is. A pirate's playground? Mermaids cavorting in pools? Plastic coral reefs? Bolitho told me that 'the maritime park never really eventuated. The Friends of Westgate Park still hold out hope for the Park to extend to the River in the longer term' (e-mail to the author, 1 May 2015).

Westgate Park was described in *The Encyclopedia of Melbourne* in 2005 as 'a rehabilitated wetland habitat' (Brown-May and Swan 2005: 267). It also includes an artificial pond readily seen by the motorist travelling east on the Westgate Freeway as well as rehabilitated bushland with endemic species of flora. It is thus an important inner-city recreation site with trails and picnic areas. Interpretation of the site and its history is limited, with signage at the main entrance of the park off Todd Road giving some information and showing maps. The Friends of Westgate Park website has much more information about the history and features of the park. Like many parks and reserves in inner-city situations, it is a place and time apart from the urban landscape and speedscape, inviting the city dweller to slow down, take a stroll and appreciate the sights and sounds of bushland, birds and wetland while trying to shut out the noise of the traffic and the sight of the scar of the Westgate Bridge.

NOTES

1. For maps of Toronto and Ashbridge's Bay Marsh, see: http://maps.library.utoronto.ca/dvhmp/maps.html. Accessed 20 August 2010.

2. For these two paradigms, see Giblett (2011: especially 15–38); for the maternal marsh of the 'Great Mother' earth, see also Giblett (1996: especially 127–51).

3. The lost wetlands of Melbourne do not rate a mention or a photograph in Heather Chapman and Judith Stillman's book entitled *Lost Melbourne* (2015). There should a complementary book to this called 'Lost and Found Wetlands of Melbourne', which would include descriptions and photographs of all the billabongs and other wetlands that have been destroyed or conserved and that make Melbourne what it is today.

Found and Founded Wetlands

Many of Melbourne's wetlands have been lost, but remnants of some remain and can still be found today. One such remnant is Bolin Bolin Billabong or Bolin Swamp on Bulleen Road in the Doncaster/Templestowe area. Unlike South and West Melbourne Swamps, named after compass points, this swamp was dignified with the Aboriginal name of Bolin Swamp or Bolin Bolin Billabong from the local Wurundjeri clan (Presland 2008: 75). Marilyn Bowler says that 'the word [Bolin] means "lyrebird", as does Bulleen, and repetition of a word in Aboriginal place names usually indicates that there were a lot of them' (e-mail to the author, 24 May 2015). Along similar lines, nineteenth-century naturalist Horace Wheelwright said that the lyrebird is 'the "bulla-bulla" of the natives' (1861: 64). Remnants of Bolin Bolin Billabong remain today, though much of it is now buried beneath the Trinity Grammar Sports Grounds (Costello 2009: 8).

In the late nineteenth century the Australian artist Arthur Streeton might have depicted Bolin Bolin Billabong, but chose instead on two occasions to place it firmly in the mid-ground, once beneath a clump of trees and subsumed within a sweeping panorama of a pleasing pastoral prospect as in his 1890 painting *Still Glides the Stream, and Shall Forever Glide*,[1] and once over the brow of a hill in the depths of a portrait of the country, as the backdrop for the recreation of the human figures engaging in leisure in the mid-ground of another 1890 painting, *Near Heidelberg*.[2]

On his imaginary mystery tour of the lost landscapes of Melbourne, Gary Presland describes Bolin Swamp as both 'low-lying swampy land' and as 'a large marshy area' (1985: 18, 1994: 25). A map of 1863 shows Lake Bulleen with the two parts of Bolin Bolin Billabong connected to each other and the Yarra River (Presland 2008: 77).

Billabongs are typically a cut-off loop of a river (or oxbow lake) that are often rejoined to the river in seasonal flooding. Bolin Bolin Billabong is no exception. On the 1863 map, the billabongs look like two internal organs in an anatomical illustration of the human body, such as the kidneys as depicted in Figure 1120 of *Gray's Anatomy* of 1858.[3] They are two internal organs of the body of the earth. They are connected to other organs, all of which are mutually dependent and vital for human and other life on earth. Wetlands are often described as the kidneys, liver or placenta of the earth for the life-giving and water-purifying functions they perform (see Giblett 1996: 135–37, 2008a: 186). Billabongs, for Kristin Otto, are 'hatcheries and feeding grounds, arks of the uncharismatic microfauna that sustain the ecological health of the river' (2005: 63). As Bolin Bolin Billabong is missing one part, and as wetlands are the kidneys of the body ecologic, the Yarra here is functioning on one kidney – not a healthy situation for the river and the broader bioregion of the Yarra catchment when many other wetlands have been lost.

Humans can live with only one kidney and Melbourne is living with only one of the kidneys of Bolin Bolin Billabong. The other one is buried beneath the Trinity Grammar Sports Grounds. Yet whereas human donors usually donate one of their kidneys so that another human, such as a family member, can continue to live, one of the Bolin kidneys has been 'donated' or sacrificed so that a school can have a sports ground. The donated Bolin kidney is no longer living and functioning as a wetland kidney in the body of the earth, but it has become a manicured sports ground, a zombie (one of the 'living dead'), inscribed on the surface of the earth. The fluid shape and dynamics of the Bolin kidney have been replaced by the mathematized spaces of sport.

Traditional cultures, including Australian Aboriginal, ancient Chinese and premodern European cultures, regard the body as an earth and/or the earth as a body with life-giving organs and processes (see Giblett 2008a: 157–90). Modern cultures regard the body and the earth as a machine with mechanical parts and processes (see Giblett 2008a: 19–36, 90–107, 125–56). Regarding the earth as a body (and a body as the earth) is one way of acknowledging and respecting the life-giving organs and processes of both, including wetlands. Humans should care for wetlands like they do their own organs and body. After all, we only have one body and one earth, one body of the earth joined in symbiosis. The human body is in symbiosis with the symbiotic earth.

Like West Melbourne Swamp (or Batman's Swamp) was in the past, Bolin Swamp 'is an important source of eels, fish, water birds and vegetable foods and a popular camping place for the Aboriginal people' (Presland 1985: 18, 1994: 25; see also Eidelson 2014: 41; Lacey 2004: 21). Like Le Mans Swamp, Bolin Swamp is habitat for the abominable swarming and sustaining creature of eels. In their book about Merri Creek, Ian Clark and Toby Heydon (2004: 31) cite the journal of early settler William Thomas, who described how Bolin Bolin Billabong was 'a place of significant economic value to Aboriginal people [...] While fishing for eels at Bolin was a seasonal activity, Aboriginal people visited the site at other times of the year, but usually between June and November'. Otto, in her book on the Yarra River, concurs and describes Bolin as 'the great Wurundjeri food source and ceremonial ground' (2005: 65). Otto includes an aerial photograph on the same page depicting 'what's left of the great Bolin-Bolin Billabong' (2005: 65). There is not much left, but there is something left worthy of conservation.

What's left and what's being rehabilitated of the Bolin Bolin Billabong still make it an important place for plants to grow and a vital habitat for animals. In their seminal article on Bolin Bolin Billabong, Karl Just and Garry French argue that

> [t]he site has outstanding natural values and supports disjunct rare plant species, many old-growth River Red Gum (*Eucalyptus camaldulensis*) trees, a high diversity of bat species and one of the most diverse and intact bird communities in the inner city.
>
> (Just and French 2010: 11)

Because of these values, Just and French go on to relate how, in the 1990s, 'research projects were undertaken to document the billabong's botanical composition [...] It was found that Bolin supported an assemblage of rare plant species, many that are of disjunct occurrence and more common in northern Victoria' (2010: 11).

Meyer Eidelson, in his book on Aboriginal Melbourne, concurs that 'Bolin Bolin is a delightful, almost secret location, which contains rare and threatened species of fauna and flora not found elsewhere in the Yarra River corridor, including one of the most intact remnant River Red Gum wetland habitats' (2014: 56). Like Westgate Park, with traffic speeding by on Westgate Bridge, most people travelling along Bulleen Road have little knowledge of Bolin Bolin Billabong. Unlike Westgate Park, which is highly visible from Westgate Bridge, Bolin Bolin Billabong is largely invisible from Bulleen Road. Eidelson concludes by emphasizing the Aboriginal significance of Bolin Bolin Billabong that 'today remains a place of spiritual and cultural inspiration to the Wurundjeri people' (2014: 57; see also Otto 2005: 197).

Bolin Bolin Billabong is part of the catchment for the Yarra River and part of the bioregion in which the city and people of Melbourne live. As part of the catchment and bioregion, Just and French relate how Bolin Bolin Billabong is

> one of only several billabongs remaining from at least 50 that were formerly scattered along the Chandler Basin, a floodplain basin of the lower Yarra River formed by an ancient lake system. In the early days of European settlement wetlands were seen by many as unclean and disease-ridden areas, and most of the billabongs were filled in to utilise the ground for agriculture, roads and sports fields. Groundwater was drained to make way for agriculture and several of the billabongs were used as tip sites and filled with garbage.
>
> (Just and French 2010: 11)

As a result of the sad and sorry history typical of many wetlands around Melbourne and around the world, Just and French relate how

> Billabong wetlands comprise some of the most endangered ecosystems in Victoria. Damming and regulation of most major river systems has greatly reduced the capacity of lowland streams to flood onto adjacent plains, often leaving billabongs stranded and dry. Unless more focus is given to these highly significant icons, they are likely to become increasingly degraded and modified over time.
>
> (Just and French 2010: 11)

Bolin Bolin Billabong, for Just and French, is one such Billabong where that focus should be directed, as '[o]f the several remaining billabongs, Bolin is the only wetland whose bathymetry and vegetation has not been significantly modified, although the hydrological processes that determine its wetting and drying cycles have been greatly altered' (Just and French 2010: 11).

Research in the 1990s not only focused on the botanic composition of Bolin Bolin but also 'investigate[d] its current hydrological regime' and 'concluded the billabong was flooding far less than historically, and an appropriate flooding regime was recommended' (Just and French 2010: 11). This is a pressing and urgent task as Just and French go on to relate how

> [b]y the late twentieth century Bolin had been greatly impacted by agricultural practices and weed invasion. Cattle were present in the wetland until recently, pugging the banks and grazing sensitive aquatic herbfields. Weeds had invaded much of the site [...] This highly modified habitat was now unsuitable for many ground foraging birds and restricted recruitment of native plant species. The surrounding floodplain had been mostly cleared and developed, although Bolin still retained a relatively intact canopy and shrub layer.
>
> (Just and French 2010: 11)

In the 1990s, Parks Victoria began a programme of restoration. In 2004, Parks Victoria ranger Cam Beardsell began an intensive programme of vegetation management. Just and French describe how this program

> included hand weeding of exotic grasses and herbs in the northern bay of the billabong, which supported the highest density of rare native flora [...] During these works additional rare flora species were discovered, many of which are absent or known only from very few other occurrences in the Melbourne region, and demonstrate biogeographic affinities with the Murray River floodplain.

Seed collected from several of the most localised species was grown by the Friends of Yarra Parklands nursery and used to enrich the current populations at Bolin.

(Just and French 2010: 12)

Just and French conclude that

[t]he management works at Bolin Bolin Billabong span at least 20 years and act as a model for restoration of billabongs elsewhere. The works that continue to progress have secured this wetland as one of the greatest jewels of the Yarra River.

(Just and French 2010: 12)

Yet what Just and French refer to as the 'exciting stormwater harvesting project to restore the natural hydrological regime to the billabong' (2010: 12), 'ended up falling in a heap and never went ahead […] it is very unfortunate, so management of the hydrology is still a pressing concern' (Karl Just, e-mail to the author, 1 June 2015). Management of the introduced species, such as carp and weeds, is also still a pressing concern. An iconic Melbourne wetland, a remnant of a much larger wetland, a wetland that can still be found when so many have been lost, should not be allowed to go to rack and ruin.

Bolin Bolin Billabong was being rehabilitated in the late 1990s and early 2000s, but much of it is now in a degraded state, though weed control and revegetation was thankfully recommenced recently in December 2014, with completion of the project scheduled by June 2018, according to signage at the site. The sign states that Melbourne Water have engaged Fulton Hogan Ecodynamics to carry out the weed control and revegetation with the Wurundjeri people 'on this site of indigenous cultural heritage'.[4] The works 'involve the removal of invasive weeds […] followed by a significant revegetation program. The goal is to improve the condition of vegetation and habitat for native birds, frogs and reptiles'.[5] When I visited Bolin Bolin on 1 July 2015, weed control and plots of revegetation had been started. Bolin Bolin Billabong is also a site of indigenous natural heritage as it is a relict billabong with 'many old-growth River Red Gum (*Eucalyptus camaldulensis*) trees' (Just and French 2010: 11) that are hundreds of years old. It should also be recognized as a site of settler heritage, because these magnificent trees with their huge branching limbs pre-date settlement, and because early settlers recognized its importance for Aboriginal people (as we have seen). It should be, in short, a heritage site for all people, for all time, something from the past that is passed on to future generations in good condition. Everyone should look after it as part of the larger Yarra River bioregion.

Billabong, like swamp, can be a pejorative term. Billabongs, as Otto bluntly puts it, are 'not some weird, nostalgic theme-park idea of the Outback' (2005: 60), as in the immortal opening line of Banjo Paterson's 1903 bushman ballad 'Waltzing Matilda': 'once a jolly swagman camped by a billabong'. Or in terms of the immortal opening line of Dorothea McKellar's jingoistic 1904 poem 'I Love a Sunburnt Country': 'They [billabongs] are part of the poetic drought-and-flooding-rain cycle of our natural landscape'. Otto estimates that, 'since [the European] settlement of Victoria, about a third of river wetlands [or billabongs] have completely disappeared and almost another third have been partly ruined' (2005: 60). Bolin Bolin Billabong would fit into both categories as one of its 'kidneys' has completely disappeared, while the other is partly ruined and rehabilitated. One part of the Billabong, the site of the Trinity Grammar sports ground, is invisible, while the adjacent and partly ruined part is visible. Melbourne is a visible city on a largely invisible site.

Banyule Flats are another case in point. For Ward they are 'the biggest billabong in the urban region' (2011: 108). The Flats comprise Banyule Billabong, Banyule Swamp and adjacent 'wet depressions', as Lacey (2004: 36) calls them. They are all remnants of the chains of the billabongs that accompany the Yarra and its tributaries. Billabongs, for Ward, are 'an ecosystem that had been, until recently, methodically and systematically destroyed. Melbourne's waterways were once all fringed with wetlands' (2011: 108). These wetlands have been described as 'the Kakadu of the Yarra Valley' (Glen Jameson cited in Ward 2011: 163). The wetlands of Kakadu are indigenous habitat, a World Heritage site, a Ramsar Convention wetland of international importance and an iconic tourist destination. On her pilgrimage on the Yarra from former delta to swampy source, Ward finds 'one of the only remnant billabongs on the Yarra [...] The last bit of Kakadu on the Yarra' (2011: 168). City-dwelling Australians tend to ignore or overlook the local wetlands on their doorstep in the southern coastal cities and value the exotic wetlands in the remote north, such as Kakadu. Both should be given equal consideration and conservation.

Yarra biographer Otto bemoans the fate and mourns the loss of the Yarra billabongs:

> The process of the ruination and annihilation of the Yarra's billabongs, lagoons, waterholes and creeks has been repeated over and over for more than a century. The stage can take decades: a waterway or wetlands [*sic*] becomes a receptacle for human sewage and rubbish, is rightly pronounced a disgusting health hazard, and the problem is solved by either filling it in, concreting it or putting it underground.
>
> (Otto 2005: 90)

Modern human beings using industrial technologies are not only the judge, jury and executioner of pronouncing the waterway or wetland guilty and executing it, but they are also the criminal who perpetrated the crime of making it into a receptacle for sewage and rubbish in the first place. The waterways or wetlands were unable to defend themselves against the charges brought against them as they had no legal standing and so were not entitled to legal representation in this kangaroo court.

Finding other wetlands

The Cheetham wetlands, or Cheetham Swamp, are 420 hectares of artificial and natural lagoons that lie on the western side of Port Phillip Bay and on the south-western outskirts of Melbourne. Aboriginal occupation and use have been well-documented; European exploration of the area is also well-documented, with Grimes's map (Shaw 1989: 203, Figure 38) describing it as 'swampy' and James Flemming ([1802–03] 1984) mentioning it in his *Journal*; European settlement is well-documented too, but it was spasmodic due to the wetlands. Waterbird inhabitation is well-documented and long-standing.[6]

The configuration of the wetlandscape and the hydrologic regime has changed over time and has even been highly modified. Parks Victoria states that

> [t]he series of ponds that now make up the migratory bird habitat and conservation area called Cheetham Wetlands were constructed in the 1920s by Cheetham Salt Pty Ltd. Sea water was fed into the shallow ponds and allowed to evaporate. Dried salt was then harvested from the floor of the lagoons. This operation continued until the early 1990s, when the site was purchased by the Victorian Government. The more environmentally important bayside part of the original saltworks now comprises Cheetham Wetlands.
>
> (Parks Victoria 2012b)

The Cheetham wetlands are an important wetland habitat. Parks Victoria states that

> Cheetham Wetlands, consisting of salt marshes and natural and artificial lagoons of Skeleton Creek, are a natural bird haven. These internationally significant wetlands provide important feeding and habitat areas for thousands of migratory birds from Japan, Siberia and New Zealand.
>
> (Parks Victoria 2012a)

They also provide important feeding and habitat areas for thousands of non-migratory Australian waterbirds, such as ducks.

According to the *Wetlands Australia National Wetlands Update 2012* produced by Parks Victoria for the Australian government's Department of the Environment and Energy, the Port Phillip Bay Western Shoreline and Bellarine Peninsula Ramsar site is

> one of 11 wetlands of international significance in Victoria listed under the Ramsar Convention. The endangered saltmarsh communities provide a valuable food source and roosting habitat for many of the native and migratory birds that frequent the wetlands, and are vital in supporting the critically endangered orange-bellied parrot. The site regularly supports more than 20 000 water birds, and more than 1 per cent of the global population of several listed species including curlew sandpipers, double-banded plovers, red-necked stints, and sharp-tailed sandpipers.
>
> (Tuohy 2012)

The update goes on to outline some of the typical pressures facing the wetlands on urban fringes:

> Given the wetlands are so close to Victoria's major population centre, many factors have combined to place pressure on the Ramsar site and adjoining lands over the years. Rubbish dumping, poor drainage, stock grazing and infestation by pest plants and animals such as boxthorn or rabbits have all taken their toll on the vegetation communities throughout the region. In addition, there are increasing demands on the use of the site for recreation and open public space for health and well-being in rapidly expanding urban communities such as nearby Point Cook. It is clear that a well-planned and integrated approach is required to sustainably manage the unique values of the Ramsar wetlands and the globally important species they support.
>
> (Tuohy 2012)

Various management agencies responded, and in 2008

> the Port Phillip Bay Western Shoreline Protection Program commenced as a partnership between Parks Victoria, the Department of Sustainability and Environment, Port Phillip Westernport Catchment Management Authority, local government and other key stakeholders, including Melbourne Water and Birds Australia. The program aimed to establish effective partnerships with stakeholders, deliver integrated and effective pest plant and animal control programs, map vegetation and site use by shorebirds, and develop community engagement programs for building stewardship within local communities.

The work of the Program was recently recognised when it was awarded a Victorian Coastal Council Award for Coastal Planning and Management in 2011. The award acknowledged the value of the conservation initiative and the establishment of successful partnerships between the various land managers to meet the challenges of wetland management. Since late 2008 the steering committee has obtained significant site investment, delivered improved pest management, informed and provided opportunities for engagement of local communities, and has also established a framework for improved cooperation across the site. The successful delivery of the project has enabled Australian Government Caring for Our Country funding to be secured until 2013. This will enable further engagement with local communities to help protect flora and fauna in this internationally significant wetland.

(Tuohy 2012)

Funding for 'Caring for Our Country' was slashed in the 2014 federal budget so these projects face an uncertain future.

More care is given to the artificial wetlands founded in the iconic Royal Park. One of the wetland areas within Royal Park (now called 'the Billabong') was constructed around 1990 as part of the staged implementation of the 1984 masterplan design (Taylor 2014: 36). Another wetland area within Royal Park, 'Trin Warren Tam-boore', meaning 'bellbird waterhole', was founded in 2005 (Freeman and Pukk 2015: 244, with accompanying photograph). In the words of an interpretive brochure, the wetland is

designed to treat and recycle stormwater run-off from the roads, rooftops and gutters of surrounding suburbs [...] It consists of two linked ponds. The 'treatment pond' acts as a natural filter, with banks densely covered by native Australian plants that treat and clean stormwater through natural biological processes. The processed clean water then goes to the 'storage pond' and is used to irrigate extensive areas of Royal Park in summer, while the remainder flows through to Port Phillip Bay.

(Royal Park 2012)

These kinds of 'environmental services' were provided by natural wetlands in the past but were not recognized and valued before they were lost. Now the urban environment is being retrofitted with artificial wetlands to serve the functions that natural wetlands had previously served.

The Royal Park artificial wetland scheme

works so successfully that abundant quantities of Class A water have been delivered; in its first productive summer the reclaimed water maintained valuable street trees and 15 hectares of public open space, including the Royal Park Public Golf Course and nearby sports fields.

(Royal Park 2012)

It is an irony of history not lost on the student of wetlands that artificial wetlands are being constructed around the world to serve the function of natural wetlands that were lost either by dredging and draining or by filling. The Royal Park wetland is a window into the past through which we can see what the lost wetlands of Melbourne might have looked like if they had been allowed to go on living. As it is also 'home to a wide range of plants and animals' (Royal Park 2012), it is also a habitat in which we may appreciate what species the lost wetlands of Melbourne supported and what 'environmental services' they provided to those species, including humans.

Unlike Perth (Western Australia), with its two or three wetland memorials and several interpretive projects – including one in which an elevated, artificial and interactive wetland was recreated out of a reflective pool in the Perth Cultural Centre; and another in which Edith Cowan University and the City of Perth mounted an exhibition in the Perth Town Hall in 2014, comprising archival maps showing the lost Perth wetlands and a virtual 3D digital view of Perth's wetlands as they might have looked in 1827 (Western Australian Museum 2015; Ryan et al. 2015) – Melbourne does not seem to have any memorials or projects. It should have them to commemorate this history and to celebrate the role of wetlands in Victorian ecology of the past, as well as their role in Victorian ecology in the present and for the future. Along similar lines to the City of Perth, the City of Melbourne could also develop an exhibition in the Melbourne Town Hall Gallery comprising archival maps of Melbourne showing the wetlands, and a virtual 3D digital view reimagining Melbourne's wetlands as they might have looked in 1835.

NOTES

1. A reproduction of this painting is available online at: https://media.artgallery.nsw.gov.au/collection_images/8/859%23%23S.jpg. Accessed 1 May 2015.
2. A reproduction of this painting is available online at: http://www.ngv.vic.gov.au/explore/collection/work/3055/. Accessed 1 May 2015.
3. A reproduction of this illustration is available online at: https://www.bartleby.com/107/illus1120.html. Accessed 1 May 2015.
4. Melbourne Water, 'Waterway Improvement Works: Bolin Bolin Billabong Weed Control and Revegetation', signage at Bolin Bolin Billabong, viewed 1 July 2015.
5. Melbourne Water signage.
6. On all three counts and European exploration, see Vines and Lane (1990).

Lost Foundations

Federation Square, on the corner of Flinders and Swanston Streets, is in, or is, the heart of Melbourne. It was created for the commemoration of the Federation of Australia in 2001 and set beside the Yarra River, whose banks were a wetland at the time of settlement and for some time thereafter. All of Melbourne's wetlands past and present are largely absent from *Nearamnew* (2001), Paul Carter's inscription in stone of the history of the city of Melbourne and the colony of Victoria in Federation Square. This absence is surprising, as the presence of these wetlands and their Aboriginal peoples is well-documented in many of the same sources that were used for the creation of the artwork, as well as in those that were used for the second chapter of *Modern Melbourne* (such as Presland 1985 in both instances).

The absence of Melbourne's wetlands and Aboriginal people from *Nearamnew* is also surprising as Carter (1987: 207–20) discusses the early history of Melbourne extensively in *The Road to Botany Bay*, again using some of the same sources as I have used in Chapter Two (such as Grant and Serle 1957), without mentioning Melbourne's wetlands, and without using Presland (1985) or mentioning Melbourne's Aboriginal peoples. Carter writes wetlands and Aboriginal peoples out of history, even out of what he calls 'spatial history' (including that of Melbourne), whether it is the writing of his books in ink (Carter 1987, 2005), or his inscription in stone on the pavement of Federation Square. *Nearamnew* does not even acknowledge the wetlands that were on its site, let alone mourn their loss or commemorate their life.

This chapter critiques *Nearamnew* and argues that it represents a lost opportunity to create a public work of art that celebrates the wetlands which were the environmental context in which the city of Melbourne and the colony of Victoria were founded, and a lost opportunity to mourn the loss of wetlands and to commemorate their role as living places of and for plants and animals, and as sources of sustenance for the local Aboriginal people and nutriment for the settlers and city-dwellers to grow their crops and graze their animals.

Melbourne's wetlands were well and truly colonized. Colonization is just as much about places as it is about people. Colonization took place in, and of, the drylands and wetlands of Australia as the history of Melbourne shows.

Colonization is just as much about nature as it is about culture. And so is decolonization. Frantz Fanon, the pioneer theorist of decolonization, argues that

> hostile nature, obstinate and fundamentally rebellious, is in fact represented
> in the colonies by the bush, by mosquitoes [from swamps], natives and fever
> [from mosquito bites], and colonization is a success when all this indocile nature
> has finally been tamed. Railways across the bush, the draining of swamps and
> a native population which is non-existent politically and economically *are in
> fact one and the same thing.*
>
> (Fanon [1965] 1967: 201, emphasis added)

In the case of Melbourne, as with other Australian cities such as Perth, colonization was also a matter of railways through the (drained) swamps (as we will see in Chapter Nine). Swamps suffered the double indignity of being drained and then having railways put through them. Swamps were drained, trained and railroaded. Colonization was also a matter of 'taming' and 'cultivating' the bush into gardens, as Graeme Davison (1986: 125) notes.

In the era of so-called postcolonialism, it is necessary to ask the following question: what process of decolonization has been carried out in cities like Melbourne in relation to the colonization of spaces and places, like wetlands, by maps (from which wetlands are absent or on which they are present but reduced to a two-dimensional surface and frozen in time), by settlers and by urban development? Not much if *Nearamnew* in Federation Square is anything to go by. The wetlands of Melbourne are absent from *Nearamnew*. Decolonization will not be fully achieved until spaces and places are decolonized, and not only external, terrestrial and extraterrestrial spaces and places, but also internal, corporeal spaces and places, especially those regions of the human body – the 'nether regions' – associated with the dark and dank regions of the earth – the nether(wet)lands.

In this chapter, I not only critique *Nearamnew* but I also propose ways of commemorating and celebrating Melbourne's wetlands. Despite its ambitions 'to dream place into being', as Emily Potter (2007: 248) puts it in her discussion of Carter's *Nearamnew*, it largely ignores the history of Melbourne as a wetland city, the history of the place of Melbourne as a wetland and the history of the wetlands on the site for Melbourne, and so, in Sophie Cunningham's (2011: 127) terms, it does not make much sense of Melbourne, at least of its wetland history and geography.

Nearamnew also largely ignores the history of its very own site, as once upon a time it was a wetland, and so it does not dream its own place into being. Federation Square is located on the south-east corner of Swanston and Flinders Streets. It is also opposite St Paul's Cathedral to the north, which was built, as Michael Cannon puts it, 'on one of the worst sites in the lowest part of the city that could have been selected' ([1966] 1976: 15). Flinders Street in the early days of settlement was a swamp (Dunstan 2000: 1). The eventual site for Federation Square was probably swampier than the site for Flinders Street and the cathedral as it was located on the lower, riverside of Flinders Street. The monumental sacred cathedral built to the glory of God and the secular monument built to the glory of the nation are both located in a swamp. They remind me of the White House, the home of the most powerful person in the world, built in a swamp (see Giblett 2016: 215–24). The monstrous swamp makes the monumental possible. The monumental represses the monstrous and maternal swamp that made it possible. The monumental sacred cathedral rises above and sublimates the sacral and slimy swamp; the secular monument paves over the monstrous wetland below and before it.

Federation Square was built over the Jolimont railyards and the Princes Bridge Railway Station, which were constructed, in turn, on the swampy banks of the Yarra between Swanston and Russell Streets. This area is described by Robyn Annear as 'the reedy swamp' (2014: 47) and explicitly documented by Kristin Otto (2005: 64). This 'enormous wetland', as Cunningham describes it, was 'fed by a stream that trickled down from Fitzroy Gardens before being absorbed into an area rich with bird and plant life' (2011: 160). This stream still trickles down through Fitzroy Gardens. Cunningham had earlier related how 'latent under the Jolimont railyards [and so under Federation Square] are the remnants of the broad wetlands that sustained the Wurundjeri clans' (2011: 25). Beneath the pavement of Federation Square lies the Jolimont railyards, and beneath them lies the swamp, with the city as a palimpsest written over previous layers, and written on the surface of the earth. Similarly, the Footscray marshalling yards were constructed over West Melbourne Swamp (or Batman's Swamp). Beneath the iconic technology of modern railways and their stations and marshalling yards lies the pre-modern wetland at the heart of the city. Colonialism in Melbourne was also a matter of railways through the swamp (as we will see in Chapter Nine).

Nearamnew largely ignores the forgotten history and lost geography of its site as a wetland and of Melbourne as a wetland city, despite Carter referring in *Mythform*, his book about the project, to Gary Presland's (1985) first book on the Kulin, the local indigenous people, and acknowledging Presland's account of them (though there is no account of the Kulin's practical use of the wetlands or of the sustenance the wetlands gave them) (2005: 11, see also 120, note 2). As a result, Carter reduces Presland's book to a source about the Kulin people. He does not regard it as an account of the specificities of their place and their practical uses of Nearamnew (the place, not the monument), and so he does not consider it to be about the wetlandscape of Melbourne. Carter abstracts place into space in *Mythform* as he does in *The Road to Botany Bay*. This is so despite invoking 'Nearamnew' in *Mythform* as a name meaning the 'place on which the city of Melbourne is now built' (Carter 2005: 11). People are also abstracted into static figures posed against the tableau of the background of Melbourne and are not respected as active agents engaged in the practices of everyday life and deriving a livelihood from the wetlands and drylands of Melbourne. People, place, practices and processes should be dreamt, thought and traced together.

For Carter,

> the precise location of this 'place' [on which the city of Melbourne is now built] is unclear: in the absence of any evidence to the contrary, it might have referred to the point on the river where it was now planned to construct Federation Square.
>
> (Carter 2005: 11)

This is idle speculation and special pleading for Federation Square. There is also evidence (to the contrary) dating from 1997 that Nearamnew does not refer to such a small, specific site, but to 'the Melbourne area' (Eidelson 2014: 5). The location of Nearamnew was not unclear for the local Aboriginal people and certainly the location of Melbourne is not unclear for all to see today. Wherever it was, the location of this place for local Aboriginal people and for early explorers, settlers, founders and chroniclers included and referred to the wetlands of the area (as we have seen). The wetlands beyond those adjoining the Yarra are absent from both Carter's accounts of the place, one written and printed in ink in *Mythform* (2005) and *The Road to Botany Bay* (1987), and the other inscribed in stone in *Nearamnew*.

The Yarra is also a dubious name as, according to Garryowen (Edmund Finn), the Aboriginal name for the river is 'Birr-arrung', whereas 'Yarra Yarra' refers, for Garryowen ([1835–52] 1967: 37–38), to the falls upstream. For some, 'yarra yarra' means 'ever-flowing'. Melbourne was founded on the banks of the dubious river Yarra, on the dubious site of Nearamnew and on its indubitable adjoining and much more widespread wetlands, but the larger place in which the city was and is now built included many other wetlands absent from Carter's accounts.

The place of, and site for, Melbourne is regarded reductively by Carter as located benignly and pastorally 'by the banks of the Yarra' (Potter 2007: 250) – as Potter puts it in writing about *Nearamnew* – like in a Constable painting, as if the rest of the site for Melbourne were a *tabula rasa*, a blank space for the grid-plan settlement to be inscribed on; a *terra nullius*, an empty land to be filled with a city, rather than a wetland traced with people and stories; and an *aquaterra fullius*, a full wetland. G. H. Haydon's depiction of *Melbourne in 1804*[1] showing the muddy and swampy banks of the Yarra River, belies a Constable-type bucolic representation of the dry and grassed banks of the Yarra. In *The Road to Botany Bay*, Carter discusses extensively the grid-plan town, including Melbourne, and how it is written over the surface of the earth with little regard for what was there in the first place, and no regard for the first, Aboriginal people who owned the place but are written out of his spatial history.

What Carter calls 'the rational principle of the grid' (1987: 203) was used to produce what he also calls 'the grid-plan town' (209), which was, like the map that preceded it and made it possible with its 'grid of longitude and latitude' (204), 'paradoxically placeless and directionless' (209). The grid-plan town was derived from the military camp which produces what Henri Lefebvre calls 'an instrumental space [...], a rectangular, strictly symmetrical space [...] with its strict grid' (1991: 244–45). It also produced what he goes on to call 'the cult of rectitude, in the sense of right angles and straight lines' (305). Through this 'cult', Lefebvre goes on to argue, 'the order of power, the order of the male is thus naturalised' (1991: 305, see also 361), and the female order of the swamps is alienated.

The grid achieved this power because it is, for Carter 'the supremely historical figure' (1987: 210), or perhaps more precisely the supreme historical figure that supersedes the pre-history of Aboriginal people and of Port Phillip Bay (both of which Carter ignores). On the one hand, the grid was 'a means of speeding up the appearance of things, for hastening the nearness of distant objects' (221), and on the other it 'shared the qualities of the explorer's track and the appeal of the picturesque view' (219). Both are necessary for capitalist 'progress' and for figuring Aboriginal people out of history and geography, out of time (past, present and future), space (place) and out of landscape. 'The rational principle of the grid', as Carter (203) calls it, was not only associated with 'the myth of progress' (215), but was what Carter calls 'the matrix of physical progress' itself, capitalist 'progress' (219). Matrix succeeds *mater*, or mother, the 'Great Mother' of the marshes. The Port Phillip colony was a colony for capitalists because, as Carter (203,) puts it, 'the rational and equal division of land into purchasable blocks was the essential precondition of capitalist settlement [...] what the grid generated was wealth' (212). The grid was a machine for producing private property and thus private wealth. Melbourne is a case in point, as Carter discusses in the above and as Cannon ([1966] 1976) documents in *The Land Boomers*.

What T. M. Perry describes in relation to Melbourne as 'the imposition on the landscape [including the wetlandscape] of the grid' (1986: 131) had a profound and devastating effect on Great Mother Earth, the *magna mater*, especially on her most fertile and vulnerable places, such as swamps. As marsh and modernity are inimical to each other, so are the grid of the matrix and the body of the *mater* (despite the fact that the former is derived from the latter, though as a mathematized abstraction). Indeed, as matrix and modernity go hand in hand, so do marsh and *mater*. Modernity and matrix are inimical to marsh and *mater*. The grid is also the supreme historical figure of the divide between nature and culture because, as Keith Thomas puts it, 'neatness, symmetry and formal patterns had always been the distinctively human way of indicating the separation between culture and nature' (1984: 256). Or more precisely, they are the patriarchal way of indicating the separation, and not the mere separation as if both could then co-exist in harmony, but the instrument of colonization of nature by culture.

The grid is composed of straight lines whose power is not just confined to the rational principle of the grid, or to the grid-plan town with its straight streets and lot boundaries, but it extends to canals, drains and railway lines. The straight line was not only 'the offspring of the intentional gaze', as Carter (1987: 222) puts it, but it was also the instrument par excellence of empire. The straight line rules, okay? The straight line subjects the unruly and recalcitrant wetland to a rationalist, linear logic. The map or plan renders the heights, depths and extension of the land as virtual two-dimensional surface of length and breadth repressing what is below, including wetlands.

The 'artificial space of the grid', as Carter puts it, 'brought the "country" into being as country, which created the dialectical boundary between town and non-town. It was through the frame of the town that the bush acquired direction, became a focus of strangeness and an object of desire' (1987: 220), became, in a word, both uncanny and the device to overcome uncanniness, including that of wetlands, the uncanny place *par excellence* (see Giblett 1996: 25–51). Town and non-town, city and country are not only in a mutually constitutive dialectical relationship, but they are also mediated by the excluded middle or third term of what Raymond Williams ([1984] 1989) called 'livelihood' (see also Giblett 2011: 239–42). Aboriginal peoples and early settlers of Melbourne found and derived their livelihoods at least in part in and from the wetlands of the city.

Although, as Carter argues, the ultimate effect of what he calls the grid-plan town's 'geometrical tendency was to iron out spatial differences, to nullify the strangeness of here and there' (1987: 221), the uncanniness of the unhomely, this was not initially performed, as he goes on to suggest, as 'a means of translating the country into a place for reliable travelling' (221), but it was performed for safe settling, to render the unhomely homely in the first place. Only then could travel be undertaken. While the elements of the grid certainly rendered, as he puts it, 'the topographical peculiarities of the country [including swamps] "level" at least in theory' (221), their initial effect was not to render travelling itself 'an activity independent of place' (221), but to make the unhomely homely.

Carter concludes that 'of course, the local topography [of Melbourne, or any other grid-plan town for that matter, such as Perth] could not be wholly ignored' (213).[2]

And Robert Hoddle, the surveyor who designed Melbourne's grid, could not, and did not, wholly ignore it. More precisely, he did largely ignore the local topography inside the grid, such as the fact that Elizabeth Street was a creek, but he could not wholly ignore the local topography outside the grid, such as the surrounding swamps. Indeed, the swamps constrained the location of his grid in the first place between West Melbourne Swamp (or Batman's Swamp) to the west, the swamp of what became Treasury and Fitzroy Gardens to the east and the swamplands to the south along the Yarra River between Russell and Swanston Streets. Robert Russell's *Map Shewing* [*sic*] *the Site of Melbourne: And the Position of the Huts & Buildings Previous to the Foundation of the Township by Sir Richard Bourke in 1837* depicts Hoddle's grid located hard up against 'Batman's Hill' and a 'flat' extending into a 'salt lake at times quite dry' (Russell *c*.1837).[3] It also depicts marshy ground along the Yarra River between approximately Swanston and Spring Streets. Maree Coote later describes this map showing Melbourne as 'official, sparse, marshy' (2012: 50). Unlike Hoddle, in *The Road Botany Bay* Carter does not wholly ignore the local topography inside the grid, such as that 'Elizabeth Street was a creek' (1987: 213). However, unlike Hoddle, he wholly ignores the local topography outside the grid, such as the surrounding swamps.

Carter, of course, was not writing a history of Melbourne in the chapter of *The Road to Botany Bay* devoted to the city (and nor am I), or a history of the lost and found wetlands of Melbourne (as I am), but he was writing 'an essay in spatial history' (as the subtitle of the original British edition of *The Road to Botany Bay*, published by Faber, proclaims) of the grid-plan town using Melbourne as an instance or case study. Spatial history is concerned with the grid-plan town written on the surface of the earth and not with what was there in the first place, the place that surrounds, constrains the location and underlies the surfaces of the earth and the plan. Spatial history is not history of place, not placial history; Carter's spatial history of Melbourne is not a history of a place of wetlands.

Carter was also writing 'an exploration of landscape and history' (as the subtitle of the American edition of *The Road to Botany Bay*, published by the University of Chicago Press in 1988, indicates) and again not a history of Melbourne, or a history of the decolonization of wetlands in the history of the present (as I am); he was surveying the surfaces of the earth as they are presented to the eye in keeping with the concept and history of landscape, so he was not encountering the depths of the land (including wetland) as they address the surfaces and depths of the body and as they are latent in the history of the city and its site. Carter thus ignores the local topography of Melbourne (just as Hoddle largely did, but could not wholly do), and repeats on the page what Hoddle drew on the map and on the ground: the writing out of wetlands, in Hoddle's case from geography and in Carter's from spatial history. Just as the grid-plan town is colonialist, so Carter's various histories of Melbourne inscribed on paper and in stone are neocolonialist.[4] Carter writes roughshod over the earth, its wetlands and their Aboriginal peoples. He is in solidarity with his Aussie mates who ride roughshod over the bush, and other writers who write roughshod over it too.[5]

In *Mythform*, Carter makes one passing reference (and Potter [2007: 254] cites it) to the fact that 'before the Yarra was banked and its adjoining swamplands were drained' there was 'a network of local [...] billabongs' (2005: 11), including where Federation Square and *Nearamnew* are located. The swamplands and billabongs of early Melbourne, however, were much more extensive than those that could be considered as the Yarra's, or to merely adjoin it, as Presland and others have documented and as we have seen in Chapter Two. Nearamnew had many other wetlands besides those adjoining the Yarra. Carter goes on to refer to 'inundations intermittently overflowing [the banks of the Yarra presumably] to feed and preserve a network of local creeks, waterholes and billabongs' (2005: 11), again without specifying where they were, including beneath Federation Square. The wetlandscape of early Melbourne was a network of swamplands far more extensive than the Yarra's and its tributary creeks, adjacent waterholes and adjoining billabongs, but extended throughout the suburbs of present-day Melbourne and the Yarra catchment.

Acknowledging and including a reference to the lost wetlands of Melbourne in *Nearamnew* would have given Carter the ideal opportunity to more extensively pursue what Potter sees as the basis for his artistic project and to produce a more productive intersection between language and space than the one he propounds as a desideratum in and for *The Road to Botany Bay* (1987: back cover). As almost an anagram and abbreviation, language + space = landscape, is the surface of the land-space laid out for the eye. Landscape does not embrace the depths of the land and wetland, nor the features of a place presented for all the senses and surfaces of the body in language + place = landplace, the language of land-place (see Giblett 2011: 59–76).

For Potter, Carter's basis for his project was that 'both poetically and materially, the ground beneath our feet is never given: it should not be assumed to be permanent and solid' (2007: 249). Indeed, as the ground beneath *Nearamnew* was neither permanent nor solid, but a wetland, why did he overlook this and the other swamps of Melbourne in designing *Nearamnew*? Was it because he bought into the triumphalist history of colonialism that drained wetlands and built cities on them? Was it because he was so concerned with the site by the Yarra for the foundation of the city and for his federalist project that he neglected the history of the foundation site for the city of Melbourne and the rest of the site for the city? Or was it that he regarded the wetlands as a matter of geography, whereas he was concerned with history?

Carter is concerned primarily in *The Road to Botany Bay*, with what he calls 'spatial history' in which 'the future is invented' and 'travellers and settlers do not so much belong to our past as we belong to their future' (1987: 294). Yet the future cannot be invented any more than the past can be changed. We can, however, imagine the future and have hope in and for the future by using what Raymond Williams called 'resources for a journey of hope' (Williams [1982] 1989, [1983] 1985: 243–69, [1984] 1989; see also Giblett 2009: 138–56). By *not* acknowledging the wetlands of Melbourne and their place in the space, place and history of Melbourne, or their role in the local Aboriginal peoples' lives and livelihoods, Carter in *Nearamnew* erases them from the past, present and future in chronology; he abstracts the wetlands into space and does not locate them in a particular time and place when he could have located the past and absent wetlands in the present and for the future.

Rather than decolonizing place and being postcolonial, *Nearamnew* is neocolonialist as it abstracts place into space. Moreover, it abstracts place from a four-dimensional locale in the Einsteinian time–space of energy and matter, through two-dimensional Euclidean geometry of length and breadth and into a three-dimensional mathematized Cartesian space, just as the map and the grid-plan town did for Carter. Cartesian space is, as Stuart Elden puts it, 'measurable, mappable, strictly demarcated, and thereby controllable', which 'underpins [not only] the modern notion of political rather than geographical borders, the boundaries of states' (2013: 291, see also 293), but also, I would add, the notions of political and geographical space within the borders of states enacted by the map and the grid plan. The map, for Carter, 'with its ability to fix even blankness beneath the inflexible […] grid of longitude and latitude, was essentially an instrument for performing geometrical divisions' (1987: 204), while the grid plan exemplified 'the principles of Euclidean geometry'. The grid measured length and breadth in two dimensions, but then superimposed this geometry onto space in three dimensions. Like the map and the grid plan, *Nearamnew* abstracts place into two dimensions of length and breadth (after all, Federation Square is roughly rectangular and is called a square) without the third dimension of depth, the deep space of the swamp beneath Federation Square and the deep time of Melbourne's swamps before Federation Square. In this regard, it is hardly surprising to learn that *Nearamnew* was designed in conjunction and collaboration with architects who are only concerned, spatially and historically, with the third dimension of the depths below insofar as they support physically the horizontal surfaces and vertical heights above.

By solidifying the original processes of the place's wetland ecosystem into the product of the dry-stone pavement of the s/Square, *Nearamnew* drains these wetlands of their significance, of their life and history, just as they were drained in actuality of their wetness and dried out. *Nearamnew* is a narrative, a nightmare repetition of wetland draining that dreams place *out* of being and into oblivion. Frequenters of Federation Square come and go oblivious to the history of the site as a wetland and of Melbourne as a place of wetlands, unless they take the indigenous tour of the area; readers of *The Road to Botany Bay* finish the book oblivious to the city of Melbourne as a place of wetlands in the past and present (as I did when I first read it), and remain oblivious unless they read other accounts of Melbourne (as I did). Because *Nearamnew* subjects place to chronological time, colonizing past, present and future; to mathematized space, colonizing place; and to the city, colonizing site, *Nearamnew* is neocolonialist. The monumental inscription in stone of *Nearamnew* represses the traces of the monstrous marsh below the city in space and before the city in time. *Nearamnew* subscribes to the dominant cultural paradigm of the patriarchal, the monumental, the chronological and the inscription (see Giblett 2011: 15–38).

Recent commentators on Federation Square, such as Coote, have critiqued 'its surface harsh like a quarry [...] There is no organic softness [...] Were it a naturally occurring landscape, Federation Square might be a gorge, or a dry, rocky outcrop' (2013: 330). It is an artificial, waterless gorge with a dry, rocky surface constructed out of stone imported from the Kimberley region of northern Western Australia. The site was once a naturally occurring wetlandscape with the organic softness and wet depressions of a moist marsh. Federation Square does not commemorate the wetland it once was but substitutes it with not only a dry gorge in its horizontal and vertical surfaces, but also with the bunker-like building of the Australian Centre for the Moving Image, with its desert camouflage and skew-whiff windows that look like they have been blasted out by a bomb. Instead of the native or natural wetlandscape of Melbourne, the horizontal and vertical surfaces of Federation Square present the desert screens of reality television news, a world away from the watery womb of the wetlands.

The repressed always returns, though, in jokes, dreams, tropes and slips of the tongue and pen. The repressed wetlands of Melbourne return in this chapter, the counter or rejoinder to *Nearamnew* by a wetlands conservationist. This chapter also engages in critical dialogue with *Nearamnew*, coming out of the transdisciplinary environmental humanities, principally ecocultural studies.[6] It dreams a phantasy design for a new surface for Federation Square that will never be built and that traces the phantoms of the Melbourne marshes and swamps in what I call temporal geography or the geography of time (past, present and future; the cycle of the seasons; the life and death, energy and matter, of wetlands; the livelihoods of people in place), and places hope in the future for wetlands. The temporal geography of Melbourne's repressed wetlands takes place in *kairos*, the now-time (*Jetztzeit*) of messianic irruption in the eternal present, rather than in *chronos*, the linear time of *Nearamnew* and *The Road to Botany Bay*, with their selective memory of the past and its triumphalist and spatial history set in stone.

With both temporal geography and spatial history (as Carter [1987: 295] puts it in relation to the latter), 'we recover the possibility of another history [and geography, I would add], our future', and our past I would also add, including remembering the history of the lost wetlands as this chapter does, rather than forgetting it as *The Road to Botany Bay* and *Nearamnew* do. Hope in the future would amount to a spatially emplaced and embodied history and a temporal geography of the past and present that relates the wetlands of Melbourne lost in the past and found in the present to the future.

The present chapter also proposes an annual performance by an Aboriginal dance company on World Wetlands' Day (2 February) in Federation Square celebrating the life and commemorating the death of the lost wetlands of Melbourne and their role in sustaining the lives and livelihoods of the local Aboriginal people. It would avow the alternative cultural paradigm of the matrifocal, monstrous *kairos* and trace. It would refuse the dominant cultural paradigm of the patriarchal, monumental *chronos* and inscription to which *Nearamnew* subscribes (see Giblett 2011: 32–34 Figure 2).

Another opportunity exists on North Wharf in the Docklands, currently under redevelopment, including the construction of an 'eco-park' at the end of the wharf which could have a 'floating wetland' with clumps of reeds and rushes. As this area was once upon a time West Melbourne Swamp (or Batman's Swamp), this site could be a rehabilitated wetland, a vital ecosystem and habitat with introduced frogs that would attract waterbirds: a wetlandscape rather than a parklandscape.[7] A children's play pool with tadpoles in the seasonal life cycle of the endemic frog species would provide a space for bodily interaction with the wetlands. Aboriginal interpretation of the former wetlands and their species would provide the pre-settlement history of the nature and culture of the place. I propose calling the constructed wetland 'Batman's Swamp', as that was once what this area was called.

History occurs in locations; history takes place in spaces and places. Geography is set in time (past, present and future), including the seasonal flowering cycles of wetlands and their seasonal wetting and drying cycles, and it participates in a circular sense of time. Spatial history for Carter 'begins and ends in language. It is this which makes it history rather than, say, geography' (1987: xxiii). Yet geography, literally 'writing the earth', begins and ends in language too, including the verbal language of the explorer's journal about his journey in time through space between places with his record of his observations of wetlands experienced through the course of his journey, and the visual language of his topographic maps making marks on paper in the scalar grid of latitude and longitude. Time and space come together anyway in the calculation of longitude, because measuring time is the means to measure space cartographically. In turn, the grid plan marks on paper or parchment, and then on the earth, the rectilinear lots and streets of the settlement and city. Temporal geography begins and ends in the language of time, including writing on the seasonal cycle of wetlands and about the succession of their flowering plants through the seasons. Understanding the meanings, metaphors, landscapes and gender politics of wetlands is part of producing a better understanding of one's place on earth and one's point in time, suspended in the present between a past one cannot return to and a future one cannot invent or know, but can hope for and have hope in (see Giblett 2009: 138–56).

Despite Potter's claim that 'the mythopoeic return of the repressed environment is a key feature of *Nearamnew*' (2007: 253), the repressed wetlands of Melbourne are not discussed in *The Road to Botany Bay* nor inscribed in *Nearamnew*, and remain largely repressed in *Mythform*, except (as we have seen) for the brief mention of the Yarra's swamplands that were near Federation Square. However, the repressed natural environment returns, literally, when Melbourne's low-lying areas return to the ephemeral wetlands that they once were, and when some of its streets revert to 'the creeks of the Yarra River' (Potter 2007: 254), as they do periodically. For instance, for Garryowen in the mid-nineteenth century, Flinders Street was 'a swamp and [...] Collins Street was so slushy and sticky' that pedestrians needed leggings or 'long mud-boots', while 'boggings' of cumbersome horse-drawn vehicles at intersections were commonplace (Garryowen ([1835–52] 1967: 44; also excerpted in Grant and Serle 1957: 36 and Lewis 1995: 33). The mud accumulating in Melbourne streets was so deep that one of the newspapers of the day advertised for one thousand pairs of stilts so that the inhabitants of Melbourne could 'carry on their usual avocations' (Garryowen ([1835–52] 1967: 45).

Elizabeth Street was more precisely, or originally, Williams Creek or River Townend. W. Lloyd Williams devotes (and entitles) Chapter Six of his *History Trails in Melbourne* to 'the stream that became a street' (Williams 1957: 53–62). The transition from stream to street was not from wet to dry, soft to hard, because what Williams calls 'the wet, muddy, and boggy Elizabeth Street' (1957: 55) occasionally resulted in the street reverting to a stream. As a joke, a punt was proposed for it in winter for 'the transit of goods and passengers' (Garryowen ([1835–52] 1967: 45). Clarence Woodhouse's panoramic view of *Melbourne in 1838 from the Yarra Yarra*, prepared in 1888 for the Centennial Exhibition, depicts Elizabeth Street as a creek with bridges across it at Collins, Bourke and other streets, eventually discharging into the river via a creek (Woodhouse 1888).[8] Garryowen remarked in the mid-nineteenth century that 'Elizabeth Street, the outlet between two hills, was a jungly chasm – an irregular broken-up ravine through which the winter flood-waters thundered along over shattered tree-trunks, displaced rocks, roots, and ruts' (Garryowen ([1835–52] 1967: 6).

81

Elizabeth Street was what Bill Newnham calls 'a gully that became a raging torrent in the rainy season' (1985: 60), and 'down which floodwaters frequently rushed' (234), as depicted in a famous photograph of 18 February 1972, the day of 'the heaviest downpour ever recorded in Melbourne' (McComb and Lake 1990: 9).

FIGURE 6: A wall of water running down Elizabeth Street, 18 February 1972. Photo: Neville Bowler/Fairfax Syndication. Reproduced from *The Age* newspaper with kind permission.

This photograph shows Royal Arcade in the background. It was first published in *The Age* newspaper and has been republished many times since (Presland 1985: 16, 1994: 24; McComb and Lake 1990: 9). Jenny Sinclair sees the flooding of Elizabeth Street as a product of

> Hoddle's refusal [in his grid plan] to notice the existing hills, valleys and streams [which] brought its own problems; the stream that ran down Elizabeth Street, for instance, did not respond well to being renamed a street and just kept right on flowing, with sometimes fatal results.
>
> (Sinclair 2010: 33)

For instance, in the 1880s, 'a sober strong man was carried off his legs by the force of the stream, and ignominiously drowned in a gutter' (Anon. cited in Otto 2005: 75).

Hoddle, unlike Carter, did not fail to notice the existing marshes and swamps, though not usually with the same disastrous results as ignoring the creeks, because the marshes and swamps were easier to attempt to eradicate with the stroke of a pen and a pump. Not so the lower end of Elizabeth Street between Collins and Flinders Streets, which was known in the 1840s as 'River Townend' or River Enscoe, and the junction between Elizabeth and Collins Streets, which was known as 'Lake Cashmore' (Annear 2014: 29, 31–32, 40–46). Williams Creek, as Miles Lewis describes it, 'flowed down Elizabeth Street, into a somewhat unpleasant watercourse', and then, 'even more seriously […], discharged into the Yarra' (1995: 32). The predominant substance at the time present on the streets in this area was mud (as Annear [2014] notes), a mixture of earth and water, the stuff of wetland, wetlands, and lowlands. 'Elizabeth Street, the lowest point of the CBD [Central Business District], is still particularly susceptible to flooding', as Cunningham puts it (2011: 118). Floods, Cunningham suggests, 'remind us of repressed rivers, creeks and billabongs' (2011: 2). Mud and floods are the return of the geographical and historical repressed of the lost and forgotten waterways and wetlands.

Potter points out that wetlands are neither permanent nor solid, and she also points out in cognate terms, they are 'neither solid nor liquid' (2007: 250). Potter goes on to give a potted (Pottered?) history of wetlands in 'the western ontological tradition', and of its inheritors in non-indigenous Australia (see also Giblett 1996). She concludes in general terms (and not in relation specifically to Melbourne, though she could have) that 'wetlands represented an obstacle' to agricultural (and she might have added urban) development, and so were 'methodically drained' (Potter 2007: 250). Unknown to Potter (email to the author, 24 May 2015) at the time of writing her discussion of *Nearamnew*, was that this is precisely what occurred in Melbourne with its wetlands, but this was presumably known to Carter as he not only mentions (as we have seen) the Yarra River's 'adjoining swamplands' and 'a network of local […] billabongs' (2005: 11), but he also refers to the page of Presland's book directly following its chapter on the lost wetland-scape of Melbourne (2005: 25).

This history of this place could have been acknowledged and included in *Near-amnew*, its lost wetlands celebrated and their loss mourned, rather than excluded, and so *Nearamnew* becomes a monument to a missed opportunity to do so, as well as a monument to a triumphalist history of a (yet another) city draining its wetlands. *Nearamnew* could have commemorated the role of the lost wetlands as living places of and for plants and animals, and as sources of sustenance for the local Aboriginal people and nutriment for settlers and city-dwellers to grow their crops and graze their animals. Melbourne needs wetland memorials and interpretive projects that commemorate this history and celebrate the role of wetlands in Victorian ecology in the past, the present and for the future.

NOTES

1. Reproduced in Arnold (1983: 14).

2. For the history of Perth as both a grid-plan town (drawing on Carter's work in *The Road to Botany Bay* [1987]) and as a city of wetlands, see Giblett (1996: 55–76, 2013a: 105–22). As Carter does not discuss Melbourne as a city of wetlands and as it was unknown to me at the time, I did not mention it in these discussions of Perth and other wetland cities, such as St Petersburg. I mention it in passing in Giblett (2016: 12) and refer to my article, 'Lost and found wetlands of Melbourne,' in the *Victorian Historical Journal* (2016, 87:1, pp. 134–55), an earlier version of Chapters Two, Four and Five of *Modern Melbourne* as indicated in the Acknowledgements.

3. Detail reproduced in Coote (2012: 10–11).

4. By contrast, Davison recently reads *Nearamnew* as both 'a post-colonial anti-monument' and 'a historical ground zero', without attempting to resolve this apparent contradiction or conundrum; see Davison (2016: 262–63).

5. See Giblett (2011: 117–34, Chapter Six: 'Riding roughshod over it: Mateship against the bush').

6. For a brief introduction to some key concepts of ecocultural studies, such as nature, landscape (especially pleasing prospects) and livelihood, see Giblett (2012: 922–33, 2013b: 111–20).

7. I develop this distinction in Giblett (2017).

8. Reproduced in Coote (2012: 16–17). See also detail of Elizabeth Street (Coote 2012: 19).

PART II

VISIBLE CITY, INVISIBLE SITE

The Paris of the South

To make sense of a city, or to at least to boost its status, one city is often seen in terms of another. Comparing one city to another is usually made by the boosters of the less-famous city in order to raise their city to a rating comparable to that of the more famous counterpart. Melbourne is no exception. Melbourne for some is 'the Paris of the south', with its faux mini Eiffel Tower atop the State Theatre Centre, its bustling Parisian-style arcades and laneways (with their small café/bar/restaurants like Paris) and its 'Paris end of Collins Street'. The comparison is not usually made, however, that Melbourne was founded, like Paris, in a swamp on the banks of a sluggish river.[1] Both the Seine and the Yarra are lazy, muddy and serpentine rivers. The banks of both rivers on which their cities were founded were also marshy.

The Paris end of Collins Street

'The Paris end of Collins Street' is perhaps an ersatz French Quarter with its high-end French and quasi-French boutiques, such as Le Louvre. Described by Maree Coote as 'a branch office of Paris', Le Louvre was 'a chiffon palace that became the temple of Australian fashion and reigned supreme for over 80 years at the so-called "Paris end of Collins Street"' (2013: 288). Lillian Wightman (1902–92), 'the Queen of Melbourne fashion', established Le Louvre in the 1930s and reigned supreme over it for 60 years. She also claimed to have coined the phrase 'the Paris end of Collins Street'. In the late 1950s, putting tables and chairs on the pavement also contributed to the creation of 'the Paris end of Collins Street' (Davison 2016: 190, 247).[2] Painters, such as Dora Wilson and Louis Kahan (reproduced in Coote 2012: 86, 110), and photographers, such as Wolfgang Sievers, depicted this section of the street in their artworks (reproduced in Davison 2016: facing 155). This café, Le Louvre and other establishments of eastern Collins Street, made this section famous as 'the Paris end' – at least in Melbourne. In Peter Carey's 1985 novel *Illywhacker* his narrator wryly comments that 'the Paris end of Collins Street' is 'famous, in Melbourne at least, for resembling Paris' (cited in Sinclair 2015: 135).

Other writers are equally as scathing or sceptical as Carey about making the comparison between the eastern end of Collins Street and Paris, at least recently. Collins Street, for Sophie Cunningham, 'was once the grandest shopping street in Melbourne' (2011: 197). For her, 'references to "the Paris end" of the street are somewhat delusional, in part because of developments such as the Sofitel', a postmodern hotel connected with the atrium-style shopping plaza of Collins Place, which, Cunningham argues, is 'devoid of [natural] light [unlike arcades] and oriented away from the street', like arcades (2011: 202). The hotel makes a selling point on its website of its location at 'the Paris end of Collins Street'. The postmodern atrium and shopping plaza inherited the modern arcade from Paris, so the Sofitel can still justifiably claim a dubious connection with Paris.[3] Yet Collins Place obliterated what Ronald Jones calls 'an area of historic building fondly known as the Paris end of Collins Street' and erected 'one of the dullest examples of monumental Modernism in its place' (2018: 92). Collins Place killed what the Sofitel continues to promote. Collins Place is the memorial to a lost place.

The comparisons to Paris may be somewhat delusional and whimsical today, and they certainly were in early Melbourne when, from 1835 to 1851, Collins Street for Annear obviously 'had no Paris end' (2014: xii) and so, she goes on to argue, 'it would be a mistake to confuse the early Collins Street with the swank boulevard of the later Victorian period' (34). Late Victorian Melbourne, from 1851, did perceive itself as legitimately calling itself 'the Paris of the south', culminating in the temporary construction of lighting towers to celebrate Federation in 1901, in tribute to Paris, commonly called 'the city of lights'. The *Argus* newspaper described how 'a new city was created [...] a veritable Paris of the South, the city of a faerie dreamland' (cited in Otto 2009: 13).[4] The Parisian 'city of lights' came south, at least for a time. The phantasmagoric city of lights is a marker of modernity, perhaps with its unfortunate culmination in the lighting of the Nazi Nuremberg rallies and its recent populist manifestation in Melbourne's 'White Night', when the facades of buildings become projection screens for animated light displays, and the streets of central Melbourne become packed with pedestrians (while cars and trams are excluded).

Melbourne is the Australian capital of modernity and 'the Paris of the south' because it is 'the undisputed fashion capital of Australia', as Coote (2013: 278) says, just as Paris was the nineteenth-century capital of modernity and remains the undisputed fashion capital of the world. Paris, for Joan De Jean, is not only 'the key capital of modernity' (2014: 5), but also 'the capital of an empire of culture' (14) and the 'capital of high fashion' (16). Indeed, for her, 'Paris *is* fashion' (144, original emphasis) and 'the most romantic city in the world' (191). Melbourne is arguably the Australian capital of high fashion and the most romantic city in Australia. In the early years of the twentieth century, for Judith Buckrich, 'in all ways Melbourne set the trend for fashion and social life in Australia' (1999: 9). Many Melburnians still like to think that it does. Similarly, for Coote Melbourne is 'the best-dressed metropolis' (2013: 278).

Melbourne has been seen not only as 'the Paris of the south', but also as the New York or Chicago of the south (or at least potentially), and more recently as the Los Angeles or Toronto of the south. In this chapter, I trace these analogues (as well as those with Berlin and London) and argue that they produce some interesting comparisons between Melbourne and other cities, which help to make sense of the city by locating it in an international urban context and in the history and culture of modernity. The comparisons, however, are not always flattering for both sides of the analogy being drawn. In the case of Paris and Melbourne, rather than showing one city in a favourable light and raising the status of the other, both cities have come to be regarded as having the same problematic aspects. This is no more so than with the founding of both cities in swamps and the siting of their slums. This is certainly the case with the designation of Melbourne as 'the Paris of the south'.

Lutetia du Sud

Paris was founded in and on the swamps of Lutetia, the original Celtic-cum-Latin name for the site and city meaning 'the filthy marsh' (Hussey 2006: 11; see also Giblett 2016: 38). 'The muddy etymology of Lutetia' is linked, for Colin Jones, to 'the Celtic word for marshland and to *lutum*, Latin for mud' (2002: 4). More specifically, Lutetia, for Andrew Hussey, is Celtic for 'the place of mud, marshes and swamp' (2006: 3, 7). The muddy aetiology of Lutetia itself is also linked to what Jones calls 'marshy and muddy land' (2002: 4). Similar descriptions were made of the site for Melbourne, such as 'swampy land' in Charles Grimes's map of 1803 (as we have seen in Chapters Two and Four). Thus, both these capitals of modernity have their beginnings, and largely deny them, in pre-modern wetlands. Both are capitals of space and place.

Walter Benjamin calls Paris 'the capital of the nineteenth century' ([1982] 1999a: 3) and notes the beginnings of Paris as Lutetia, the 'filthy marsh' (14).[5] Melbourne is the Australian capital of the nineteenth century and, like Paris, it is a marshy city built on the banks of a marshy river. Both capitals also have their beginnings, and largely deny them too, in their environmental history of this and previous centuries. Both are capitals of time, space and place. The city marks a moment in time and makes a place in space. 'Marvellous Melbourne' was also 'Marshy Melbourne', and Melbourne is not only 'the Paris of the south' but also *Lutetia du Sud*, 'the filthy marsh' of the south.

Time, space and place come together in what Benjamin calls 'a dialectical image' for, as he goes on to elaborate, 'while the relation of the present to the past is a purely temporal, continuous one, the relation to what-has-been to the now is dialectical: is not progression but image, suddenly emergent' ([1982] 1999a: 462). *Lutetia du Sud* is the image of the what-has-been, of Melbourne as marsh, related dialectically to the now of recognizability, of Melbourne as metropolis. This image is situated between the filthy marsh and the miry city. *Lutetia du Sud*, Melbourne as marsh metropolis, is a dialectical image of Melbourne of the past in the now. Rather than the past being absent, the past is present.

Benjamin elaborates further that 'in the dialectical image, what has been within a particular epoch is always, simultaneously, "what has been from time immemorial"' ([1982] 1999a: 464). Wetlands in general have been from time immemorial when the world was wetland. *Lutetia du Sud*, in particular, has been from time immemorial and it has been in the particular epoch of the beginnings of the history of Melbourne. 'The dialectical image', for Benjamin, is 'the primal phenomenon of history' ([1982] 1999a: 474). Wetlands in general are the primal phenomenon of history from its beginnings (see Giblett 2018b: 3–20). *Lutetia du Sud* in particular is the primal phenomenon of the history of Melbourne. Of course, the vast majority of the residents of Melbourne are oblivious to its lost wetlands, its ghost swamps (as Carter's *The Road to Botany Bay* [1987] and *Nearamnew* [2001] attest, and of which they are symptomatic), but, as Benjamin (1999b: 809) says of the hetaeric stage of the swamp world, 'the fact that this stage is now forgotten does not mean that it does not extend into the present. On the contrary: it is present by virtue of its very oblivion'. The same could be said of *Lutetia du Sud*. It extends into the present and is present by virtue of its very oblivion in Melbourne today (as *Nearamnew* and *The Road to Botany Bay* again attest). This statement not only could have served as the epigraph for *Modern Melbourne* (as it could have for *Cities and Wetlands* [Giblett 2016]), but it is also the motto for my discussion of the absence and absenting of wetlands from Melbourne (as it was for the cities discussed in *Cities and Wetlands*), and for their ongoing presence in the present by virtue of their very oblivion: Melbourne is a city of ghost swamps (as we saw in the four previous chapters).

The early Bohemian era of Melbourne in the 1890s drew an explicit connection with Paris when Marcus Clarke ([1874] 1972), in a short piece of journalism devoted to 'The Café Lutetia', signalled the importance for Bohemian Melbourne of the Café de Paris attached to the Theatre Royal in Bourke Street. For Clarke, the café 'became the resort of Upper Bohemia' ([1874] 1972: 337). When the Café de Paris changed its name to Café Lutetia, Clarke wrote that 'the Café Lutetia was a part of our existence. Its revelries, its follies went to make up our life'

(340, see also the photo on 341 and the note on 463). Clarke drew a parallel between Parisian Bohemian life and Melbournian Bohemian life, but he did not explore the meaning of the word Lutetia, nor draw the parallel between Paris and Melbourne, with both being former wetland cities, or between the underworlds of both cities that were figured in swampy and sewery metaphors.[6]

Other similarities with Paris have been drawn. In the 1870s and 1880s, Collins Street was described as 'having all the sophistication of a Parisian boulevard' (excerpted in Flannery 2002: 16). Yet, unlike the boulevards of Paris – which were created by blasting a way through potentially seditious neighbourhoods as part of Baron Georges Eugène Hausmann's authoritarian redesign and militarized management of the city – the boulevards of Melbourne were created as part of the initial city design of Robert Hoddle's grid-plan town. Arguably this design was authoritarian and reactionary too. Whereas Hausmann's redesign of Parisian boulevards was designed to clear the slums by clearing a way through them, Hoddle's design of Melbourne, with 'wide streets and large lots', was designed to 'prevent slums' appearing in the first place, as Cunningham (2011: 201) puts it. In this respect, he failed spectacularly as slums eventuated.

Others also drew the same parallel between Melburnian and Parisian boulevards and made other comparisons between the two cities in the nineteenth century. In 1885, George Augustus Sala, the minter of the moniker 'Marvellous Melbourne', suggested to his readers that

> you might, without any very violent stretch of the imagination, fancy on a fine night that Bourke St was one of the Paris boulevards instead of being a highway hewn not fifty years ago out of the trackless Bush and that you were a *flâneur* [...] who had just strolled into the nearest passage to saunter from shop to shop.
>
> (excerpted in Flannery 2002: 328)

Sala's imaginary Melburnian *flâneur* would go strolling and sauntering in the arcades of Melbourne, just like his Parisian counterpart who not only strolled and sauntered through the arcades (or 'passages' in French and German) of Paris, but also went 'botanizing' on its boulevards for unusual or rare species of the human race.[7] 'The trackless Bush' that preceded the design and construction of Melburnian boulevards was probably roughly equivalent in the minds of the urban designers of the Parisian boulevards to the labyrinthine slums of Paris. Both were inhospitable territory through which a highway was hewn, or a boulevard blasted, opening up both spaces for ready ingress and egress by wheeled transportation. Just as the so-called 'trackless Bush' was traversed by the dreaming tracks of indigenous owners, so the slums were crisscrossed by the trails of local walkers.

Arcades

In his monumental history of the arcade as 'a building type', Johann Geist defines an arcade as 'a glass-covered passageway which connects two busy streets and is lined on both sides with shops [...] The arcade is the organising force of retail trade' ([1979] 1983: 4). It is hardly surprising, then, that the shopping arcade gave rise to the department store, the atrium, the galleria and the shopping mall as traced initially and partially by Benjamin in *The Arcades Project* (*Passagenwerk*) ([1982] 1999a) and as traced more extensively and globally by Pierre Missac in *Walter Benjamin's Passages* ([1987] 1995). Nor is it surprising that the arcade's building materials of glass and iron were used in market halls, railway stations and exhibition buildings (such as the Crystal Palace), as also traced by Benjamin. Geist acknowledges that Benjamin, in his work on Paris as the capital of the nineteenth century, was 'the first to recognise the arcade as a phenomenon of the century and to view it in context' ([1979] 1983: 115). Or more precisely contexts, such as the heyday of industrial capitalism, the rise of consumerism associated with what Marx called 'commodity fetishism' or what Benjamin called 'the phony spell of a commodity' (1973: 233), and the development of the *flâneur* as the representative figure of the arcades, and of the detective novel as the quintessential genre of the nineteenth-century city.

Tim Flannery's anthology of writings about the birth of Melbourne in a marsh and about the nineteenth-century city of Melbourne, with its boulevards and arcades, as 'the Paris of the south' is the antipodean analogue to *The Arcades Project*, with a similar edge of political critique. Benjamin is the *flâneur* of culture who went botanizing in the bog of books in the Bibliotheque Nationale, where he collected specimens of species to array, display and study in his cabinet of curiosities called *The Arcades Project*, with its convoluted taxonomy of genuses arranged alphabetically. Flannery is the *flâneur* of nature who went botanizing in the stacks of the State Library of Victoria where he (or his research assistants) also collected specimens for his cabinet of curious informants, arranged chronologically in *The Birth of Melbourne* (2002), unlike Benjamin's ([1982] 1999a) thematic arrangement in *The Arcades Project*.

On several occasions in his work on Paris as the capital of the nineteenth century collected in *The Arcades Project*, Benjamin cites an anonymous *Illustrated Guide to Paris* from 1852, which describes how

> [t]hese arcades, a recent invention of industrial luxury, are glass-roofed, marble-paneled corridors extending through whole blocks of buildings [...] Lining both sides of these corridors, which get their light from above, are the most elegant shops, so that the *passage* [French] is a city, a world in miniature,

in which customers will find everything they need. During sudden rainshowers, the arcades are a place of refuge for the unprepared, to whom they offer a secure, if restricted promenade – one from which merchants also benefit.

(cited in Benjamin [1982] 1999a: 3, 15, 31, 873)[8]

Geist ([1979] 1983: 54) reiterates that the arcade is always a promenade. The arcade is a place for strolling and for display, for displaying both the stroller and the objects of visual consumption for sale to the stroller in a mutually regarding, if not narcissistic, positioning of the subject of the stroller and the object of the commodity. Parks and gardens, such as the Royal Botanic Gardens in Melbourne (as we will see in the following chapter), were landscaped to create promenades for displaying flora and vistas as objects of visual consumption forming the background and context for the stroller to display him or herself.

As the *Illustrated Guide to Paris* claims, the arcade was invented in Paris. Geist relates how 'the first building which deserves the designation "arcade" stood in Paris at the Palais Royal' built in 1629 by Cardinal Richelieu ([1979] 1983: vii). From France, the arcade was exported to England, which, in turn, exported the arcade to its colonies, such as Australia. In discussing Benjamin's work on the arcades of Paris, Missac wonders 'if the arcades were indeed a defining characteristic of nineteenth century Paris', as 'there were arcades in Italy and Germany as well, and they were especially numerous in England, which exported them to Australia' ([1987] 1995: 178). An endnote at this point refers to the fact that 'Melbourne had at least ten arcades, built between 1853 and 1912' (Missac [1987] 1995: 219, note 5).[9] Arcades were a defining characteristic of nineteenth-century European cities and their colonial diasporas. Melbourne is no exception. The arcades of Paris contributed to Benjamin's conclusion that Paris is the capital of the nineteenth century; Melbourne's arcades support the claim that Melbourne is the Australian capital of the nineteenth century and of high modernity (though, of course, Sydney had a few, most notably the surviving Strand Arcade, and Adelaide and Brisbane have their eponymous arcades, but the flat topography and the expansive and extensive rectilinear grid of Melbourne made it more conducive to the construction of arcades).

One of the most famous arcades in Melbourne was Cole's Book Arcade that 'ran through from Bourke to Collins Street' (Newnham 1985: 43). Cole's Book Arcade, for Coote, was 'the most famous Melbourne landmark of his [E. W. Cole's] time' (2013: 198). Peter Maltezos describes how

in 1906, Cole's Book Arcade was extended all the way through to Collins Street alongside Howey Place. E. W. Cole paved and built a beautiful glass and iron ornamental roof for Howey Place, at his own cost, which still stands proudly today.

(Maltezos n.d.)[10]

Howey Place now joins with 'Collins234 Boutique Place' on Collins Street and forms an L-shape with the back of Capitol Arcade on Swanston Street and joins up through a labyrinthine passageway with the Manchester Unity building arcade on the corner of Swanston and Collins Streets. Cole's Book Arcade 'was said to be the largest bookshop in the world, with nearly two million volumes on the shelves' (Lewis 1995: 91). By contrast, Powell's 'City of Books' in Portland, Oregon, currently 'the largest used and new bookstore in the world', according to its website, 'occupies an entire city block and houses approximately one million books'.[11] Cole's Book Arcade was closed in 1928 and demolished in 1932 (Chapman and Stillman 2015: 16–17).

Melbourne's most famous surviving arcades and the ones that are most redolent of Paris are the Royal and Block Arcades. The Royal Arcade was 'constructed with very delicate cast iron roof trusses' (Garside and White 1963: 80). It was 'opened in 1869' and is presided over by the 'tall wooden figures of the giants Gog and Magog [...] with their bizarre colouring [and] fantastical appearance', as described by Bill Newnham (1985: 42–43).[12] Royal Arcade is also presided over by 'Father Time', described by Newnham as 'an eight-foot high, bearded but emaciated figure, wearing a long red toga and grasping a rather wobbly-looking, traditional scythe' (1985: 43). Statues are usually found in official and private places, not in the semi-public spaces of arcades, what Geist calls 'public space on private property' ([1979] 1983: 4). Photos of European arcades do not seem to show them (such as in Geist's monumental work on arcades), nor does Benjamin mention statues in arcades. The statues in Royal Arcade seem to be an Australian innovation and deviation from the norm.

The Block Arcade, 'with its glass domed roof' (Newnham 1985: 33), 'heavy cast iron trusses' (Garside and White 1963: 83) and mosaic tile floor was built between 1892 and 1894, during the depression of that decade. Glass and iron are the two defining materials out of which arcades were built. Arcades were not possible without the modern development of iron (cast and wrought), a long time after the development of glass. Melbourne's arcades were also not possible without the city's well-developed iron foundries, and so the structural use of iron was made here 'earlier and more extensively than in other parts of Australia' (Lewis 1995: 55; see also Davison 1978: 48). Writing in the 1960s (and it still applies fifty years later), Janet Garside and Deborah White stated that the Block Arcade is 'Melbourne's most lavish Arcade of all' (1963: 81). Writing (in German) in the 1970s (and it still applies forty years later), Geist stated that the Block Arcade is 'today Melbourne's most elegant arcade' ([1979] 1983: 365).

The Block Arcade is L-shaped and joins Collins and Elizabeth Streets. A laneway joins the arcade to Little Collins Street, nearly adjacent to Royal Arcade, so it is possible to traverse on foot 'the Block' from Collins to Bourke Street, 'the epicentre of nineteenth-century life in the city', as Robyn Annear (2014: 30) puts it, mainly via arcades and a laneway. Royal Arcade is T-shaped with the long, upper cross bar of the 'T' traversing 'the Block' from Bourke Street to Little Collins Street, and the short central leg of the 'T' opening through a narrow passageway, or what Geist calls 'a lateral wing' ([1979] 1983: 364; see also Garside and White 1963: 80), onto Elizabeth Street, which was added in 1903 with wrought iron roof trusses, unlike the main arcade with its cast iron trusses. Sauntering through this passage is like travelling in a time machine back to what I imagine Parisian arcades must have been like in the nineteenth century with their display of commodities in their cluttered shop windows and their inviting and intimate interior spaces.

Centreway, comprising an arcade and laneway between Collins Street and Flinders Lane, was built in 1912. Geist describes it as 'a continuation of the Block Arcade in the direction of the [Flinders Street] train station [...] Centreway is supplemented by the Port Phillip Arcade today, which was built in 1962 and which leads directly to the station' ([1979] 1983: 366). The laneway of De Graves Street is nearby to both arcades, and a pedestrian subway under Flinders Street connects it to the station.

Cathedral Arcade is also L-shaped and is the entry to the Nicholas Building on the corner of Flinders Lane and Swanston Street. As Cunningham describes, Cathedral Arcade 'still has its original leadlight, barrel-vaulted ceiling (Melbourne's first)' (2011: 170–71).[13] If Cunningham 'were compelled to sum up Melbourne in a single building, it would be this one, with its striking terracotta and dark-green faience glaze façade' (2011: 170). Kristin Otto waxes even more lyrical than Cunningham when she describes how 'the Nicholas Building's intimate L-shaped shopping arcade is entirely – wall and ceiling – glass-paned and -panelled' (2009: 345). She goes on to effuse that it is an 'imagining of a crystal space – ethereal, glittery, modern, electric-age [...] This incandescent Cathedral Arcade, with its vaulted Luxfer fire glass ceiling, bathes one in the paradisical glow of shopping delight' (345), and so on. Or, as Benjamin puts it, 'the phantasmagoria of the marketplace' bewitch one under 'the phony spell of the commodity' ([1982] 1999a: 14). For Benjamin, 'modernity' is 'the world dominated by its phantasmagorias' ([1982] 1999a: 26). Phantasmagorias were a form of magic lantern show popular in the nineteenth century. Benjamin ([1982] 1999a) notably explored phantasmagoria in his work on nineteenth-century Parisian passages, or arcades, especially in relation to the Crystal Palace and World Exhibitions (as we will see in relation to Melbourne in Chapter Eleven).

The *Illustrated Guide to Paris* (cited in Benjamin [1982] 1999a: 3, 15, 31, 873) goes on to describe how the arcades of Paris open onto 'the inner boulevards' of the city on the Seine, just as Royal Arcade opens onto the inner boulevard of Bourke Street and the Block Arcade opens onto the inner boulevard, or 'block', of Collins

Street between Elizabeth and Swanston Streets of the city on the Yarra. Henry Handel Richardson in 1910 described 'the "block"' as 'that strip of Collins Street which forms the fashionable promenade' (cited in Arnold 1983: 41). The arcades are an inner place to promenade, opening off the inner boulevard into an interior space through which to walk into the even more interior space of the shops. In the case of Melbourne, the narrower, inner boulevards of Collins and Bourke Streets of the Central Business District [CBD] are distinct from the wider, outer boulevards of Royal Parade, Flemington Road and St Kilda's Road outside the CBD.

The sky bridge is another sort of passageway that is an inheritor of the arcade. In the case of Melbourne, a four-storey pedestrian bridge was constructed over Little Bourke Street in 1963, connecting the Bourke and Lonsdale Street sections of the Myer department store. The bridge's official and grandiose title was 'the Myer Department Store Aerial Crossover' (Lewis 1995: 137). The shopping arcade is a glass-covered passageway connecting two busy streets, whereas the pedestrian sky bridge is a glass-sided passageway crossing a busy street and connecting two sections of a department store, and now connecting Myer department store with Emporium Melbourne. Later, a glass-sided passageway was constructed over Little Lonsdale Street connecting two sections of the Melbourne Central shopping mall. With the two sky bridges, labyrinthine passages of store departments and small shops were created in the precinct between Bourke and La Trobe Streets.

Melbourne's centre was, for Miles Lewis, 'one of the great colonial city centres of the nineteenth century' (1995: 12). Melbourne's centre, or more precisely its 'central business district' (because a grid-plan town has no centre as such), for Lewis 'quickly became the quintessential expression of early nineteenth century planning with an emphasis upon broad, rectilinear streets [laid out by Hoddle] with little provision for gardens and open space' (1995: 12). No provision could be more precise. Parks and gardens were later constructed on the outskirts of the central grid.

Parks and gardens

Today, Melbourne's parks and gardens, like those of Paris, are a defining feature of the city and provide valuable amenities. For Coote,

> the key to Melbourne's liveability lies in two major design elements. First, the garden wedges. Great chunks of green were designed into the city plan by our prescient founding fathers – vast tracts of open space that break into the metropolis bringing sanity, clean air, negative ions, shade, shelter, grace and spring.
>
> (Coote 2013: 101)

The second factor for Coote is the width of the city's main streets so designed for the turning circle of a bullock train, like many other Australian towns and cities of the time. Later they fortuitously provided sufficient width for trams and traffic.

Melbourne's parks and gardens around the CBD, especially on the south side of the Yarra River, certainly provide valuable amenities, as Coote indicates, but they are not the result of prescient design by the 'founding fathers' of the city, as she wishfully thinks (2013: 101). They are more the result of a series of happy accidents or serendipity coming to fruition over nearly a decade for the founding designers who were bequeathed the site by the settlement founders, John Batman and John Fawkner (who contended for paternity rights). Robert Hoddle did not include any parks and gardens in his grid of 1836.[14] Only a decade later in 1846 did La Trobe 'set aside' areas outside the grid for parks and gardens, such as that for the Royal Botanic Gardens.[15] Coote acknowledges later that 'Melbourne's green wedges are attributable to Governor La Trobe' (2013: 133), though he was Superintendent of the Port Phillip District at the time and did not become Lieutenant Governor until Victoria became a colony in its own right in 1851. Certainly this was a prescient initiative, but it was hardly a valuable urban feature envisaged and incorporated into a design for a city before the fact of the city. Like most creative design endeavours, the incorporation of parks and gardens into the city was the result of a process of evolution, rather than of a single miraculous conception.

Like Melbourne's parks and gardens, its railway stations, Exhibition Building and Queen Victoria Market – 'the only substantial nineteenth-century market buildings remaining in the central area of Melbourne' (Cole 1980: 47), 'the oldest' market in Melbourne (Cunningham 2011: 45) and 'one of the features [*sic*] of the city' (Newnham 1985: 120) – were also later constructed on the outskirts of Hoddle's central grid. Railway stations, exhibition buildings and market halls built in the nineteenth century were invariably constructed of iron and glass, like their counterparts and precursors in London, Paris and other European cities, such as Berlin. Market halls, such as Queen Victoria Market, also 'employ the arcade's method of spatial access', as Geist ([1979] 1983: 33) puts it, with long rows of stalls and passageways between them. In addition, Benjamin ([1982] 1999a) and the writers whose quotations he gathers together in *The Arcades Project* note the similarities between these iconic architectural designs and structures of modernity.

Market halls

Rather than writing about the market hall of Paris, Les Halles, in *The Arcades Project*, Benjamin has most to say about the market hall in his recollections and memories of his childhood in Berlin. *Berlin Childhood around 1900* (1950), for Missac, is

'Benjamin's most accomplished work' ([1987] 1995: 41) and 'the author's masterpiece' (162). For Carl Skoggard it 'has emerged as a modern classic of German literature' (2015a: 300). Berlin's Markt-Halle that Benjamin remembers as a child is not so much a marker of modernity, with its iron and glass architecture and passageways (depicted in a photograph from 1899 and reproduced in Benjamin [(1950) 2006: 70]), as it is an avenue to pre-modernity via the women who run the stalls and who lead him back from the present patriarchal capitalism and the agricultural mother earth to the past of the great goddess of the swamps that preceded the city of Berlin, another marshy metropolis like Paris and Melbourne, and another dialectical image.[16]

Recollecting his Berlin childhood, Benjamin relates how in Markt-Halle,

> [b]ehind screened-off partitions [...] reigned the lethargic women: priestesses of commerce-minded Ceres, market women supplying all the fruits of field and tree, all edible fowl, fishes and mammals, procuresses, inviolable wool-clad giants communicating from stall to stall among themselves by means of a flash of their big sweater buttons, a slap on the apron, or perhaps a bosom-heaving sigh. Weren't things seething, swelling, and bubbling up beneath the hems of their skirts, wasn't this the truly fertile soil? Did not a market god himself toss wares into their laps – berries, shellfish, mushrooms, lumps of meat and cabbage – an unseen presence for those who yielded themselves to him [...]?
> (Benjamin [1950] 2015: 42–43)[17]

Skoggard, the translator into English of this edition of Benjamin's *Berlin Childhood*, comments on this passage that

> Benjamin's dream-vision of a seething, female-centred fertility cult in the market owes something to Johan Jacob Bachofen, who in *Muttererrecht* (Mother right) [1861] was the first to hypothesize an early matriarchal civilization. Benjamin showed a lively interest in this work in the early 1920s and would later write a long essay (in French) on Bachofen [...] In Bachofen's second phase of culture, a lunar matriarchy arises, based on agriculture and featuring chthonic mystery cults [...] In the third phase, Dionysus ousts Demeter as the dominant deity.
> (Skoggard 2015b: 204–05)

Benjamin reprises all three phases in his saunters through the market hall; a journey in space can also be travel in time. A different deity presides over each phase, though Skoggard neglects to mention that the early matriarchal civilization focused specifically on, and was presided over by, the matrifocal great goddess or mother of the swamps and marshes, what or who I am calling in the case of Melbourne, Mother Marsha Melba.

As a result, a different economy presides in each phase. The modern market hall enacts the tension between the popular sphere of the marketplace and the semi-public and private sphere of the market or 'civil society' (commodity exchange, social labour, corporations and non-government organizations). The latter can never erase the traces of the former phase with its deities and economy. Nor can the city erase the traces of the marsh in which it was founded – whether it is Paris, Berlin or Melbourne. Perhaps Melbourne is the Berlin of the south, with its Queen Victoria Market with its earthy smells of fresh fruit and vegetables and the fetid smells of fish, meat and cheese that lead the market-goer back to the marshy Melbourne from which the city sprang. Queen Victoria Market is a reminder not only of the pre-modern marsh, but also of the modern cemetery, because 'much of today's market is built on Melbourne's first formal cemetery' (Cunningham 2011: 47; see also Lewis 1995: 47). Beneath the market lies the grotesque lower urban stratum of mortal human remains.

Flannery introduces excerpts from the English journalist George Augustus Sala reporting from Melbourne as 'a vast metropolis sprung from nothing in a single lifetime' (2002: 326). Yet the birth of Melbourne, like the birth of Paris and Berlin, was not from nothing, nor was it instantaneous; it was not created *ex nihilo*, like the God of the biblical book of Genesis in the beginning. Melbourne, for Michael Cannon, 'sprang into being as one of the great cities of the world almost over-night' ([1966] 1976: 12). Melbourne, like Paris and Berlin, sprang into being out of something and out of some-where and some-when. It sprang out of the mater-nal marshes of its indigenous peoples and out of the brainbox of its city fathers and founders. A vast metropolis sprung from the arranged marriage and shotgun wedding between the maternal marshes and the masculine minds of the found-ing fathers. The masculine machine out of which the city sprang was the Hoddle grid, which was where, for Cunningham, 'the embryonic city lived' (2011: 197).

The urban underside

Melbourne is haunted by its ghost swamps. One way in which the absent wetland is present by virtue of its very oblivion is in the tropes for the urban underside. Or to put it in Freudian terms, the repressed wetland returns in figures of speech for the urban underside (see Giblett 2016: 3–32). Melbourne is no exception. Besides, or behind, the Parisian glories of Melbourne, including the arcades and boulevards of Bourke and Collins Streets, Melbourne had, like Paris, its dark and seamy underside in the slums of and off Little Bourke Street.[18] At the same time as Sala was extolling the virtues of 'Marvellous Melbourne', Hume Nisbet was excoriating the vices of monstrous Melbourne:

Little Bourke Street is a world apart from the city of Melbourne, and the race which occupies its crowded courts seems to have no connection with the other people who by day or night promenade along the pavements of Bourke St proper. Few Victorians who look with just pride upon the vast, clean-kept streets and lofty buildings of their monster city know or dream of the life so far removed from all their ideals of home comfort which is seething quietly a few feet away from where they are walking and laughing in happy ignorance.

(Nisbet excerpted in Flannery 2002: 336)

The founding fathers gave birth not only to the monumental city of the arcades and boulevards of Bourke and Collins Streets, but also to the monstrous city of the slums off Little Bourke Street redolent with what Nisbet (excerpted in Flannery 2002: 337–38) called 'the damps and chills of foulness underground', which was 'a vast territory of horrible dens of infamy'.

For Nat Gould, too, 'on an ordinary Sunday, and also on Saturday nights, Bourke Street is the favourite promenade of the masses. Thousands of people of all ages and sexes promenade up and down with monotonous regularity' (1896: 127). Henry Kingsley is less complimentary than Gould about 'the black swarming masses' whom he saw at the east end of Bourke Street in 1858 (Kingsley excerpted in Arnold 1983: 27). Swarming creatures are an abomination (as we saw in a previous chapter). Similarly, Henry Newton Goodrich in 1864 described the 'swarming inhabitants' of Melbourne (Goodrich excerpted in Arnold 1983: 29). 'Promenading' puts a positive spin on public perambulation on the fashionable promenade in the central city, whereas 'swarming' implies that the masses' mode of propulsion in the sub-city slums was subhuman, or even reptilian in keeping with the biblical interdiction against swarming creatures.

At the same time as Sala was praising the virtues of 'Marvellous Melbourne', and as Nisbet was excoriating the vices of monstrous Melbourne, and after Kingsley described its swarming masses, Fergus Hume, in his best-selling detective novel and 'the first popular Melbourne novel' (Arnold 1983: 7–8) *The Mystery of a Hansom Cab*, first published in 1886, was evoking vividly, like Nesbit, the Dantesque 'Infernal Regions' (179) 'off Little Bourke St' (178). Like the epic hero descending into the underworld to slay monsters and return home triumphant, 'the detective led the way down a dark lane, which felt like a furnace owing to the heat of the night' (178). The infernal distress of the slums of Bourke Street can be contrasted with what Marjorie Clark (cited in Arnold 1983: 69) in 1927 described as 'the cool charm of its [Collins Street's] arcades'. Worse for the detective entering the slums of Bourke Street, it was 'like walking in the valley of the shadow of death' (Hume: [1886] 1999: 180). The narrator comments, '[a]nd, indeed, it was not unlike the description in Bunyan's famous allegory what with the semidarkness, the wild lights and shadows' (180). Hume combines Dante's *Inferno* (1472), Bunyan's *Pilgrim's Progress* (1678) and the biblical Psalmist, as Bunyan is drawing on Psalm 23: 4 (as we will see shortly), in an omnibus and ominous grab bag of tropes for the urban underworld.

As an aside here, these pages are excerpted and reproduced as a quintessential depiction of the 'mean streets and back alleys' of late nineteenth-century Melbourne as depicted in crime fiction for the anthology *Literary Melbourne*, edited by Stephen Grimwade (2009: 187–90). The reference to 'the valley of the shadow of death' is later misquoted by Grimwade as 'the shadow of the valley of death' (2009: 244). This misquotation gives a new nuance to the idea of death-valley transposed here from the remote deserts of California to inner-city Melbourne. Both are deadly places. As Cannon puts it, 'the Angel of Death came early and stayed late in the Melbourne of 1892 and 1893' ([1966] 1976: 42), with 'epidemics of influenza, typhoid and measles [...] which [...] killed thousands' (43). It is only a hop, skip and a jump from Bunyan's and the Psalmist's 'valley of the shadow of death' to Hume's alley of the shadow of death and Grimwade's shadow of the valley of death.

The detective's journey into the urban underworld is not only physical but also moral and allegorical. The detective novel is a secular allegory of literal and spiritual descent and ascent, of degradation and salvation, just like the sacred allegory of Bunyan's *Pilgrims Progress* (1678). Arcades are secular, architectural passages between the material and the spiritual, just as allegory is a sacred, textual passage from the material to the spiritual. Baudelaire, for Benjamin ([1982] 1999a: 228–387), was a writer of secular allegories that bore traces of the sacred textual passage from the material to the spiritual.

In the case of Sherlock Holmes, the detective's journey also includes an allegorical descent into the Bunyanesque 'Slough of Despond' of Great Grimpen Mire in *The Hound of the Baskervilles* (1902; see Giblett 1996: 170–72, 2019b: 103–04). Flinders Street in 1845 was described as 'that slough of despond' (cited in Annear 2014: 40). The swamp outside the city in the country, or inside the city in the muddy streets or slums, is a secularized satanic space. Perhaps it is fitting that the *flâneur* is a creature of the arcades, which Geist describes as 'a secularised sacred space' ([1979] 1983: vii). The swamp is a secularized satanic space for the detective, whereas it is a sacred space for indigenous, traditional peoples. The secularized satanic space of the swamp could be the native or natural swamp of the country, or the feral or cultural 'swamp' of the slums of the city, in which the latter is used as a figure for the former (see Giblett 2016). The commonplace responses of dread and horror that were projected onto the native quaking zone of the swamp were displaced onto the industrial quaking zone of the urban underside. These writers are 'placist' in that they ascribe to the lower regions of an artificial place

100

(the city) characteristics that were previously ascribed to a place not made with human hands (jungle, abyss, nether-land, swamps, etc.). The negative connotations that attach to the latter (horror, disease, melancholy, monstrosity) are applied to the former in placial discrimination.

In *Pilgrim's Progress*, Bunyan takes the fourth verse of Psalm 23 referring to the valley of the shadow of death for his text and sermonizes on how 'Christian must needs go through it, because the way to the Celestial City lay through the midst of it' (65). Typically the detective in the modern city must go through the valley of the shadow of death of the underworld of the slums in the monstrous, grotesque underside of the city in order to protect the upper city of the upper ten thousand living in the upper world of the crystalline celestial city. Or the hero of the modern epic of the novel, such as Jean Valjean in Hugo's *Les Misérables* (1827), must descend into the underworld of the sewers of Paris (see Giblett 2016: 35–58). The modern hero of the tourist can even follow in Valjean's footsteps and go on a tour of the sewers of Paris in the Seine underworld. Although Melbourne does not have such an official tour of its sewers, 'a small group has for several decades mounted regular unlawful explorations of Melbourne's stormwater drains and tunnels', in what Otto calls 'a Yarra underworld' (2009: 175). Cunningham also comments that 'while Melbourne does not boast Paris's hundreds of kilometres of underground tunnels, it does have Anzac, a cavernous drain under South Yarra where many parties have been held over the years' (2011: 147).

Later in *Pilgrim's Progress*, Christian is informed that 'the valley [of the shadow of death] itself' (67) is

> as dark as pitch: we also saw there the hobgoblins, satyrs, and dragons of the pit; we heard also in that valley a continual howling and yelling, as of a people under unutterable misery, who there sat bound in affliction and irons; and over that hung the discouraging clouds of confusion; Death also does always spread his wings over it. In a word, it is every whit dreadful, being utterly without order.
>
> (Bunyan [1678] 2008: 69)

As the underworld is a monstrous place itself inhabited by monsters, so is 'the monster city'.

In a similar vein, Little Bourke Street for Hume, in *The Mystery of a Hansom Cab*, has its 'weird and grotesquely horrible' inhabitants (220). In a word, they are monstrous. Little Bourke Street contrasts with Bourke Street proper, not only in the type of inhabitants, but also in the mode of illumination. Bourke Street is described 'as the brilliantly lit street' (178) highlighting the members of the crowd caught in 'the full blaze of the electric light' (176). By contrast, while Little Bourke Street is lit by 'sparsely scattered gas lamps' with their 'dim light' (180), the lanes have no lights or lamps so they are dark, or 'not quite dark, for the atmosphere had that luminous kind of haze so observable in Australian twilights, and the weird light was just sufficient to make the darkness visible' (180). Typically, the fictive detective of the modern city enlightens the benighted, brings light to darkness and illuminates the crepuscular gloom of crime and grime.

The play of light and darkness between the overworld of the boulevard and the underworld of the backblocks in *The Mystery of a Hansom Cab*, creating 'the semidarkness, the wild lights and shadows' (as we have seen), is typical of the phantasmagoria of the modern capital(ist) city. Benjamin ([1982] 1999a: 26) saw modernity dominated by its phantasmagorias exemplified both by the arcades of Paris and by the figures of the poetic *flâneur* and the fictional detective. The *flâneur*, for Benjamin, 'abandons himself to the phantasmagoria of the marketplace' ([1982] 1999a: 14), typically in the light-filled arcades opening off the well-lit boulevards, while the detective abandons himself to the phantasmagoria of the metropolis in the dark and dingy slums also opening off the well-lit boulevards. The slums of Bourke St are also hot and can be contrasted with what Marjorie Clark in 1927 described as 'the cool charm of its [Collins Street's] arcades' (cited in Arnold 1983: 69). Benjamin made a connection 'between flânerie and the detective novel' in that the detective is 'preformed in the figure of the *flâneur*' ([1982] 1999a: 441–42). The detective pursues traces left by dwelling, whereas the *flâneur* pursues traces left by walking.

Edgar Allan Poe is an important early writer of detective fiction. For Benjamin, in 'Philosophy of Furniture' (1840) Poe is 'the first physiognomist of the domestic interior' ([1982] 1999a: 9); in 'The Man of the Crowd' (1840), Poe is the first physiognomist of the foreign or feral interior of people massing in the exteriority of the street. The eponymous man of Poe's story is of the crowd, not merely in it; he experiences the crowd as an interior and comforting place, as well as an exterior and alienating space. Like Poe, Hume as a writer of detective fiction is the physiognomist of the inner spaces of dwellings and the inner spaces off streets, the exterior interior as it were.

For Lucy Sussex in *Blockbuster!*, her 'biography' of the book *The Mystery of a Hansom Cab*

> Hume was a *flâneur*, a term defined by Baudelaire as 'a person who walks the city in order to experience it'. To stroll through Melbourne today is to experience both its present and its past [...] Through *Hansom Cab* we saunter into a lost place, Marvellous Melbourne.
>
> (2015: 2)

Marvellous Melbourne is lost in the past and cannot be experienced in the present except in what Benjamin called a dialectical image in which past and present are overlaid, such as in the monuments (buildings and memorials) of Marvellous Melbourne which are visible for all to see. By contrast, the traces of Melbourne's wetlands are largely invisible, but are present (in the present) by virtue of their very oblivion. To stroll through Melbourne today is to experience both its present and its past, because Marvellous Melbourne is a lost and found place. In sauntering through the city and reading the city, we can read it, and its wetlands also, as a lost and found place.

Like Poe for Benjamin, Hume for Sussex had 'an important role in establishing detective fiction as a publishing category', as he is 'one of the most influential crime writers of all time' who wrote 'the biggest-selling crime novel of the nineteenth century, and one of the most important Australian books ever' (2015: 7). Sussex traces the etymology of the word 'detective' and how it literally means 'de-roofing', so 'a detective raises the roof, figuratively' (2015: 9). The detective in the detective story, and the detective storyteller, raises the roof of dwelling spaces, looks inside and reveals what is inside to the reader. The detective and detective-story reader are positioned as snooping voyeurs.

Sussex also traces how this uncovering and de-roofing had a demonic function and cites how Dickens in *Dombey and Son* (1848), pleaded for 'a good spirit who would take the house-tops off' (cited in Sussex 2015: 9–10). David Grann similarly traces how 'the term "to detect" derived from the Latin verb to "unroof," and because the devil, according to legend, allowed his henchmen to peer voyeuristically into houses by removing their roofs, detectives were known as "the devil's disciples"' (2017: 57). In the 1891 Sherlock Holmes story 'A Case of Identity', Conan Doyle has Holmes describe the detective's work of unroofing in similar terms (though without the etymology and the theological overtones). The detective in the detective story, and the detective storyteller too, performs these socially useful, but morally ambiguous, roles of the good, or demonic, spirit. Both were *flâneurs* who entered 'the city's central hell [of] the slums', as Sussex (2015: 60) puts it in relation to Hume and *The Mystery of a Hansom Cab*. As with the circles of Dante's hell, or inferno, the city has a centre, and its centre is the lower depths of its slums and sewers, the grotesque lower urban strata. Seemingly, the most secularized literary genre of the detective story about the modern city has strong theological undertones.

When Hume arrived in Melbourne in 1885 the city was what Sussex (2015: 58) calls 'a bustling, go-ahead metropolis, the wealthy commercial capital of the country built on gold money [...] [as well as] the largest urban centre in Australasia, [and so for all these reasons] "The London of the South"', according to some citizens. Like Melbourne, London was also a swamp city built on the banks of a marshy river.[19] London and Melbourne are not only commercial capitals but also the classic cities of nineteenth-century detective fiction, with Conan Doyle's Sherlock Holmes as inextricably associated with London as his contemporary Hume is with Melbourne.[20] More specifically, *Hansom Cab*, for Sussex, was 'intimately tied to Marvellous Melbourne and its fall. The novel depicted the city at its glorious zenith, but with overtones of foreboding [...] [of] the 1890s depression' (2015: 209).

Marvellous Melbourne

The development of 'Marvellous Melbourne' in the late 1880s was the culmination of an uneven process that had been occurring for some decades before that. For Archibald Ritchie writing in 1860,

> the Melbourne of 1852, then but a very inferior English town, unpaved, unlighted, muddy, miserable, dangerous, has become transformed into a great city, as comfortable, as elegant, as luxurious (it is hardly an exaggeration to say it), as any place out of London or Paris.
>
> (Ritchie cited in Serle 1963: 369)

Much of Melbourne from the 1860s was paved, lighted, dry, congenial and safe as befitting an iconic city of modernity, though, like London and Paris, it also had its unpaved, unlighted, muddy, miserable and dangerous places as depicted by Hume, and as befitting a demotic city of modernity.

However, rather than the London or Paris of the south, or both for one real estate spruiker (cited in Davison 1978: 138), Melbourne for one writer from Geelong in 1850 was 'perhaps destined to become the New York of the future United States of the South' (excerpted in Grant and Serle 1957: 66; cited in Lewis 1995: 31 and Annear 2014: 231–32). Along similar lines, Richard Horne in 1859 'hailed Melbourne as "the New York of the Southern Hemisphere"' (cited in Davison 1978: 230). Melbourne for Francis Adams had 'something of London, something of Paris, something of New York, and something of her own' (excerpted in Flannery 2002: 330–31). Like Berlin, Paris and Melbourne, New York was founded in marshes, but this is probably not what these writers had in mind in making the comparison.[21] Nor were they probably referring to New York's grid of plots and streets north of Washington Square (Homberger 2002: 26). New York, for Richard Sennett, is 'a grid city par excellence' with 'no fixed edge or centre' (1994: 359), like Melbourne. New York was later given Times Square as, or at, its dubious centre as Melbourne was given City Square (as we will see later in this chapter).

Perhaps Horne and the Geelong writer were referring to the Dutch city south of Washington Square with its irregular pattern of streets that bore some organic relationship to the topography and shape of the island. Or perhaps they were being prescient about New York becoming the economic and cultural capital of the United States in the late nineteenth century and the world capital of the twentieth century. Some likenesses with Melbourne, albeit within the narrower compass of Australia, are warranted, though comparison with other cities as national capitals is also warranted, such as London, Berlin, Paris and Washington DC (another 'swamp city'),[22] because Melbourne was the political capital of the newly federated Australia from 1901 to the establishment of Canberra as the national capital in 1927 (see Otto 2009: 1–31). Comparison is also warranted between Melbourne and Toronto as Melbourne is the state capital of Victoria and Toronto is the provincial capital of Ontario.

The Geelong writer certainly did not see Melbourne as 'the Paris of the south' because for him/her Melbourne has 'no boulevards' (excerpted in Grant and Serle 1957: 65; cited in Lewis 1995: 31). Newnham defends Hoddle and his grid on the basis that 'the broad central streets of the city are Melbourne's only memorial to its first planner, Robert Hoddle' (1985: 67). Unfortunately, the name 'Hoddle' is associated more recently by Cunningham (2011: 4) and others with the 'Hoddle Street massacre' in which seven people were killed and nineteen injured by a lone ex-army sniper in 1987. Although Collins and Bourke Streets may not have qualified as boulevards for the Geelong writer, such 60-metre-wide tree-lined avenues as Royal Parade and St Kilda Road did qualify as boulevards for Lewis (1995: 31, 98). St Kilda Road for Newnham is 'one of the loveliest [roads] in the world' (1985: 67).

The Geelong writer, however, was generally critical of the Hoddle grid plan, perhaps for good reason:

> Melbourne has no large central square, possesses no main arterial streets, conducting to the heart of the town, ventilating its back lanes and carrying health to its crowded quarters, has no suburban roads, giving easy access to the country, no boulevards, no great lines of communication uniting public buildings.
>
> (excerpted in Grant and Serle 1957: 65; cited in Lewis 1995: 31)

Melbourne, in other words, in terms of the trope of the city as the human body, is deformed and diseased. The lack of a central square is a product of the rectilinear grid-plan as it has no defined centre, unlike the radial city radiating out from a central hub.

City centre

Although Melbourne in the nineteenth century did not have a central square on its surface, it did have a central circle in its depths and on its surface. The Myer department store is located in almost the exact centre of Hoddle's grid on two blocks of wetland that Batman bought and sold in 1838, 'believing them to be worthless swamp', as Coote (2013: 90) puts it. Coote (2013: 90) reproduces the plan of the Hoddle grid showing the two blocks of the worthless swamp and site of the Myer department store as a black spot. The wetland is a black spot on the landscape, whether it be the grid-plan town or the gentleman's park estate, and a blot in the ledger of both.[23] The modern city is three dimensional, not only above the surface of the earth in its monumental structures, soaring heights and glittering facades, such as the department store (an icon of modernity), but also behind these visible aspects and beneath the city in the depths of the monstrous swamps, slums and sewers in the grotesque lower earthly and urban strata. The Myer department store was located in the mire of Melbourne, as it was in Perth in Wellington Street on the edge of the Northbridge wetlands.

The trouble with the grid plan is that one size fits all and so it is written over the land (wet and dry) with scant regard for what was there in the first place, except for major geophysical features, such as rivers, in Melbourne's case the Yarra on the banks of which Hoddle's grid was located in parallel. The 'plan' for Melbourne, as Asa Briggs calls it, 'paid little attention to physical features' (1963: 286), such as its wetlands (as we have seen in Chapters Two and Four). The grid-plan town is a rigid grid-iron, as Robin Boyd ([1960] 2010: 47) indicates. Briggs goes on to point out that 'such grid-iron development took no account of physical contours, and allowed for neither crescents [...], nor squares' (1963: 287). In Hoddle's grid, according also to Annear, 'no space was allowed for a public square, considered a breeding ground for the spirit of democracy' (2014: 18). In this respect, Melbourne is similar to Hausmann's Paris. Yet, according to Graeme Davison, Hoddle did propose 'a public square on a site near the present State library but nothing came of it' (2016: 261). Hoddle's proposal was revived during the centenary of the city in 1935, but nothing came of that either (Davison 2016: 243). The lack of a central square thus haunted Melbourne for some time until 'City Square' – '(well, it's a rectangle, really)', as Cunningham (2011: 168) points out, like Fed 'Square' – was carved out on Swanston Street between Collins Street and Flinders Lane.[24] Davison describes it as 'a cramped little rectangle opposite the Town Hall' (2016: 261). Cunningham relates how 'the Melbourne City Council started buying up land near the Melbourne Town Hall in 1966 to create space for a central plaza, and many of the city's Victorian buildings and arcades were lost in the process' (2011: 167). City Square is currently a building site for a new underground railway station.

One arcade to be lost in the process, in the march of 'progress', was Queen's Walk with what Cannon calls its 'wonderful lead-light cupolas sheltering a shopping arcade' ([1966] 1976: 8), which was for him the epitome of 'Marvellous Melbourne'. Perhaps the 'wrecking' (as Cannon [(1966) 1976: 304] later calls it in a caption to a photograph)[25] of 'Queens [Walk] Arcade' in 1966 to make way for City Square marks another point in the architectural demise of 'Marvellous Melbourne' and the inception of postmodern Melbourne in the same place, and at the same time. The two cities continue to coexist side-by-side, which makes Melbourne a more interesting city than Perth, where most of the old city has gone and the postmodern predominates. City Square, for Newnham, was 'the city's first major square' and 'one of the most important projects undertaken by the Melbourne City Council' (1985: 58). It was opened in 1980 by Queen Elizabeth II and cost $25 million.

Yet 'the true centre' of the city of Melbourne socially and culturally, not geometrically, for Jenny Sinclair is at 'the intersection outside Flinders Street Station' (2015: 23). This for her is 'a place everyone passes through one way or another' by road or rail. And by foot, as it is no place to stop, except at the foot of the steps to the station under the clocks, 'the traditional Melbourne meeting place', as Otto (2009: 334) points out, or across the road at what Sinclair calls 'the postmodern jumble of Federation Square' (2015: 23), with what she later calls 'the crazy starburst [vertical] surfaces of [the buildings of] Federation Square', based on Voronoi diagrams (113–14). Fed Square is now one of the central meeting places in the city. The city now has a central square on its surface. Under the clocks outside Flinders Street Station is more like a passageway to somewhere else and not the most congenial place to meet. The city also did have the central circles of its slums, like the Dantesque circles of hell and the Biblical and Bunyanesque valley of the shadow of death in its depths, but they are not its heart. Its heart is the maternal marshes on which it was built.

The writing of the grid-plan town on the surface of the earth after the filling or draining of its marshy or swampy depths is preceded by the drawing of the grid plan on the surface of parchment or paper or drafting film. The Geelong writer goes on to describe how Melbourne

> has its river; but the lines of houses on the banks, instead of gracefully sweeping round with the stream, run off at a tangent from it. In short, the only skill exhibited in the plan of Melbourne is that involved in the use of square and compasses.
>
> (excerpted in Grant and Serle 1957: 65; cited in Lewis 1995: 31)

The drafting instruments of tee-square and set-square slide over the surface of the plan and reproduce relentlessly the rectilinear grid, irrespective of the graceful curves of a river and the irregular shapes of wetlands that lay beneath and beside the city in reality.

Rather than the New York or Paris of the south, Melbourne has been seen variously as 'the Athens of the South' (Roe 1974: 81), as 'the Chicago of the south'

(Briggs 1963: 286), 'a sort of Queen Anne Chicago' (Lewis 1995: 9), and even as 'the Chicago of the Newest World' (Roe 1974: 11), the newest world of Australia, newer than the new world of the Americas. The fact that Chicago was only founded five years before Melbourne points to the haste in which boosters seized on any outlandish comparison and possible exemplar. Just as Boston as the capital of Massachusetts in the United States wanted to be the 'Athens of America', so did Melbourne as the capital of Victoria want to be 'the Athens of the south'. Boston and Chicago, like Melbourne, were built on waterside swamps and marshes;[26] Boston and Chicago, like Melbourne, were the centre of a railway network for the transport and export of pastoral and agricultural produce; Chicago and Melbourne were slaughterhouse cities; all three were also port cities; Boston, like Melbourne (both unlike Chicago), are state capitals with larger aspirations to preside over the north-east corner of the United States and the south-east segment of Australia, respectively. Chicago, however, was the home of steel-framed skyscrapers well before Melbourne built any. Melbourne, as Davison sums up 'the phenomenal city', 'had its slums and smells as well as its skyscrapers and fine suburbs' (1984: vii). Skyscrapers and fine suburbs do not seem possible without slums and smells.

Rather than the New York, or Chicago, or Paris, or Berlin, or Athens of the south, Melbourne, for Flannery, is 'the Los Angeles of the south, with its crowning glories a racetrack on top of the Yarra's old billabong at Albert Park' (2002: 22), the former South Melbourne swamp. Former Premier Jeff Kennett may well 'probably be remembered', as Flannery (2002: 22) puts it, for this and other monumental constructions of Los Angelean hypermodernity, such as tolled freeways. Yet, rather than the Los Angeles, or Paris, or Gotham (New York) of the south, Melbourne is more the Toronto of the south (as I have suggested in Chapter Three), not only because both cities were founded next to wetlands and developed ports on those wetlands, and because both are provincial or state capitals, but also because both cities developed industry adjacent to their port wetland and river delta sites around the same time in the late nineteenth century, the heyday of industrial capitalism.[27]

NOTES

1. For Paris, see Giblett (2016: 35–58, 'Paris: or, Lutetia, "The Filthy Marsh"').
2. Davison (2016) refers variously to Maurice Ress (190), Leon Ress (caption to Wolfgang Sievers' photograph facing 255) and the latter's unnamed wife as the instigator of this innovation (247).
3. Missac ([1987] 1995: 147–97) traces the architectural lineage from the arcade to the atrium. Missac was a friend of Benjamin in Paris in the 1930's.
4. For the illuminated city of Melbourne as an ephemeral fairyland during the celebrations of Federation in 1901, see also Lewis (1995: 90).

5. As do his editors; see Benjamin ([1982] 1999a: 56, 83, 959 note 12, 1038).

6. See Giblett (2016: 35–58, 'Paris: or, Lutetia, "The Filthy Marsh"').

7. The literature on the *flâneur* is now huge. The classic discussion is by Benjamin ([1982] 1999a: 416–55, convolute M, 'The *flâneur*'). For a recent French discussion of the *flâneur* in the context of the history of Paris, see Hazan (2010: 315–339, 'Flâneurs').

8. This *Guide* seems to have been plagiarizing Eduard Devrient, who is also cited later by Benjamin ([1982] 1999a: 42).

9. In this note, Missac ([1987] 1995: 219, note 5) refers to Geist's monumental book on arcades which refers ([1979] 1983: 581 note 497), in turn, to the article on Melbourne's arcades by Garside and White (1963: 80–84). I bought a copy of Missac's book in 2016 from the Collected Works bookshop in the Nicholas Building above Cathedral Arcade, a fitting location to come across a book about Benjamin's work on Paris's arcades with an endnote about Melbourne's arcades. It might have been sitting on the shelves for twenty years waiting for someone writing about these topics to find it and buy it. Objects have a life of their own, often a serendipitous one as in this case, as Benjamin well knew. Sadly, Collected Works bookshop closed in 2018. Serendipity in research, as in life, is a rare and valuable phenomenon.

10. See also Otto (2009: 95–99), who incorrectly has 'Howey Court' (95) rather than Howey Place.

11. See http://www.powells.com/locations/powells-city-of-books. Accessed 1 May 2015.

12. For the biographical and biblical background to Gog and Magog, see Coote (2013: 96–97).

13. Garside and White (and so Geist) do not mention Cathedral Arcade, Capitol Arcade and the Manchester Unity building arcade, nor do they show them on their maps of Melbourne's arcades.

14. As Hoddle's grid shows, and as reproduced by Coote (2013: 28–29).

15. As Coote (2013: 123) later points out.

16. For the history of Berlin as a marshy metropolis, see Giblett (2016: 97–113).

17. For a slightly different translation by Howard Eiland, see Benjamin ([1950] 2006: 70–71).

18. For the slums and sewers of Paris, see Giblett (2016: 35–58).

19. For the history of London as a swamp city, and as Sherlock Holmes's city, see Giblett (2016: 59–81).

20. Conan Doyle and Hume were both born in 1859; see Sussex (2015: 12).

21. For the history of New York as a marsh metropolis, see Giblett (2016:145–62).

22. For the history of Washington as a swamp city, see Giblett (2016: 215–24).

23. For the black spot of a wetland as a blot on the landscape of the gentleman's park estate and in his ledger, see Giblett (1996: 4–8).

24. For the city square 'saga', see also Lewis (1995: 132).

25. The caption refers to 'Queen's Arcade […] now the site of the City Square'. Cannon's book has separate index entries for 'Queens Arcade' and 'Queens Walk' when he is referring to the same site (Cannon [1966] 1976: 332). According to Garside and White, 'Queen's

Arcade was built between Little Bourke Street and Lonsdale Street' (1963: 80–81) in 1853, whereas 'Queen's Walk' arcade was built in 1889 between Swanston and Collins Streets.

26. For the history of Boston as a marsh metropolis, see Giblett (2016: 163–81) and for the history of Chicago as a swamp city, see Giblett (2016: 225–37).

27. For the history of Toronto as a marsh metropolis and swamp city, see Giblett (2014: 133–52, 2016: 197–213).

Nature on Display

The Royal Botanic Gardens Melbourne (RBGM), now the Melbourne Gardens and part of what is now called 'Royal Botanic Gardens Victoria', are a site where the distinct contribution of both the sciences and the arts/humanities to the formation and development of the Garden over time can still be seen today. The sciences are evident in the formal garden beds and named floral species. Nature is displayed here as taxonomic natural history in a botanical garden as if it were specimens in a cabinet of curiosities. The arts/humanities are expressed in the pleasing prospects of lawns, lakes and avenues of trees. Nature is displayed here as landscape in a public park as if it were scenes in a panorama. Landscape (whether it be in landscape painting, landscape writing, landscape architecture, landscape design or landscape gardening) and natural history are two different, competing discourses of nature. Despite their obvious differences, both disciplines and discourses put nature on display. Both also entailed the destruction of the pre-contact wetlands on the site. In response, and drawing on more recent understandings of nature, including the value of wetlands and the need to conserve the ones remaining and restore the ones that have been lost, wetland restoration in the Gardens could work in concert with an environmental work of art. This could consist of a multimedia diorama of archival maps and photographs of the Gardens that acknowledge the contribution then and now of the sciences and arts/humanities to the Gardens and the history and geography of their site.

Nowhere in the Gardens is the history of the contribution of the sciences and arts/humanities to the Gardens' development and of the destruction of the wetlands on the site acknowledged or displayed. The Melbourne Gardens are a place where this forgotten history could be remembered and a site where the lost geography of the site and its wetland could be restored. Wetland restoration could be accompanied by an interpretive diorama of archival maps and photos as an environmental work of art that creates a dialectical image, a visible reminder and expression in the now of what has once been and is now lost.

Scientific and/or artistic gardens?

The Melbourne Gardens are a classic case of the sciences versus the arts/humanities. The struggle between the sciences and humanities in and over the Melbourne Gardens came to the fore under the third and fourth directors of the Gardens. The third director was a botanist who thought that the Gardens should be scientific and taxonomic, whereas the fourth director was a landscape gardener who thought that the Gardens should be aesthetic and picturesque, and perhaps not even botanic gardens at all, but an urban or public park in keeping with other public parks being developed in many places around the world at about the same time as a marker of modernity. In the mid-nineteenth century across Europe and North America there was a movement away from the formal botanic garden and the private rural park towards the informal public urban park.[1] The Melbourne Gardens got caught up in this shift, but stayed resolutely with their original name of the Royal Botanic Gardens Melbourne, until recently when they were renamed Melbourne Gardens, whereas in Perth (Western Australia) Kings Park and Botanic Gardens embrace both traditions in the same site.

Melbourne also has a Royal Park, which 'has long been regarded as iconic Melbourne parkland', as John Taylor (2014: 35) puts it,[2] whereas the Melbourne Gardens have long been regarded as an iconic Melbourne garden, or even as 'Melbourne's garden', as Crosbie Morrison (1957) puts it. Royal Park also has its own reconstructed wetlands (one of which is called 'the Billabong'), whereas the Melbourne Gardens have their own constructed dryland made out of drained wetlands (or billabongs), their Ornamental Lake made out of a 'lagoon' (or billabong), and no reconstructed wetlands as yet, though it has some replanting of local wetland vegetation and floating islands.[3] Melbourne, unlike Perth, has the luxury of both a Royal Botanic Gardens and a Royal Park, and so can maintain the distinct traditions and features of both, at least in name. However, on the ground, over time, the Melbourne Gardens did take on the form and function of a park, as well as maintaining some of the traditional functions of a botanic garden. If the Melbourne Gardens have become 'arguably the most expertly created gardens in the world', as Maree Coote (2013: 124) suggests, then this is more a product of historical and geographical contingency over time, than of planning before the fact – just like the provision of space for the Gardens in the first place (as we saw in the previous chapter).

The struggle between the scientific and the aesthetic continues in the Melbourne Gardens to this day, though in a different register. Science has triumphed over the humanities, botany over beauty, at one level through the development of seed banks, such as the one at Kew Botanic Gardens in London, to which the Melbourne Gardens sends duplicate seeds collected from around Victoria for a project funded by the UK and Victorian governments (Tim Entwisle, director of RBGM, e-mail to the author, 27 June 2016). This offshore shipment is certainly valuable for the conservation of plant species, though it is largely invisible to the average garden goer who enjoys the triumph of the humanities over science, beauty over botany, in the landscapes of the Gardens that are visible to him or her, just as they are to the average garden goer at Kew Gardens. With the development and use of the Internet, though, the seed bank project is visible to the net surfer and virtual garden goer if they are prepared to drill down far enough into the 'Science' page of the Melbourne Gardens website (Royal Botanic Gardens n.d.b).

It is much easier for the net surfer to see the triumphalist history of the Gardens on the 'Our story' webpage that trumpets the transformation of the 'swampy site into the world-famous landscape we know today' (Royal Botanic Gardens n.d.a), a topic to which I return below by recounting the sad and sorry story of the loss of the wetlands on the site. I propose that the Gardens should revise this section of their website and relate their history and the geography of their site in less triumphalist and more wetland-friendly terms and tones that acknowledge, respect and remember the wetlands that have been lost and that made the Gardens possible.

Wetlands were on the site prior to the establishment of the Gardens. They were later aestheticized into an ornamental lake as part of the landscaping of the Gardens into a public urban park. The Gardens have long been subjected to the competing disciplinary demands of science and the humanities, botany and aesthetics. Despite their disciplinary differences, both botany and aesthetics are ocular-centric. They privilege the sense, the subject and the technologies of sight, including taxonomies, herbariums, promenades and prospects, over the original wetlands on the site that were anti-aesthetic and that required or elicited a multisensory and embodied appreciation via immersion, or semi-immersion, and engagement – with the sense of smell in particular.[4]

One place and way to do so in the Melbourne Gardens would be by restoring the Ornamental Lake into a wetland and reconnecting it to the Yarra River via a swale under Alexandra Avenue, which skirts this river and currently divides it from the Gardens. This environmental artwork would be a visible expression of the contribution of the sciences and humanities, botany and aesthetics, natural history and landscape architecture to the history of the Gardens. It would also be a visible expression of the geography of the site and its broader bioregion, including the other lost and found wetlands of Melbourne. Scientific natural history and botanic gardens, the aesthetic landscaped park and the restored wetland would co-exist and co-habit on the site as living reminders of the genealogical 'history of the present' (in Michel Foucault's [1977: 31] terms) of the Gardens and their site. Wetland restoration would also reduce evapotranspiration, provide filtering services and make the Gardens more sustainable in the age of climate catastrophes.

Some steps have already been taken in this direction. The current director of the Gardens, Tim Entwisle (e-mail to the author, 27 June 2016), relates how 'in the past few years there have been extensive plantings of local plants around what we call Long Island, turning at least part of the lake and its edge into something celebrating if not reproducing the original vegetation' (and so not reproducing an adequate habitat suitable for a suite of waterbirds, including waders, as native wetlands with their shallow water do). There have also been extensive plantings of local plants in the eastern corner of the lake. Both sets of plantings, however, have not changed the edge of the lake into a wetland, as the edge of the lake is still steep-sided and stone-lined in keeping with the European idea of a lake with a clear line of demarcation between land and water. This planting is not a wetland as a wetland has no edges, but rather sloping sides that segue from land to water with no clear dividing line between them in keeping with the wetland's rising and falling waters; its wetting and drying cycles; and its shallow, saucer-shaped geomorphology. Entwisle and his team have been constrained by, and give preference to, the Guilfoylean design concept. Removing a section of the 'Northern Lawn' adjacent to the eastern corner of the Lake, grading a gradual slope to a shallow depth below water level in this area, planting it with wetland plants, removing the bluestone wall and allowing the water to flood into the area would be the next step in restoring a more authentic wetland to the Gardens.

In the meantime and to date, it is certainly laudable how, as Entwisle goes on to describe,

> we employ floating islands and various 'wetlands' to treat storm water these days, getting up to 40% of our irrigation from non-potable sources. This water flows into Ornamental Lake (the lake formed [in part] when the river was rerouted), pumped up to what we call Guilfoyle's Volcano (with the energy off-set through solar panels) and then flowing down through the Fern Gully back into the lake. The floating islands absorb nutrients and the plant material on these is harvested from time to time.
>
> (Entwisle, e-mail to the author, 27 June 2016)

Floating islands are located in both Guilfoyle's Volcano and the Ornamental Lake.[5]

The restored vegetation and the new water regime function, however, to provide 'environmental services', rather than to be a fully functioning wetland in its own right. It is as if the wetland has to justify its existence and earn its keep in terms other than its own. Again, Guilfoyle's landscape design and its subsequent interpretation and extension over the last century have guided decision making. Although, as Entwisle notes, 'the floating islands and some of the recent additions to encourage wildlife and help conserve water challenge key elements of that original design, so compromises are made from time to time' (e-mail to the author, 27 June 2016).

These 'environmental services' and replanting are vestiges of the original wetlands on the site. Entwisle argues that 'changes over the last decade, particularly around Long Island, have reclaimed at least the echo of the swamp and its vegetation' (e-mail to the author, 27 June 2016). The wetland that was reclaimed from the river and the lagoon has been re-reclaimed partially in re-vegetation for the provision of mere 'environmental services'. As billabongs are, as Kristin Otto puts it, 'shadows and echoes of the river' (2005: 63), Entwisle's echo is, in fact, an echo of an echo. To hear it requires a garden goer curious enough to leave the sealed pathway and walk across the lawn to bend down and read the excellent ground-level signs dotted around the site at various points at the north-eastern corner of the Ornamental Lake, which describe the wetland vegetation replanting, the floating islands and the wetlands that were once on the site. Only then would the garden goer hear the echo of the forgotten history and the lost geography of the Gardens and their wetlands.

Rather than re-reclaiming an echo of the swamp in the lake, restoring the Ornamental Lake (or portions of it) to a fully functioning wetland and creating a multimedia diorama of archival maps and photographs of the Gardens could work in concert with each other in order to provide the context of the history of the present and the geography of the past of the Gardens and their site in order to enable the garden goer to see and appreciate the dialectical image of the wetland and the lake.[6] The restored wetland and a multimedia diorama would together form a kind of double (or stereoscopic) dialectical image that would act in concert and be mutually reinforcing. These environmental works of art would emphasize a mode of thinking, feeling, sensing, designing and making that is attuned to environmental change and inherently collective in nature.

One without the other would be inadequate. The restored wetland would require interpretation and contextualization to make sense of it (as the 'floating islands' do have signage), and the diorama would require wetland restoration to make it more than mere window-dressing and touristic display of a lost and forgotten wetland and world. The restored wetland would be a living memorial (and not a dead monument) to the lost wetlands of Melbourne that were destroyed. It would also be a reminder of the living wetlands of Melbourne that can still be found to this day in various sites in and around the city in the Yarra River bioregion, such as Banyule Billabong and Bolin Bolin Billabong, and it would promote their conservation (as we have seen in previous chapters).

Two directors, two directions

The Melbourne Gardens were subjected to competing scientific and aesthetic imperatives right from their beginnings in 1845. Baron Ferdinand von Mueller, the government botanist from 1853, was director of the Gardens from 1857 to 1873. He subscribed to the scientific side, whereas the garden-going public generally supported the aesthetic side. Geoffrey Serle describes von Mueller as 'no artist entertainer but a scientist and an educator' (1963: 366), who 'made the Gardens a museum of botany for the next sixteen years' under his directorship. More recent historians and commentators have been less polite and more acerbic about von Mueller. Jill Roe describes how

> Australia's most famous nineteenth-century botanist, Baron von Mueller, [...] set up Melbourne's now beautiful Botanical Gardens like a scientific market gardens, or a nursery: he cared nothing for landscapes and patterns of colour, being far too busy revealing the facts of Australia's flora.
>
> (Roe 1974: 84)

In other words, he only cared for science and nothing for aesthetics, though he did care for, and promote, recreation.

Similarly, a century before Roe, for Anthony Trollope, visiting Australia in 1870 during von Mueller's directorship, the Melbourne Gardens were more scientific than those in Adelaide and Sydney, 'but the world at large cares little for science [...] The gardens at Melbourne are as a long sermon from a great divine, – whose theology is unanswerable, but his language tedious' (1876: vol. I, 26). Perhaps Trollope, as the novelist *par excellence* of nineteenth-century provincial clergy who delivered long and boring sermons in tedious terms, was well-qualified to detect the same propensities in von Mueller. For Trollope, who was also a landscape writer,[7] von Mueller has 'made these gardens a perfect paradise for science for those given to botany rather than to beauty [...] But the gardens though spacious are not charming [...] The Baron has sacrificed beauty to science' (1876: vol. II, 36). Von Mueller's successor, William Guilfoyle, arguably sacrificed science to beauty, botany to aesthetics.

Later commentators, however, have seen the Gardens as balancing botany and beauty over the course of their history. For Bill Newnham, in his biography of Melbourne, the Gardens have 'since [their founding] won great praise for their beauty and scientific interest' (1985: 152, see also 153–55). Beauty and scientific interest have been competing imperatives for the Gardens, and especially for their third and fourth directors, von Mueller and Guilfoyle. Von Mueller inclined more to the scientific side and Guilfoyle to the aesthetic side. Both sides are valuable, but so too were the wetlands on the site, which were destroyed to create the scientific and aesthetic Gardens. Restoring the anti-aesthetic wetland in the Gardens would provide greater balance to botany and beauty, the scientific and aesthetic, as well as display the forgotten history and lost geography of their site.

During the early directorship of Baron von Mueller, in the words of Richard Pescott, director of the Melbourne Gardens from 1957 to 1970, in his history of the Gardens:

> The public was expecting continuous floral displays, sweeping lawns and vistas, a beautiful landscaped setting as in the English style it knew. Instead Mueller developed the Gardens as a scientific and educational institution [...]. This type of garden made no concession to the needs of a general public wanting a pleasant venue for recreation [...]. In reality aesthetic concerns gave way to scientific exactitude.
>
> (Pescott 1982: 79)

Aesthetic concerns gave way early on to scientific exactitude in both theory and practice, more than in practice alone, only to make a comeback later in practice.

Pescott later highlights in his history (and in his tortuous syntax with some additional commas):

> the fundamental differences between Guilfoyle's philosophy of the function of a botanic garden and his background in the English landscaping tradition and that of von Mueller and his European background [in the Linnean taxo-nomic tradition]. Von Mueller was a botanist first and foremost, and for him a botanic gardens [sic] was essentially for the teaching and forwarding of botan-ical science, the juxtaposition of plants being based on scientific requirements, and 'a healthy locality for recreation' being a secondary consideration. Guil-foyle was a horticulturalist and, while agreeing with von Mueller on the scien-tific purpose of a botanic gardens [sic], he considered such requirements were to be balanced by recreational and aesthetic ones in the design of the gardens.
>
> (Pescott 1982: 101)

The phrase, 'a healthy locality for recreation', is von Mueller's own, though in his original context he did not regard it as a secondary consideration, as indicated when Pescott (1982: 37) cites von Mueller earlier.

Commentators have tended to overstate the differences between the two direc-tors when it comes to recreation, claiming that von Mueller was against recreation and Guilfoyle for it. Both were for it. At issue between the two directorships was what sort of recreation was appropriate for a botanic garden. Guilfoyle was more

117

for the recreation of the stroller promenading through the park and taking in the pleasing prospect of the landscape gardens, whereas von Mueller was more for the recreation of the serious student (amateur or professional) of botany examining the specimens of flora displayed in the botanic gardens.

Other accounts have highlighted the differences between the two directors on the more solid and visible ground of garden layout. The 'Biographical sketch of W. R. Guilfoyle' in *The Jubilee History of Victoria and Melbourne* (1888) highlights their differences by describing how

> the gardens, which under the regime of his predecessor, Baron von Mueller, had been more in the nature of a scientific herbary than a recreation ground and botanic garden combined ... underwent a rapid transformation. The prim geometrical polygons, still straight lines, and angular monstrosities were ruthlessly invaded, and out of chaos was educed order and beauty.
>
> (excerpted in Grant and Serle 1957: 149)

Guilfoyle transformed von Mueller's formal, geometric, scientific and continental garden, a kind of taxonomic grid of species in garden form, into an informal, landscaped and picturesque English garden, a kind of picture of pleasing prospects in garden form.

The Gardens, for von Mueller, were the living book of botany as a branch of natural history arrayed in taxonomic display (to reuse Foucault's terms), whereas for Guilfoyle they were the living aesthetics of picturesque and beautiful flora displayed in landscapes (Foucault 1970: 135, see 132–33 for the privileging of sight and the denigration of the other senses in and by natural history). The Melbourne Gardens, for von Mueller, were what Foucault (1970: 137) calls 'the inevitable correlative' of natural history that operated 'within a taxonomic area of visibility' found in scientific botanic gardens (and natural history collections). The botanic garden is a natural history collection writ large on the land (and wetland) in the landscape of garden beds and the building of the herbarium. The botanic garden inscribes natural history on the surface of the land (and wetland). Draining and/or filling the wetland creates the surface of inscription on which the botanic garden/natural history collection writ large can be inscribed. Under von Mueller, as Morrison puts it, 'the gardens became, with humourless teutonic thoroughness, a living text-book of systematic and economic botany, with garden beds for pages' (1957: 26).

By contrast, for Guilfoyle the Gardens were the inevitable correlative of landscape aesthetics within a picturesque area of visibility, which were found in pleasure and leisure parks and gardens that were initially and exclusively private (and largely rural), and later became public (and mainly urban). Guilfoyle also transformed the park and garden-goer from von Mueller's active educational and recreational subject of natural history discourse absorbing scientific knowledge, such as a student of native flora or an amateur botanist, into a more passive stroller promenading in the Gardens and appreciating them aesthetically as the subject of the gaze of the Gardens' landscaped features. The Gardens also became the backdrop for the human drama of the display of the fashionable attire worn by garden-goers in keeping with the dominant discourses and everyday practices of conspicuous consumption of the heyday of industrial capitalism in the late nineteenth and early twentieth centuries.

Following the Guilfoyle revolution beginning in 1873, in 1883, Richard Twopeny cited 'Professor S_ of Melbourne University', who said that 'the Botanical Gardens are not scientific gardens like Kew [Gardens in London], but capital places to walk and sit about in' ([1883] 1986: 114). Yet, in keeping with the fashion of the day, the Gardens were not just a desirable place in which to leisurely walk and sit, but they were also a place in which to promenade in a much more overt performance of the cultural display of class rivalry and solidarity, conspicuous consumption and fashionable dress. Even from the beginning of von Mueller's directorship in 1857, 'the Melbourne Botanic Gardens' were described as 'everyday acquiring additional importance as a place of public promenade' (cited in Pescott 1982: 40). Thus, despite von Mueller's preference for scientific and educational purposes, some members of the public in his day were using the Gardens solely for promenading and leisure (shock, horror).

This importance increased under Guilfoyle until in 1875 the Moonlight Concerts in Gardens were described as having 'groups of brightly dressed promenaders stroll[ing] about the paths' (cited in Pescott 1982: 127). This fashion was to persist for at least a decade, for in 1886 'the Botanical Gardens (Melbourne's pride)' were regarded as a 'public promenade' (cited in Briggs 1963: 309). By day the Gardens were a place in which nature was put on display (a nature albeit aestheticized in terms of the English landscape aesthetic) in the full glare of daylight; by night the Gardens were a place in which culture was put on display (a culture albeit aestheticized in terms of fashionable attire in a display of conspicuous class consumption) in the flickering glow of gaslight. As either foreground, by day, or background, by night, the Gardens were an object of sight and the garden goer the subject of sight. Subject and object were divided and made mutually constitutive by natural history and aesthetics, whereas the abject horror of the wetland was the excluded middle or third term between them that makes both possible (for the abject, see Kristeva 1982: 1–2). Wetlands are the excluded middle or third term between land and water that makes both possible (see Giblett 1996: especially 3–24).

By the early 1880s, the Gardens had become pleasure gardens for Richard Twopeny, who later concurs with 'Professor S_ of Melbourne University' that the

Botanic Gardens have 'no great scientific pretensions as their name would imply, but are merely pleasure grounds, decked with all the variety of flowers which this land of Cockaigne produces in abundance' ([1883] 1986: 116). Cockaigne is 'a land of plenty in medieval myth, an imaginary place of extreme luxury and ease where physical comforts and pleasures are always immediately at hand'.[8] The Gardens for Twopeny, under Guilfoyle's directorship, had not only ceased to be scientific and taxonomic, but had become mythic and otiose, if not Arcadian in the sense of an idyllic, pastoral paradise lost.

The Gardens, for A. Sutherland writing in 1888, were certainly 'picturesque' as 'the eye wanders with satisfaction' over 'an English meadow' (cited in Roe 1974: 110). In other words, the implicit masculine gaze wanders with pleasurable satisfaction over the aestheticized and feminized surface of the land in landscape pornography. The wetland depths of the land are glossed over. At the time that von Mueller's directorship was terminated in 1873, one contemporary writer commented that 'the gardens themselves did not feed the hunger of the eyes', as Morrison (1957: 28) puts it. In other words, they did not feed the desire for visual satisfaction figured orally. Under Guilfoyle's directorship from 1873 to 1909, the Gardens fed and satisfied hungry eyes. They also fed and satisfied the desire for harmony, that desideratum of Romantics for the musical ear and of organic machinery in the pastoro-technical idyll (see Giblett 2008: 22). Guilfoyle, for Morrison, 'planned the vast landscape that has made the gardens [into] an [sic] harmonious whole' (1957: 12).

Recent writers and commentators concur with Guilfoyle's preference for landscape aesthetics. For Jenny Sinclair,

> the gardens, at least, are 'human scale.' The gardens are designed to provide a new vista at each turn, a reproduction of lush New South Wales landscapes loved by the early gardens director, William Guilfoyle: patches of forest beside rolling grassy hills, rainforest gullies and tracks passing between high straight tree trunks or massive bushes with dark, glossy leaves.
>
> (Sinclair 2015: 86)

Guilfoyle was singing from the song sheet of the English landscape garden aesthetic of the eighteenth century, with the work of Humphry Repton ([1803] 1980) as the first landscape gardener, if not landscape architect (composed in concert with William Gilpin's [1794] landscape aesthetics of the picturesque). Sinclair (2015: 60) previously bemoans the loss of West Melbourne Swamp (or Batman's Swamp) (as we have seen in Chapter Two), but here she glosses over the fact that the landscaping of the Gardens involved the loss of a wetland, or more precisely its transformation into an ornamental lake as a wetland had no place in a landscaped park.

'Useless marshes'

Indeed, for the Gardens to take place from their beginnings, a wetland had to be drained. The Melbourne Gardens website describes the site pejoratively as 'swampy' (Royal Botanic Gardens n.d.a). Sophie Cunningham, in her recent book about Melbourne, says that 'where the gardens now stand was once wetlands [...] The wetlands were drained by Charles La Trobe in 1846 so that the gardens could be developed' (2011: 56–57). For Serle, 'the parks and gardens [...] [of Melbourne] were one of La Trobe's great legacies, especially the Botanic Gardens' (1971: 275). The draining of wetlands was another of his legacies, including the draining of wetlands to create parks and gardens (Serle does not comment on this legacy). In 1845, La Trobe had reserved what Newnham calls 'a lovely stretch of land which became the Royal Botanic Gardens' (1985: 114), or more precisely, a lovely stretch of land including wetlands and drylands.

In his descriptive and pictorial record of the Gardens, Morrison presents a triumphalist history of how 'a chain of useless marshes – they could scarcely be called swamps for they supported no vegetation taller than scrubby tea-tree'(1957: 10), but were nevertheless in his words 'an unmanageable, pestilent swamp' (10), were 'transformed into a chain of lovely lakes' (10). From useless marshes of scrubby (a pejorative term in the lexicon of Australian botanical description) tea-tree (melaleucas) and recalcitrant, 'pestilent' swamp (though the swamp was the habitat for 'pests'), through 'waste land' as Morrison (1957: 21) puts it, to 'lovely lakes' marks the triumphal transformation of the site for the Gardens from wetlandscape through wasteland to parklandscape. This transition also marks the transformation of Melbourne as a city of wetlands into what Morrison calls 'this city of gardens' (1957: 9). Where the Gardens now are, wetlands once were: making gardens meant losing wetlands.

Melbourne is a city of gardens, even 'one huge garden', for Morrison (1957: 9), and 'Australia's garden city', for Kornelia Freeman and Ulo Pukk (2015: 9). It developed in parts, including the Melbourne Gardens and its leafy suburbs, into a Garden City, in Ebenezer Howard's (1902) later terms, in which there was no room for swamps and other wetlands. For his Garden City, Howard envisaged a flat, dry site, a *tabula rasa*, on which to inscribe his bucolic vision of a pastoro-technical idyll. He did not envisage the swampy sites on which many modern cities, such as Melbourne, took place, as Morrison (1957: 10) also notes. Howard saw the Garden City as combining the best of the country and the city in what he called 'a healthy, natural and economic combination of town and country life' (1902: 2), though the country for him was construed in narrow terms as 'the bosom of our kindly mother earth' (1902: n. pag.).[9] There was no room in Howard's country for the womb of our great mother earth of wetlands who sometimes kindly creates and nurtures, and sometimes unkindly destroys (see Giblett 2011: 21–38).

Robert Hoddle's plan for the proposed Gardens which he presented to La Trobe in 1846 shows a 'lagoon' in a generally marshy area (indicated in accordance with cartographic convention) and with a very similar triangular shape to the current Ornamental Lake located on the horseshoe bend of the Yarra River (Pescott 1982: 14). The Yarra River, as Morrison puts it, 'in those days meandered considerably south of its present course' (1957: 21). 'The main lagoon', as Pescott describes it, 'in essence was part of the main course of the river' (1982: 92). The 'marshy lagoon' or 'swampy ground', as Morrison (1957: 21, 28) variously calls it, was more precisely a billabong in Australian terms, many of which dotted the course of the river at the time of British settlement (as we have seen in Chapter Four; for further discussion of a billabong, see Otto 2005: 61 note). The most recent account of Melbourne's parks and gardens, by Freeman and Pukk, describes how 'three lakes [...] were natural billabongs of the Yarra River' (2015: 62). Howard Gritten's two paintings of *Melbourne from the Botanical Gardens in 1867*, both housed in the State Library of Victoria (one on permanent display in the Cowen Gallery), show the serpentine course of the river at that time.

One of Gritten's paintings of 1867 clearly shows the billabongs. Coote describes this painting as depicting 'an Arcadian paradise' (2012: 54–55). Like the biblical paradise, there is a serpent in the garden, specifically in the serpentine billabong. The lagoon or billabong depicted in the painting is the habitat for the slimy serpent Satan. The modern city initially keeps the monstrous marsh (and marsh monster, such as Satan) at bay on its outskirts, and even contains it within a landscaped garden (both of which this painting depicts). The billabongs were inclined to fill up and empty out with the rising and falling waters of the river during flood and drought in the variable cycle of the seasons with their 'freshets', that lovely archaic word for fresh flushes, or flash flows.

Under the directorship of John Dallachy, the second director of the Gardens, one of the major 'improvements' of 1850–51 was what Pescott calls 'the deepening and excavating of the lagoon which prior to this time had been no more than a swampy backwater on the river, and certainly not an ornament of the Gardens' (1982: 23). Pescott denigrates, or blackens, the lagoon as a 'swampy backwater', or black water, by subscribing to the European landscape aesthetic in which wetlands have little or no aesthetic value, especially ornamental value, and are indeed anti-aesthetic.[10] The deepening of the lagoon, for Pescott, was designed 'to overcome problems of siltation from the run off of excess water from the neighbouring slopes and from periods of flooding of the [Yarra] river which occurred with monotonous regularity for many years' (1982: 23). The river in the seasonally variable land of 'drought and flooding rain' (in the words of Dorothea Mackellar's [1904] poem 'I Love a Sunburnt Country') was recalcitrant and wild, and needing to be tamed.

Dallachy was an 'improver' who made, or who wanted to make, 'Nature move to an arranged design', as Raymond Williams (1973: 124) puts it in relation to the class of 'Improvers'. In other words, Dallachy wanted to make the Gardens work like clockwork, as an organic machine in keeping with the pastoro-technical idyll of the nineteenth century. Maintaining a wetland would have filtered the run off from the Gardens. In addition to Dallachy's deepening of the lagoon in the Melbourne Gardens, as Pescott goes on to relate,

> the margins of the lagoon were defined with paths [...] which were bordered with shrubs and flowers [...] While this policy of exhibition was accepted at the time, it came under criticism from a subsequent director, Guilfoyle, many years later.
>
> (Pescott 1982: 23)

Exhibition implies a static tableau constructed for the display of living botanic specimens in its open-aired cabinet of curiosities, whereas Guilfoyle was much more interested in the dynamic and pleasing prospects of the broad vistas of an ornamental lake and sweeping lawns, inviting the gaze to wander pleasurably, and the legs to stroll leisurely, over the landscape. In both cases, plants are made to perform set-pieces as stage properties in the static tableau of parks and gardens set up for the strolling garden goer in a dynamic arrangement as entertainment for his or her visual pleasure, just like performing seals in an aquarium.

Ornamental lake

The process of completely cutting off the lagoon from the river and creating an ornamental lake was achieved under Guilfoyle's directorship. A plan from 1875 at the beginning of Guilfoyle's directorship charts this process.

The lagoon ceased to be a billabong and became an ornamental lake. Guilfoyle, for Newnham, 'converted the old swamp into a lovely lake' (1985: 155).[11] In evangelical terms, Guilfoyle converted the evil, satanic or pagan swamp into a good, saved, Christianized lake. Guilfoyle landscaped the Melbourne Gardens into what Serle calls 'lasting beauty' (1971: 275). He certainly did that, but he also ensured that the old swamp did not last, or certainly that its beauty – like the beauty of West Melbourne Swamp (or Batman's Swamp), for George McCrae (1912: 114–36, especially 117–18), in the early twentieth century looking back to the mid-nineteenth century – did not last. For Pescott,

> Guilfoyle saw the lagoon as a focal point of the overall scheme of landscape and, as such, it would need a lot of work, for although the Yarra flowed through it

in parts, it was swampy and rush covered, not the attractive Ornamental Lake
we are used to admiring today.

(Pescott 1982: 107)

Ornamental is okay, even good, whereas swampy is not; ornamental is attractive
and admirable, swampy is unattractive and not admirable; vast vistas of lawns and
water are good, rush-covered wetland isn't; open expanses of water are good, closed
confines of wetland vegetation are not. This moralization of the landscape in general,
and of wetlands in particular, has been going on for a long time (see Giblett 1996).

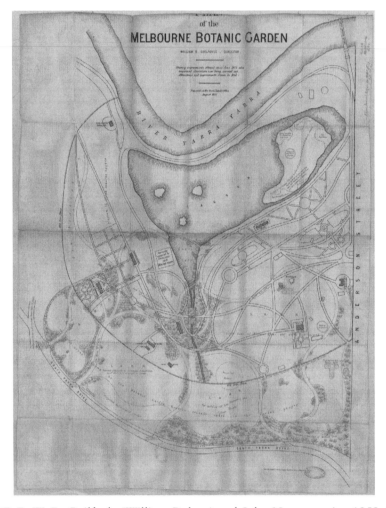

FIGURE 7: W. R. Guilfoyle (William Robert) and John Noone, active 1858–88, and
Victoria Department of Lands and Survey 1875, *Plan of the Melbourne Botanic Garden*,
photo-lithographed at the Department of Lands and Survey by J. Noone, Melbourne.

Moreover, for Pescott, 'Guilfoyle was following the English style of gardening, many of the proponents of which insisted that a water feature, even if artificially produced, was a necessity' (1982: 108, see also 143–47, 189). 'A water feature' meant 'a sheet of clear water', and not a rush-covered swamp. Similarly, McCrae, in the early twentieth century, extolled the aesthetic virtues of West Melbourne Swamp as 'a beautiful sheet of water' (1912: 117), expressing the typical preference of settlers for open water over closed swamps. A similar settler view of wetlands prevailed in Canada, a settler country like Australia, and persists to recent times (see Giblett 2014: 30–33).

In addition, for Pescott, 'the work done in the lagoon resulted in a splendid sheet of water which proved to be not only ornamental but became a magnificent area for waterfowl' (1982: 110). Presumably the native lagoon had also been a habitat for waterfowl, and for other waterbirds too. Restoring the Ornamental Lake to a wetland would provide a habitat for a suite of waterbirds, including waders, and not just waterfowl.

Finally, for Pescott, the Ornamental Lake that Guilfoyle created 'should be considered the central feature of the Gardens' (1982: 141). The lake ornamenting the Gardens is the central feature; the water feature is central. In conclusion, for Pescott, 'the Royal Botanic Gardens in Melbourne are paradise gardens of the best English tradition' (1982: 147). They are not the infernal swamps of paradise lost.[12] They are, for Pescott, 'the dominant feature of Melbourne' (1982: 199). The Yarra River and wetlands were the dominant (water) feature of Melbourne at the point and moment of European contact (as we have seen in previous chapters and as we will see in the following chapter). Eventually the lagoon was cut off completely from the river when, 'around 1900' (Freeman and Pukk 2015: 62), 'the Yarra River was straightened and the lagoon took on new dimensions', as Pescott (1982: 119) describes it. A map of 1910 shows both the old, curved and new, straightened courses of the river (Otto 2005: 86).

The Melbourne Gardens were thus participating in the worldwide, nineteenth-century phenomenon of the creation of public urban parks. Heath Schenker argues that public urban parks were 'stylized representations of rural countryside' in both of which 'marshes were drained' (2009: 5). Guilfoyle's aim with the Melbourne Gardens, as was Frederick Law Olmsted's aim with Central Park in New York in the 1850s, was to produce what Schenker calls the 'melodramatic landscape' of an urban park with its 'monumental, picturesque rendering of Nature' (2009: 134).[13] Such a picturesque parklandscape did not permit a monstrous, grotesque maintaining of nature in a swamp to persist. Nature in a swamp needed rendering for landscape architects and landscape gardeners into picturesque parklandscape. Guilfoyle, like Olmsted, operated within the patriarchal paradigm of mechanized nature and mathematized knowledge, and against the matrifocal paradigm of embodied knowledge and maternal marshes (for the two paradigms in tabular form, see Giblett 2011: 32–34, Figure 2). In the melodramatic landscape of a public urban park, a moralized melodrama of good grass, water features and an ornamental lake versus bad swamp, wetland vegetation and a local lagoon was played out.

Ornamentation and features are two characteristics of the 'featurism' that Robin Boyd refers to as 'the Australian ugliness' in his famous book of this title, first published in 1960, well before Pescott's history of the Gardens. Boyd, of course, applied his critique of Australian ugliness to architecture, or more precisely to built architecture, and the built environment more generally, and did not apply it to landscape architecture and the natural environment, though it can be applied to them. In Boyd's view, 'two of the most civilized pieces of urbanity in the world' – for the Melburnian thinking of his or her city – are 'Alexandra Avenue where it skirts the river and the shady top [or 'Paris'] end of Collins Street' ([1960] 2010: 11). Alexandra Avenue is built in part on the reclaimed wetland of the lagoon in the Melbourne Gardens, and it now divides the Ornamental Lake from the river. Restoring the Ornamental Lake to a wetland could involve rejoining it to the river via an under-road swale beneath Alexandra Avenue, and restoring the overflowing cycles of the river and fluctuating levels of the wetlands. Alexandra Avenue would thus not only skirt the river to the north but also brush across the wetland to the south and double its urbanity by acknowledging that Melbourne is, or was, a city of wetlands.

Restoring the Ornamental Lake (or portions of it) to a wetland would reverse the Australian ugliness of featurism. Boyd gives a definition of featurism as 'a nervous architectural chattering avoiding any mention of the landscape' ([1960] 2010: 20). The same could be said of the landscape architecture of Alexandra Avenue and the Ornamental Lake, as they avoid any mention of the wetlandscape that preceded them. Featurism, for Boyd, 'by definition stands for the subordination of the whole and the accentuation of selected separate features' (2010: 245). The water featurism of the Ornamental Lake subordinates the site of the Melbourne Gardens to the accentuation of this selected separate feature, whereas the lagoon was once upon a time an integral part of the site and the bioregion of the Yarra River and its attendant billabongs. Boyd's ([1960] 2010: 244–45) final discussion of featurism critiques ornament and ornamentation as its key characteristics, and as characteristics of the Australian ugliness more generally. So much for the Ornamental Lake being a 'thing of beauty'. I am reminded of the *Tao-te-Ching* and the opening line of Chapter Two in which the sage Lao Tzu says that 'when the world knows beauty as beauty, ugliness arises'. Indeed. I say no more.

The Ornamental Lake is a trace of the wetland that once was there. Restoring the Ornamental Lake (or a portion of it) to a wetland would be a reworking and re-reading of the history of the present and the geography of the past of Melbourne to the city of wetlands it once was in part on this site. Where buildings and streets are now, wetlands once were too, but these have physically destroyed those wetlands, whereas the Ornamental Lake is a trace of the 'lagoon'. Beneath and before the city, the wetlands were; beneath and before the Ornamental Lake, the wetland was and still is. The Ornamental Lake has not extinguished physically the wetland that was once there. Restoring it to a wetland would rework and re-present the trace of what it once was.

Restoring the Ornamental Lake to a wetland would also reduce evapotranspiration, provide filtering services and make the Gardens more sustainable in the age of climate catastrophes. The history of the wetlands in the Gardens has been elided by converting the lagoon (actually, a billabong) into an ornamental lake. By proposing that it be converted back into a wetland, from its saved Christian status to its lost pagan past, I am composing or developing a dialectical image of the past (wetland), present (lake) and future (restored wetland).

Restoring the Ornamental Lake (or a portion of it) to a wetland and creating a diorama of the history of the present and the geography of the past would be a double (or stereoscopic) dialectical image, a visible reminder and expression of the Gardens' history and geography, a living memorial to the lost wetlands of Melbourne and the opening statement in a dialogue between botany and beauty; science and aesthetics; and the sciences and humanities on this site, in this place, in an environmental work of art.

NOTES

1. For the public urban park, see Elborough (2016); for the private rural park (the gentleman's park estate), see Giblett (2011: 77–94).

2. For Taylor (2014: 35), the iconic status of Royal Park as 'Melbourne parkland' is to Melbourne as 'Kings Park [is] to Perth,' without mentioning that the latter is also a botanic garden.

3. See Taylor (2014: 36) and Bolitho (2015). I discuss the last two points in greater detail later in this chapter.

4. For the aesthetics (or not) of wetlands, see Giblett (1996: especially 25–51).

5. See the photograph of the former in Freeman and Pukk (2015: 88).

6. I am grateful to Warwick Mules for this suggestion.

7. See Giblett (2011: 124–26).

8. See https://en.wikipedia.org/wiki/Cockaigne. Accessed 1 May 2015.

9. See also Giblett (2016: 237).

10. 'Denigrate' literally means 'blacken'; see Giblett (2013: 100).

11. Freeman and Pukk (2015: 63) say that Guilfoyle 'transformed the lagoon into a lake'.

12. For the swamp as hell and as the home of satanic swamp monsters (including Satan in Milton's *Paradise Lost* [1667]), see Giblett (1996: 183–84 and 2018: 52–53).

13. For Central Park, see Giblett (2016: 149–53).

Streams of Living Water

The city of Melbourne is situated in the Yarra River catchment and bioregion. Looking down from a plane coming in to land at Tullarmarine Airport, the Yarra River snakes its sinuous course through the city. The city was founded next to it, and it was also founded between it and wetlands. The early city depended on the river for fresh water until it ruined this source by blowing up the falls near Queens Bridge to allow greater access by ships, also destroying the immediate source of fresh water by permitting penetration by salt water and making the lower river estuarine. Fresh water then had to be sourced further upstream above Dights Falls in Studley Park in Heidelberg. The city today still depends on water from the upper catchment of the Yarra.

Lower downstream, the river was straightened out to such an extent that below Punt Road Bridge the river is not really a river at all, certainly not a natural river, but an artificial canal and a cultural river, or even a cultured river. Like the ghost swamps and other phantom wetlands of Melbourne that have disappeared or been landscaped into lakes, the Yarra, and its tributaries, is a ghost or phantom river buried in drains beneath streets and rerouted from its original course in canals. It has also been used as an open sewer and as a border of economic and cultural division between the upper-class south side and the lower-class north side of the river. The river has had a rocky road in the life and story of Melbourne.

The Yarra Riverkeeper Association, a not-for-profit organization, has done a valiant job over many years of being a voice for the river and trying to get it better appreciated and protected. Fortunately, the recent Yarra River Protection Bill (2017), passed into legislation in the Victorian State Parliament, not only affords greater protection for the river but also recognizes the importance of the river for the traditional owners. Both should also lead to greater recognition of, and appreciation of, the river and its importance to non-indigenous people. As with recent court cases in India and New Zealand, the Yarra River Protection Bill 'recognizes the Yarra and its environs as a discrete, integrated living entity', as the environmental lawyer Bruce Lindsay puts it (cited in Meadows 2018: 15).[1] *The Guardian* newspaper reported in 2017 that 'in a world first a New Zealand river has been give the same legal rights as a human being', based on traditional indigenous Maori concepts of personhood and legal status (Ainge Roy 2017: 12).[2]

The Yarra River was both what Maree Coote, calls 'the source of life' and 'the centre of enterprise' for colonial Melbourne, and today 'Melbourne's central scenic asset' (2013: 153). The river is not only what she later calls 'the jeweled necklace of Melbourne' (248), or what I have called above a cultured river, but it also has pendant natural pearls and precious stones of billabongs hanging off it (as we have seen in previous chapters).

Early days, early river

The Yarra River was a determining factor for the location of Melbourne in the first place and is a defining feature and prominent landmark of the city today. In 2004, John Landy, the then Governor of Victoria wrote in his 'Foreword' to Geoff Lacey's book about the middle Yarra from Heidelberg to Yarra Bend that 'the Yarra is the defining feature of the City of Melbourne' (2004: vii). It certainly is that today from the air, but this is to overlook the wetlands which were also a defining feature of the site in the past and are largely invisible today, but are still present by virtue of their very oblivion (as we saw in previous chapters). They are also still present in some instances in the form of billabongs in the middle Yarra as a defining feature of the city today. Landy concludes by belatedly acknowledging 'the complex mosaic of billabongs and swamps' (2004: viii) found today along the middle Yarra. Lacey documents these extensively. They were also dotted along the lower Yarra at the time of British settlement, including in the Melbourne Gardens (as we have seen in previous chapters).

Others besides Landy have also focused on the Yarra River and largely ignored the billabongs and other wetlands. Melbourne, for Melbourne biographer Bill Newnham, is 'built around the Yarra River' (1985: 5). Melbourne is also built on, between and around swamps, billabongs and deltaic marshes. Rivers and swamps were both defining features and prominent landmarks of the site for Melbourne and its early history and geography. In 1985, on the 150th anniversary of the founding of Melbourne in 1835, Rear-Admiral Brian Murray, the then Governor of Victoria, wrote a 'Foreword' to Newnham's 'biography' of Melbourne in which he largely ignores marshy Melbourne and waxes lyrical about the pleasing aesthetic qualities of the Yarra River and surrounding hills. For Murray,

the place where Melbourne now stands was then [in 1835] the site of a bright, flowing river flanked on either side with a wilderness of reeds, scrub, tea-tree, wattle, she-oak and gum. The hills on either side were wooded and gently undulating.

(Murray 1985: x)

'England's green and pleasant land' of pleasing pastoral prospects transplanted holus-bolus to the banks of the Yarra, is contrasted with, and devalued compared to, the scrub and wetland wilderness in accordance with the conventions of the European landscape aesthetic and its hierarchy of value.

Perhaps Murray did not read the book for which he was writing a foreword, as Newnham says in his chapter devoted to 'The river' that 'today [in the 1980s] the Yarra is a quiet, well-ordered stream; but when named [by Europeans as such] it was a twisted, cantankerous river' (1985: 137). Both men were probably referring to the lower Yarra as the middle and upper Yarra can be a dull, turbid river and not Murray's 'bright, flowing river'. Yet the middle and upper Yarra is still flanked by billabongs and Murray's description of 'a wilderness of reeds, scrub, tea-tree, wattle, she-oak and gum' (1985: x) gives an idea of what the lower Yarra would have looked like to European eyes in 1802, 1803, 1835, 1839 and even 1884. Along similar lines to Murray, an 1839 land sales advertisement described 'the beauteous banks of the Yarra' and 'the lovely Yarra' (cited in Newnham 1985: 13).

Murray seems to be following in the footsteps of Rolf Boldrewood and Henry Kingsley. Boldrewood described the 'Yarra' in 1884 as a 'noble stream' (cited in Arnold 1983: 17 and McLaren 2013: 41). In 1858, Henry Kingsley looked back over 22 years to the time before European settlement when 'the Yarra rolled its clear waters to the sea through the unbroken solitude of a primeval forest, as yet unseen by the eye of a white man. Now there stands a noble city' (cited in Arnold 1983: 25). Similarly, Henry Gyles Turner evoked 'the limpid Yarra stream' (cited in Roe 1974: 97). Kingsley does not mention the fate of Boldrewood's 'noble stream' of the Yarra. Presumably the noble stream and noble city could not co-exist. The noble city was built on the banks of the noble stream, but in becoming a noble city, it turned the noble stream into an ignoble one, at least in some places where industry developed along the river and polluted its waters (as we will see later in this chapter).

Other places were, or later became, neighbours of a noble stream. A century after Kingsley, in 1962, Joan Lindsay of *Picnic at Hanging Rock* fame, described how, when she lived in Toorak, 'at the foot of the street lay the unspoiled reaches of the Yarra' (cited in Arnold 1983: 65). She also described some of the nearby residents, such as Arthur Streeton, 'a painter who loved the river' (65). Toorak was not always so, for, as Coote puts it, 'the damp south side of the Yarra was avoided for decades' (2012: 52). Arthur Streeton lived in South Yarra/Toorak for four years and painted the river in its lower and upper reaches. He painted the lower Yarra in panoramic view from his studio in South Yarra/Toorak in three almost identical versions (Coote 2012: 74–75). Lacey takes the title of his book, *Still Glides the Stream* (2004), about the middle reaches of the Yarra from one of Streeton's paintings of the area (and he, in turn, took this title from Wordsworth – 'Still glides the stream, and shall forever glide'). The middle Yarra was the river of artists, especially the Heidelberg artists, and it was the birthplace of *the* Australian nationalist landscape paintings of the 'Heidelberg School' (see Otto 2005: 159–63; Giblett 2011: 131–32). The lower Yarra was also the river of artists, but usually when it was crossed by bridges, such as Princes and Westgate Bridges, and they were depicted as the backdrop to the river (as we will see later in this chapter).

Melbourne, for Newnham, was 'created on a site with few natural advantages'(1985: 36), some of which were provided by the Yarra River, such as drinking water, while the wetlands had some of the natural advantages, such as feed and water for stock. Melbourne certainly had a few aesthetic advantages, such as the pleasing prospect from Batman's Hill. Newnham also waxes lyrical about enjoying 'the silver and misty grey of the river' (1985: 150). Presumably the ease of access to the fresh water that the river provided was a natural advantage initially, as were its grassy banks and the meadows in the marshes with their provision of feed for horses, cattle, sheep and other domesticated animals. Along similar lines to Newnham, Robyn Annear describes the Yarra River as the 'greatest natural asset' of the city (2014: 20). The wetlands were also once a great natural asset.

The official history of the city of Melbourne (Lewis 1995) published nearly forty years after the first edition of Newnham's biography of Melbourne was one of the first publications to acknowledge the importance of both the river and the wetlands as defining features of the early city. The executive summary describes 'the Yarra River and its swampy marshes' as 'the original topography' of the site for the city, referring primarily to the municipality of the City of Melbourne in the river's lower reaches, but this also applies to some of the suburbs in its middle reaches in other municipalities of the greater Melbourne metropolitan area (Lewis 1995: 2). The river and wetlands are defining features of the city early and late, present and absent, centre and periphery, urban and suburban.

For all these reasons, for 'Yarra biographer' Kristin Otto, as Sophie Cunningham (2011: 117) calls her, 'it's because of the Yarra River that the city of Melbourne has to be precisely where it is' (Otto 2005: 17). Yarra River pilgrim Maya Ward, who walked from 'the mouth' of the river at Point Gellibrand to its 'headwaters' on Mount Whitelaw, concurs with Otto that 'Melbourne is where it is because of this river' (2011: 27).[3] Melbourne is also *what* it is, a city and a port, because of this river. Without this river, Melbourne as it is today was not, and is still not, possible. The Yarra provided, and still provides, fresh water for human habitation and a safe harbour for ships, and it did provide a means of waterborne transportation for the surrounding countryside for goods going up or down stream.

A river is not only 'a natural highway', as Lewis Mumford (cited in Mauch and Zeller 2008: 1) put it (as if it were a passive road on which vehicles move), but a river is also 'a road that moves', as Blaise Pascal (cited in Blackbourn 2008: 23) said, as the river is an active road whose downstream flow moves vessels along its course providing some motive power for their propulsion. Rivers, as Christof Mauch and Thomas Zeller put it, are 'themselves agents, providers of energy [not only of hydroelectric power generation, but also in their own movement *à la* Pascal] and resources, and a driving force in history' (2008: 7). The Yarra is an active agent, energy provider, life source and driving force in the history in and of the past and in the present life of Melbourne.

Rivers have value both as means and power of transportation, not to mention as habitation and source of life-giving water essential for humans, plants and animals, and as safe anchorage – a pre-requisite for 'all the great historic cultures', as Mumford (cited in Mauch and Zeller 2008: 1) puts it. The Yarra is no exception for the great historic culture of Melbourne. The Yarra River is to Melbourne what the Seine is to Paris, the Thames is to London, the Hudson is to New York, the Neva is to St Petersburg, the Mississippi is to New Orleans, the Charles is to Boston, the Don is to Toronto, the Swan is to Perth and the Potomac is to Washington. Great or small, clear or muddy, long or short, mighty or measly, these rivers belong with their historic cities as their couple and with their greater or lesser historic cultures. One is not possible without the other. Like Melbourne, these river cities were also, or are still in some cases, wetland cities.[4] All these cities neglect the care of their rivers and wetlands to their peril, as New Orleans found out in the aftermath of 'Katrina'.

The Yarra bioregion

The Yarra River and Melbourne wetlands are part of the Yarra River catchment, and this catchment is the defining feature of, and biogeographical context for, the city of Melbourne and for its original owners and users and current residents and dependents. As Greg Barber (cited in Ward 2011: 67), the Mayor of the City of Yarra from 2003 to 2004 and the first Greens mayor in Australia said, 'everybody lives in a catchment'. As well as in a watershed, everybody also lives in an air-shed; everybody lives in a bioregion; everybody lives with the plants and animals of the bioregion. There is no other place to live. To live is to live in a bioregion. The bioregion is home. The bioregion is a broader sense of habitat than one's own dwelling place or space. The bioregion is also the basis for one's livelihood in a broader sense than one's job or other source of income. For Ward (2011: 24–25), 'almost all of greater Melbourne lies in the Yarra River bioregion [...] It was all home'

(93), as she goes on to point out, for the local Aboriginal people, and it should be regarded, and loved and cared for as such, by all non-Aboriginal people too. Not surprisingly, the territory or homeland of the local indigenous people corresponds with the river's catchment (as Otto [2005: 11] points out). As Ward (2011: 37) puts it, 'the Yarra is a Songline […] A Songline is a path of the Dreaming, a narrative of the ancestors, which mapped the land in song' (44) (and did not map it on paper.) The Yarra is a song to be sung, not a feature to be mapped, or a resource to be exploited, or a wild watercourse to be tamed.

Newnham says that Yarra Yarra means 'flowing flowing' (1985: 137). It is a verb, a doing word, not a noun, a naming word. Yarra is not really the indigenous Aboriginal name for the river. 'Birrarung' is the name for the Yarra River in the language of the Woiwurrung people (Murphy and Kelly 2019: n.pag.). This name gave rise to 'Bearbrass', 'one of the names by which Melbourne was known in its early days', as Annear (2014: xi) argues. Something is certainly lost in translation. A cultural mistranslation could have arisen from an early settler pointing at the river and asking an Aboriginal person, 'what do you call this?' and expecting the name of the river in reply and getting instead the verb for the activity of the river. A cultural mistranslation could also have arisen from pointing at the falls and asking, 'what do you call this?' and receiving in reply the name of the falls. 'The Falls' were 'called by Aborigines *yarro yarro*'. Annear (2014: 10) relates how 'one of the earliest white arrivals took that to be the name of the river itself and so it became the Yarro Yarro or Yarra River'. Part of the cultural mistranslation could also be in the figure of speech of synecdoche operating in the minds of early settlers in which the part is taken for the whole. The question of 'what do you call this (place)?' that elicited the response of the activity of the water or the place of the falls was taken as the name for the river. The name of Yarra has stuck.

The course and composition of the Yarra River have been the subject of critical commentary and engineered change since 1835. In his history of the port of Melbourne, Yarnasan describes 'the Yarra's sinuous and shallow course' (1974: 11) and the river as 'shallow and narrow' (26), and so eminently unsuitable initially as a port. Along similar lines, the lower Yarra in 1886 for Mark Kershaw (cited in Matthews 2005: 265) was 'as sinuous as a snake in spasms. Its banks are of mud, and its stagnant waters a mixture of sludge and filth'. The sinuous course of the river in those days was a survivor of pre-contact days, but the foul composition of the river was 'man'-made and a product of colonization, as was its eventual straightened course (as we saw in Chapter Three). Cunningham describes how 'the river has lost several of its more meandering loops over the 175 years of white settlement: it's straighter, wider and an entire three kilometres shorter than it was when Europeans first arrived' (2011: 116–17). For Richard Twopeny, writing in 1883 in 'A walk round Melbourne', below the city the Yarra 'presents many points of resemblance to the monotony of the Suez Canal' ([1883] 1986: 117). Indeed, the Yarra below the city *is* a canal, Coode Canal. It is hardly a river at all except in name, but an artificial channel (as we saw in previous chapters).

The Yarra was not exempt from 'canalization' because, as Mauch and Zeller put it, 'canals came to be seen as the ideal means of transporting goods [especially in the age of barges before the advent of steam railways], rivers were increasingly engineered to resemble artificial waterways' (2008: 3). Canals were what they go on to call 'smooth, predictable, and in effect, shorter rivers' (3). If a river is a natural highway that moves (as Mumford and Pascal might have together put it), then a canal is an artificial highway that moves quicker than a river, because it moves over a shorter distance as a canal is straight whereas a river meanders. A canal is also an artificial drain that moves wastes to the sea quicker than rivers do. Rivers, in one early-twentieth-century reductionist view of Pittsburgh's rivers, are 'the natural and logical drains and are formed for the purpose of carrying wastes to the sea' (cited in Collins et al. 2008: 47). This is like saying that the human body is a natural and logical drain formed for the purpose of carrying wastes through the digestive tract from the mouth to the other end. This view neglects or ignores all the other life-giving functions of the river and the life-giving organs of its wetlands. It neglects the life-giving water that the river supplies and the food that it nourishes.

Recent writers about Melbourne and the Yarra River have remarked on the canalization of the river, the destruction of Melbourne's wetlands by prominent constructed landscapes and landmarks, and the forgetting of wetlands by Melburnians. Coote writes:

> the broad Yarra floodplains and wetlands were tamed, narrowed and absorbed into the changing urban design. This allowed generations of Melburnians to forget that these soggy waterholes, billabongs and creeks were everywhere: in, near or under today's Alexandra Gardens, Botanic Gardens, Federation Square, [and so on...] and dozens more locations around the city.
>
> (Coote 2012: 44)

Coote is discussing at this point H. Nash's depiction of the opening of the original Princes Bridge in 1850 which also depicts the Yarra floodplains.[5] Coote later discusses Ludwig Becker's *Melbourne from Across the Yarra* painted in 1854, which shows what she calls 'the grassy, muddy verge, and the breadth of the Yarra's floodplains' (2012: 50).[6]

Beside its shallow and sinuous course, the flow-rate and muddiness of the Yarra also came in for comment. In the 1970s, John Bach described the Yarra graphically and disparagingly as 'a torturous muddy stream meandering sluggishly through fetid mud flats' (1976: 267). Other, more recent writers on the river have followed suit. The Yarra River, for Jenny Sinclair, is 'named for its motion, but for most of its length it shows few signs of moving at all'; it is 'a muddy, sluggish river' (2015: 54). A few pages earlier she referred to 'the muddy Yarra and its streams' (51). Similarly, the Yarra, for Cunningham, is 'an erratic river. One day its flow is slow and sluggish – it's been as low as 17 million litres per day – but during times of flood up to 97,000 million litres has coursed through its beds' (2011: 160). The Yarra famously, as Otto relates,

> flows upside down. The explanation for the river's famous muddiness [...] is that it carries its bed turgidly on the surface, the clear water flowing underneath. Too thin to plough, too thick to drink [...] Australian rivers are noted for their turbidity – that is, they are silt-filled; i.e. muddy – and the Yarra is an Australian river.
>
> (Otto 2005: 3)

So it is hardly surprising that it is turgid and turbid. The Yarra not only flows upside down, but also for Roe 'float[s] upside down' (1974: 89). Boyce also refers to 'the Yarra's murky waters' (2011: xv).

The muddiness or murkiness of the Yarra has increased with urban development for, as Ward puts it, 'the tilling and building of the European settlers broke the plant roots that once held all the soil tight, and ever since the water has looked like mud' (2011: 61). Two cultures of nature clashed over the use of the land and the river.[7] For one culture of nature the river is sacred and to be respected. The river is, as T. S. Eliot puts it referring to the Thames, 'a strong brown god – sullen, untamed and intractable' (cited in Blackbourn 2008: 11). The river for the other culture of nature is secular and to be broken, tamed and made tractable. Otto contrasts

> the amount of mud and silt disturbed by, say, a thousand people who 'touch the earth lightly' as compared to a million people in the same space who sit down hard on it, churn it, use it, readying it to wash away.
>
> (Otto 2005: 9)

The river's muddiness cannot be blamed on the river alone. The river does not live alone irrespective of the peoples who live on its banks, live by its billabongs and within its catchment, and who impact upon it.

Early visitors were not impressed with Melbourne and the Yarra River. Melbourne, for novelist Anthony Trollope in the nineteenth century, was

> not a city beautiful to the eye from the charms of the landscape surrounding it [...] Though it stands on a river which has in itself many qualities of prettiness

in streams, – a torturous, rapid little river, – with varied banks, the Yarra Yarra by name, it seems to have but little to do with the city [...] But it is not 'a joy for ever' to the Melbournites, as the Seine is to the people of Paris.

(Trollope 1876: vol. II, 29–30)[8]

Yarra was a source of water to early Melburnians and it has only become a source of joy to later Melburnians, like the Seine for Parisians.

The Seine of the south

Yet the Seine has not always been a source of joy for Parisians. The water of the River Seine is described by Hussey as 'the dirty-green water' (2006: 4) with a 'marshy swamp on the Right Bank' (7), which is what he also calls 'the stinking and greasy bank' (13). This makes the River Seine sound like 'the great grey-green, greasy Limpopo River' of one of Rudyard Kipling's *Just So Stories* (1902). Perhaps Julian Green's translator had Kipling's line in mind when he translated Green's description of the Seine in flood, '*vert jaunâtre*', into 'grey-green' ([1983] 2012: 77). Colin Jones, in his biography of Paris (why not of the Seine as well? [see Backouche 2008]), concludes that 'land, water and mud thus had a more dramatic relationship with the city's history than in recent times' (2002: 4). Perhaps it would be more precise to say that the city had a more overt, dramatic relationship in the past with land, water and mud, whereas in recent times it has had a more covert relationship with them. Similarly, Melbourne, as 'the Paris of the south', has had a more overt, dramatic relationship in the past with land, water and mud, whereas in recent times it has had a more covert relationship with them. Melbourne also had marshy swamps on the right and left banks of the Yarra.

Walter Benjamin occasionally discusses the Seine in relation to Paris in *The Arcades Project* ([1982] 1999a). With Melbourne being regarded by some as 'the Paris of the south' (as we have seen in Chapter Six), the Yarra River bears some comparison with the Seine. Benjamin figures the Paris of Baudelaire's poems as 'a sunken city, and more submarine than subterranean' ([1982] 1999a: 10). Benjamin goes on to describe how 'the chthonic elements of the city – its topographical formation, the old abandoned bed of the Seine – have evidently found in him [Baudelaire] a mold'. Paris rests, or floats, on the old bed of the Seine. One of Benjamin's 'Convoluts' (l) in *The Arcades Project* is devoted to 'The Seine, the Oldest Paris' (Benjamin [1982] 1999a: 796–99). Likewise, this chapter of *Modern Melbourne* is devoted to the Yarra, the oldest Melbourne. Melbourne rests or floats on what Otto calls 'the river's old bed' (2005: 5), as the course of the river has been rerouted on several occasions in pre-historic and modern times. The Yarra is, as Ward (2011: 85) puts it, 'a very old river, more than 100 million years [old] in parts, which means it was here in Gondwanan times […] This river was old before the Himalayas rose' (178). The old Yarra is what Tony Birch (2015: 108–09) calls a 'ghost river' in his novel of this title set on 'the river' around Dights Falls in the late 1960s. One of the vagrant river men who lives under a bridge by the river and tells stories about it relates how 'she's still there, under this one. The old ghost river'. He calls the river 'their *mother*' because she 'took such good care of the men'.

In George Turner's prescient 1987 science fiction (SF) novel, *The Sea and Summer*, set in the mid-twenty-first century and centuries later – a kind of Australian counterpart to J. G. Ballard's classic SF novel *The Drowned World* (1962) (in the US, Turner's novel was published as *Drowning Towers*) – anthropogenic global heating ('the greenhouse effect') has melted the Antarctic ice caps, drowning low-lying areas of Melbourne and creating a new mouth of the river 'where the Yarra now debouched some distance to the north, at the foot of the Dandenongs [Ranges]' (3); 'Our placid old Yarra was long ago forced over its banks by the rising tides' (22, see also 'Postscript', 364). In the novel, 'an old riverbed' (3) of the Yarra, referring to the riverbed of the late twentieth century when the novel was written, lies beneath the riverbed of the mid-twenty-first century when the novel is set. The ancient bed of the Yarra lies beneath both.

Melbourne is certainly 'one of the stars of this book', according to Turner's biographer Judith Buckrich (1999: 167). The Yarra River is one of the stars too. It is certainly one of the actors and agents, or actants, that has a character to portray and a role to play in the novel. The higher, hillier parts of 'the drowned city' (Turner [1987] 2013: 204) have become, or soon will become, 'islands in the intricate delta of the Yarra' (103). After 'a storm tide […] pushed the river back for miles […] the lower streets had been submerged' (157). During winter, 'the river would rise and a surge of filthy water would overflow its banks' (177). Flash floods carried 'stinking messes of mud and rubbish' into low-lying areas and buildings (178). The combination of 'black mud' and 'dirty water' produced 'a brown lake' (179), no longer the 'Blue Lake' of George McCrae (as he described West Melbourne Swamp [or Batman's Swamp] in Chapter Two).

Unlike Ballard's *Drowned World*, in which the wetlands on which the city of London was founded return, in Turner's novel there is no mention of the wetlands in which the marshy metropolis of Melbourne was founded.[9] In some areas that were marshy, such as the southern side of Flinders Street east of the railway station, Turner writes: 'the river regularly overflowed here' to rot the disused rolling stock and railway sleepers ([1987] 2013: 290). 'Rotted was the word, for the area smelled foul when the water shrank to quagmires between floods' (290). This is hardly surprising considering the area was a marsh (as we have seen in previous chapters).

The Yarra River, in Turner's dystopian vision, seems to be no better than it was in the nineteenth century, as it has reverted to carrying 'a filthy, garbage-brown flood [that] didn't quite stink but threw up the smell [...] of Swill decay', the offensive odour of the unwashed lower classes ([1987] 2013: 191). The parlous state of the river is reiterated later during a clandestine raid that involves some of the characters wading through 'the filth in the water' and the 'stinking rubbish carried down from the backblocks', which included 'soft slops of slime that touched and clung' (298). The open sewer of the river smelled bad enough from a distance, but immersion in it involved tactile and immediate sensory experience on the surface of the body.

Arguably, the water of the Yarra has always had a distinctive and not necessarily offensive smell. In *Ghost River*, 'the scent of the water' (Birch 2015: 24) that came from the river was a pleasant smell, as was the smell of its water on the surface of the body. Sniffing his arm after swimming in the river, one of the central characters discovers that 'the water smelled like nothing he'd expected. It was a rich scent, the same that was given off by the back garden after he'd watered' the bed of tomatoes (34). In other words, it was a moist, vegetable smell, the scent of living beings, and of death, decomposition and new life. The water could look bad, but that did not necessarily make it bad. In *Ghost River*, 'the water was the colour of strong black tea and didn't smell all that different, except on hot summers when a stink rose from its surface' (6). The water could also smell bad and probably was bad. A stink is offensive and probably the result of water pollution.

Marvellous Smellbourne

Lucy Sussex describes how, in the late nineteenth century, 'the polluted Yarra [was] full of abattoir, industrial and human waste' (2015: 58). These wastes were not only drained into the Yarra River, but also deposited into what Michael Cannon calls the 'foul swamps on the outskirts of the city, such as the "abominably malodourous" Port Melbourne Lagoon' ([1966] 1976: 18). The polluted river, the foul swamps and what Cannon calls 'the badly drained slums' (43) earned 'Marvellous Melbourne' the ironic title of 'Marvellous Smellbourne', as Sussex (2015: 59) relates. It could have had the more apt title of 'Malodourous Melbourne', as the reality-check counter to grandiose 'Marvellous Melbourne' (Roe 1974: 85; Briggs 1963: 291; Serle 1971: 279; Otto 2005: 69). This comment arose out of the polluted state of its streams and sewers.

So bad were the sanitary conditions of Melbourne in the 1880s that a 'Royal Commission on the Sanitary Conditions of Melbourne' reported in 1889 in graphic detail about the parlous state of the rivers, creeks and wetlands, and of the perilously polluted water in the Yarra and Maribyrnong Rivers, Merri and Moonee Ponds Creeks, West Melbourne Swamp (or Batman's Swamp) and the Albert Park and Port Melbourne Lagoons, as well as how in 'certain suburbs' the 'air is tainted with evil odours from noxious trades' (Grant and Serle 1957: 186–87). These evil odours, or bad air, were thought to cause disease according to the mistaken miasmatic theory of the day. Toxic air pollution from noxious trades, then as now, can cause disease.

As a result, and at this time, the Yarra River downstream was, as Otto (2005: 10) puts it, 'once known as one of the filthiest rivers in the world. Yet over the past one hundred years its [upper] catchment has provided some of the world's best drinking water'. The lower Yarra also lies within the entire catchment of the river, though not for drinking water – that is within the upper catchment. The Yarra River catchment includes all the forests, bush, billabongs, street drains, suburban gardens, sporting fields and streams from which water (good, bad or indifferent) runs into the river.[10]

The stink of the streams, sewers and slums arose from what I have called the feral quaking zone of the water of sewers, polluted streams and wetwastelands (see Giblett 2009: 1–16). This zone and its smells need to be distinguished from the native quaking zone of the water of the river and wetlands and their smells. The two waters are intertwined in practice and in the present, but can be distinguished in theory and in the past so that native waters are not blamed for feral waters, so that the evil and ills of the feral river are not blamed on the innocent and healthy native river.

Stink occurs in the air and arises from the water. The salubrity of both air and water needs to be distinguished. In *The Arcades Project*, Benjamin ([1982] 1999a: 797) quotes Victor Hugo, from *Les Misérables* (1827), who describes how 'Paris is between two layers, a layer of water and a layer of air'. The layer of water is the underground aquifer 'furnished by the bed of green limestone', on which Paris rests and which may give the water of the Seine its greenish tinge. Hugo concludes that 'the layer of water is salubrious; it comes first from heaven, then from the earth. The layer of air is unwholesome, it comes from the sewers' (cited in Benjamin [1982] 1999a: 797). Similar things were said about Melbourne and the Yarra (as we will see later in this chapter). Benjamin earlier cites a poem by Baudelaire that describes the way in which '[t]he gutter, dismal bed, carries along its foulnesses, / Carries, boiling, the secrets of the sewers; / It slaps in corrosive waves against the houses, / Rushes on to jaundice and corrupt the river Seine' (cited in Benjamin [1982] 1999a: 446).

The same could be said, and was said, about the air and water of Melbourne and the Yarra. Like the Seine for Baudelaire, Hugo and Hussey, Geoffrey Serle describes the Yarra as 'the stinking river' (1971: 272). The river of mists became the river of miasmas. 'The Yarra was "a common sewer" – inky black with foul gases emanating from it', as Serle (1971: 279) goes on to relate. Instead of a stream of living black water – as it was for William Westgarth (excerpted in Grant and Serle 1957: 38), who, in his *Personal Recollections of Early Melbourne and Victoria* (1888), evoked 'the dark, deep still Yarra' – the Yarra had become a drain of dead black water polluted by industry. Instead of mist rising from the river, 'the city often stank to high heaven', as Serle (1971: 279) adds. For one visitor to Melbourne, in around 1861 so they were presumably referring to the lower river, 'the Yarra was nothing but a festering, stagnating ditch' (cited in Serle 1963: 370). 'All about the town' at that time, as Brown-May (cited in McLaren 2013: 29) put it recently, were 'pools of stagnant filth'. Brown-May is following in the footsteps of Friedrich Engels ([1845] 1987: 42, 45, 71) in the mid-nineteenth century, who not only described the 'great towns' of industrial capitalism in England as, and as having, stagnant pools literally and materially, but also metaphorically and morally. From these pools of stagnant filth arose smells offensive to the nose for both Brown-May (cited in McLaren 2013: 29) and Engels ([1845] 1987: 71, 78, 81, 89).

With the Yarra River the city created a nuisance, injurious to health and offensive to eyes and nose, to the senses of sight and smell similar to West Melbourne Swamp (or Batman's Swamp). At the end of the nineteenth century, 'Garryowen' (Edmund Finn) noted the transition in how the Yarra (hardly a river in some places) had

> flowed through low, marshy flats, densely garbed with t-tree, reeds, sedge, and scrub [...] The waters were bright and sparkling; [...] how different in aspect and aroma from the Yarra of to-day – a fetid, festering sewer, befouled midst the horrors of wool-washing, fell-mongering, bone-crushing and other unmentionable abominations!
> (Garryowen ([1835–52] 1967: 37; also excerpted in Flannery 2002: 351)

Rivers and wetlands can be indistinguishable from each other and the distinction between them is an artificial one. Some wetlands have through-flows of water above or below ground.

Not much had changed from Garryowen's day in the late nineteenth century to the late 1960s, if the novel *Ghost River* is anything to go by: 'the skinning sheds oozed their own rivers – of blood and animal fats – into the water, while wrecking yards bled dirty oil and spent fuel. The industrial drainpipes were large enough [to ride a bike through] the pitch-black rancid air' (Birch 2015: 112). The narrow, open sewer of the river downstream and 'the grime of the city' (113) contrasts on the following page with the river upstream, where it 'widened into billabongs, the home to thousands of birds' (113). Remnants of the billabongs remain but the open sewer of the river was cleaned up, its industries relocated.

Spatial divides of the colonial city

The Yarra River divides Melbourne into the north and south side of the city. Grant and Serle describe how 'one of the most fundamental social divisions' was determined by 'which side of the river one lived on' (1957: 204). Graeme Davison argues that the Yarra by the time of 'Marvellous Melbourne' in the 1880s 'had become the boundary – almost a *cordon sanitaire* – between middle-class and working class Melbourne' (1978: 147). It also separated the clean from the dirty, with this distinction applying also to the class difference that kept them apart spatially and economically. The Yarra was also a *cordon* un*sanitaire* between middle-class and working-class Melbourne due to its unsanitary state.

Davison goes on to relate how

[f]rom their secure ramparts, upper-class Melbourne looked down over the river flats upon an inner ring of dismal working-class suburbs. Collingwood, Richmond and South Melbourne conspicuously lack the fresh atmosphere, softening foliage and wide vistas of the hillside suburbs. Their low, flat terrain and soggy soil made drainage poor and enteric diseases a potential hazard. Collingwood, the classic working-class suburb [with] its blighted environment and endemic poverty gave it the highest death rate in the metropolis. But other parts of the flat were scarcely better – the riverside areas of South Melbourne were [...] beset by swampy ground, seasonal floods and pervasive stench [...] Here, as in most parts of the unsewered city, household wastes and seepage from cesspools were permitted simply to run away through open drains into the [Yarra] river [...] Furthermore, since the 1850s the riverbank had been used by noxious industries such as tanning and wool washing; the hides of newly slaughtered animals were left to dry in the sun and their entrails thrown in the river, a double pollutant of air and water.

(Davison 1978: 150; see also Otto 2005: 200)

For Davison, 'the most salubrious suburbs in [...] Melbourne were located [...] on the picturesque hillsides on the city's fringe ([...] Hawthorn, Heidelberg), while the poorest [suburbs] were located in dense, low-lying areas close to swamps and river flats' (2016: 82).

Melbourne thus enacted the archetypal spatial, ethnic and class hierarchy of the colonial city. For Frantz Fanon, the pioneer theorist of decolonization, the archetypal colonial city was divided between the 'Settler's Town' basking on the hillsides, and the 'Native Town' 'wallowing in the mire' ([1965] 1967: 30), as it is in E. M. Forster's *A Passage to India* (1924) on the mud flats of the Ganges in Chandrapore (Forster [1924] 1936: 9). Melbourne followed suit, with the upper classes' suburbs basking on the hillsides and the workers' suburbs wallowing in the mire on the mud flats of the Yarra, while the 'Natives' wallowed in the mire of Fitzroy and Treasury Gardens and along the Yarra.

In George Turner's *The Sea and Summer*, the rich and oppressive 'Big Sweet lived on high ground well above the coastline and the river' ([1987] 2013: 86), and well above the poor and oppressed Swill. By this time, the river had no sides. In Birch's *Ghost River*, 'the high side of the [Yarra] river [is] where the moneyed people live' (2015: 12, see also 7). One character in this novel says to another, 'things are different on the other side of the river' (92). Neither had ever been to the other side. John McLaren also remarks on how Melbourne was, 'from its beginning, [...] marked by class and its indicators: the mud of Collingwood and dry shoes of Toorak, the mansions on the hills and the miserable blocks and tenements on the low lands' (2013: 233). Melbourne from its beginning was marked by hierarchical spatial indicators of class, with higher places indicative of the upper classes and lower places indicative of the lower classes. Class and space mutually reinforced each other with congruence between the levels of both.

Mud, mud, inglorious mud

As with other modern cities, the problem of mud in the nether lands of the slums was to confront urban planners and sanitary engineers in Melbourne and to challenge them to come up with a solution. In 1853, a government committee painted what Davison calls ironically 'this pretty picture' of 'a space upward of one hundred square yards [...] occupied by a green putrid semi-liquid mass [...] to form a fetid putrescent mass of tenacious mud' (1986: 124–25). This slimy mud was neither solid nor liquid, but somewhere in between (for a discussion of slime in these terms, see Giblett 1996: 25–51). The space in which it was located was in the city block bounded by Bourke, Little Bourke, Elizabeth and Swanston Streets. It was only a block away from the desirably fashionable and properly clean 'Block' between Collins and Elizabeth Streets with its Block Arcade.

This 'pretty picture' of slimy mud located between the solid and liquid could equally have been painted (and was) of the slimy mud of the western front in World War I. The mud of the lower-class suburbs of the modern city has been likened to the mud of World War I trench warfare (and vice versa) (see Giblett 2016: 78). It is hardly surprising then that both places end up looking, smelling and being the same because both were the product of class warfare fought against the earth, against both the lower earthly and class strata. One writer to portray graphically and poetically the horror of the 'mud hell' of World War I trench warfare was the Melbourne artist Penleigh Boyd of the famous Boyd family:

> Mud [...] [is] the chief enemy and misery of the soldier. Mud, soft and deep that you sink into, vainly seeking a foothold on something solid; or stiff and cling-ing, gripping boots so firmly as sometimes to drag them off. Mud [...] clings to men's bodies and cracks their skins, and the slimy horror of it soaks their souls and sucks their courage.
>
> (Boyd cited in Otto 2005: 163)

Unlike many other writers, including Australian ones, writing about World War I trench warfare, Boyd did not comment on the smell of the mud.[11] Soldiers mobi-lizing to the western front could smell it before they could see it.

'The horror of slime' was not only to afflict the minds, noses and bodies of soldiers in World War I, but also to exercise the minds of philosophers, such as Jean-Paul Sartre in *Being and Nothingness* (1969; see Giblett 1996: 39–46). Slime is the excluded third term between being and nothingness, solid and liquid, earth and water that makes both pairs possible. Similarly, 'slimy monsters' living underneath the city in the liminal zone between the surfaces and the depths were to trouble the imagination of poets, such as Charles Baudelaire: 'A soul in torment descending [...] / into an echoing cavern [...] / of vigilant slimy monsters / whose luminous eyes enforce / the gloom' (cited in Benjamin [1982] 1999a: 353).

Slimy monsters live between solid and liquid, land and water, in mud and in slime, both underground in the sewers and aboveground in the slums. Fergus Hume, in *Mystery of a Hansom Cab* (1886), reported the monstrous found in Melbourne's slums (as we have seen in Chapter Six). No slimy monsters have been reported in Melbourne's sewers yet, though they have been in other cities, at least in urban mythology and postmodern fiction and film, including luminescent Baudelairean alligators in the gleaming phosphorescent waters of the sewers of Chicago and New York.[12]

Coats of arms

Rivers, such as the Yarra, are a divide within a city, as well as a means of provid-ing ingress and egress for waterborne transportation within the city, and they are a barrier for land transportation cross-river until they are traversed by punts or surmounted by bridges that unite, or at least permit and enable union, across the great divide of the river. The river divides and unites even by virtue of making the division. The river is the glue that holds the two sides of the city together. Without the river, the city would not have a place marker, a place to mark its place in space. Without the river, the grid-plan town would not have a place in which to be placed. As a means of transportation and a source of water, the Yarra, like the Seine, 'expressed a kind of paradox', as Isabelle Backouche puts it: 'while the Seine split the urban space, it also brought the city's inhabitants together on a daily basis and constituted a space of Parisian identity whose trace is still visible in the city's coat of arms' (2008: 28). Most Melburnians would not go to the Yarra on a daily basis and many identify as coming from the north or south of the river (thus acknowledging at least some role for the river as a place marker), but all Melburnians are brought together and united on a daily basis by drinking its water in one form or another.

Unlike Paris, however, Melbourne's coat of arms does not constitute a space of Melburnian identity in which a trace of the Yarra River and Melbourne wetlands is still visible. Paris's coat of arms bears a trace not only of the river (which it straddles by depicting a boat floating on water with the city figured as a vessel in which people live), but also of the marsh in which it was founded in its motto 'it floats but it does not sink' (Horne 2002: illustration following 138). Paris floats on marshes, as does Melbourne. Melbourne's coat of arms does not depict the Yarra, nor does its motto bear a trace of the marshes and swamps in which the city was built and on which it floats as an ark for human and other life floating on the river and its floodplains.

Melbourne's first coat of arms was adopted in 1843 and depicted two lions rampant holding a crest divided into quadrants with, as Coote describes it, 'a golden fleece, a whale, a bull and a ship, representing Melbourne's key export trade in wool, oil and tallow. It was surrounded by a heraldic crest' surmounted by 'a demi-kangaroo' (2013: 76). Melbourne's coat of arms went through various incarnations with the two lions being replaced in 1910 by two female figures representing the motto of the city, 'Peace and Prosperity', who lean on a crest depicting the Southern Cross constellation supported on 'a compartment' of green sward. The Yarra River and Melbourne wetlands are absent from the coat of arms. The only gesture to the nature of the locale, besides the surviving demi-kangaroo, is the inclusion in 1973 of the Victorian floral emblem of the pink heath (Coote 2013: 77).

Drinking water

The Yarra is a ghost or phantom river in the present and in the future, not only in the sense of being ancient and having an old, underlying course, but also in the sense that it is now a dead river, as the upper catchment is dammed and the lower course is an estuarine canal. With the breaking of the rock barrier at Queens Street in the early days of settlement, salt water intruded upstream where previously there had been fresh water, with devastating impact on the freshwater ecology of the river. The middle course was also a dead river of polluted black waters.

Melbourne, for Coote, is 'one of only six cities in the world with a water resource this good' (2013: 181). The upper catchment is where drinking water comes from today. In 1891, this area was called 'the "wild, weird territory at the head of Yarra Yarra"' (Anon. cited in Otto 2005: 37). The natural advantage of the lower Yarra as a source of drinking water was soon obliterated, but the upper Yarra is still a natural advantage to Melbourne as a source of fresh water. Newnham relates how, 'away in the hills at its source, the Yarra River provides Melbourne with some of the purest and softest water in the world' (1985: 151). 'Source' implies a single origin (like a malt whiskey distillery), whereas the Yarra River has a variety of wetland sources (because it once had a number of accompanying swamps and billabongs). As Ward puts it, 'the branching headwaters bubble up in swampy hollows among mountain forests, protected by the closed water catchment of the Upper Yarra Dam' (2011: 33). By contrast, the branching lower-waters at the other end of the river once spread out in deltaic marshes.

The Yarra begins and ends in wetlands. The Yarra River not only still has a wetland origin, but it also once had a wetland destination in what Ward describes as 'a shallow delta' where the river 'seasonally flooded the low-lying land' (2011: 45). Otto describes how

> Melbourne is crowned with more than 140,000 hectares of forest set aside for water catchment, and that's where ninety percent of its supply comes from, some of the most beautiful water in the world [...] There are less than half a dozen cities on earth with a comparable system.
>
> (Otto 2005: 43)

She goes on to list them.

Melbourne's excellent drinking water helps to make it one of the most liveable cities, if not the most liveable city, on the planet, though it is a feature not often remarked upon by residents in surveys, nor is it highly regarded in surveys of the liveability of cities. Good drinking water fades into the background. Only when drinking water is bad does its quality (or lack of it) becomes noticeable. The high-quality of Melbourne's drinking water is, however, under threat from logging in the Upper Yarra Dam catchment area, permitted by the very managers who are supposed to protect it. Both Ward in *The Comfort of Water* and Coote in *The Melbourne Book* (2013) come to the same conclusion independently of each other (Ward 2011: 319–20; Coote 2013: 181). The Victorian government recently announced plans to introduce legislation to form the Yarra River Trust, with responsibility for water quality along the whole length of the river from source to outflow. The Yarra River Trust could operate along the lines of the Swan River Trust, though without suffering the same fate because the latter was starved of funds by the Western Australian government and absorbed into the Department of Parks and Wildlife.

Troubled bridges over waters

Modern industrial cities were the principal perpetrators of the crime against wetlands or waterways and the executioners of the wetland or waterway in the sentence pronounced against them. These cities not only served a juridico-legal warrant against wetlands and waterways and then tried and condemned them, but they also carried out a military operation against them as they divided and conquered. Modern industrial cites divide land from water by dredging and draining wetlands and turning them into drylands, by landscaping wetlands into lakes and by rerouting rivers into canals. They also cross divides, such as building bridges across rivers, joining, if not uniting, both sides of the river. These cities have the power of both making divisions between land and water and of crossing divisions between land and water.

Melbourne is no exception with its treatment of its wetlands and waterways. Nor is it with the construction of its bridges. The Yarra River created the banal divide of North and South Melbourne; bridges across the Yarra joined the north and south side of the river around central Melbourne. Like the famous bridges of Paris crossing the Seine and joining both sides of the river and city together with a common focal point, Melbourne has several bridges crossing the Yarra. The most prominent of these bridges in the Central Business District (CBD) and the most-used by pedestrians is the Princes Bridge, crossing the river as the continuation, meeting point and beginning (and end) of Swanston Street and St Kilda Road.

The first Princes Bridge was 'completed in April 1850' and 'its official opening took place on 15 November as part of the Port Phillip District's separation celebrations' (Annear 2014: 48; see also Newnham 1985: 138–39). 'The new (and current) Princes Bridge opened in 1888' and was, according to Otto (2005: 56–57), 'claimed as the widest bridge in the world'. Grand urban traffic and pedestrian bridges are a marker of modernity that connect two sides of cities and traverse divisive and obstructive rivers. The natural highway of the river is crossed by the cultural or artificial highway of the bridge. The arterial river, drawing life-giving water from its upper catchment, is crossed with a bridge and an arterial road drawing the life of the city together. The two arteries are literally at cross-purposes with each other.

Princes Bridge, for Coote, 'features in many [art] works' of Melbourne as it was 'serving as the only major landmark for a time' (2012: 20). Yet the river itself was, and still is, a landmark but one that is impossible to depict in its entirety in a single landscape view because of its immensity. The landmark of the bridge gave shape and definition to the landscape (viewed or painted). The Princes Bridge is a landmark made by human hands whereas the river is a landmark not made by human hands. The river was made by superhuman beings in Aboriginal story and geological forces in European science. The Princes Bridge continues to serve as a landmark worthy of note and depiction, as does the river. The bridge crossing the river also provides a focal point for landscape painting. The bridge turns landscape into landmark.

In Coote's (2012: 44–45) survey of 'the art of being Melbourne', five paintings depicting the old and newer Princes Bridges are reproduced on pages 20–21, four on page 23 and another on page 32, and then these same paintings reappear frequently throughout the book in chapters devoted to individual painters and their paintings. The bridges (old and new) are some of the main characters in the story of Melbourne, with the river relegated to a supporting role. The bridges (and occasionally the river) appear in multiple guises in the story of Melbourne at different times of night and day, in different moods and tones for over a century since the opening of the first bridge in 1850. H. Nash depicted the opening of the first Princes Bridge in 1850 (discussed above). In 1857, in somewhat lurid and Gothic tones, Ludwig Becker depicted 'Old Princes Bridge […] by Moonlight' and by gaslight (Coote 2012: 48–49). The glimmering gaslights of Princes Bridge are also depicted in Becker's twilit 'Melbourne from across the Yarra' of 1854 (50–51). Coote describes the bridge as the 'star of this painting,' and also 'the new star of the town' (50). Perhaps the river is the old (and fading) star of the city, like the marshes of Dame Marsha Melba.

Many other painters depicted the bridges. Henry Gritten depicted the old bridge in two paintings of c.1856 (Coote 2012: 52–53). Henry Burn also depicted the old bridge in a painting of 1861 (58–59). Frederick McCubbin depicted the new bridge in paintings of 1908 and c.1910 (68–69). Arthur Streeton painted the new bridge in 1888 in a painting called *Between the Lights, Princes Bridge*, in which the bridge for Coote (2012: 72) 'stars' and which for her makes 'the crossing look […] its most idyllic yet' (72). The mood is provincial, almost rural, a truly rare glimpse of a pastoral Melbourne, now long departed' (72). Streeton's view is a bucolic vision of a pastoro-technical idyll in which the city and the river are shown singing in harmony, but the river has since been rerouted and polluted by modern industry.[13]

The mood changes with the turn of the twentieth century. In 1905, Laurence Wilson painted a view of Melbourne with the new bridge dominating the painting

(Coote 2012: 76–77). In 1913, Jessie Traill etched the bridge as 'a monument' (82). A monument to what is not clear, but it certainly was a monument to modernity, to Melbourne itself and to the triumph of modern technology over premodern wetlands, such as the Yarra floodplains. Other painters were not so triumphalist. In 1923, Clarice Beckett painted the bridge in brown tones with accompanying reflections in the murky river. In 1933, she painted it again in 'myriad tones of grey offered up by Melbourne's famous weather' (94) or infamous weather, certainly notoriously changeable. In 1935, Cristina Asquith Baker painted the bridge in steely grey tones (100). In 1951, Charles Blackman painted the bridge at night in oily black tones (108). In 1963, Harold Freedman depicted the bridge in the mid-ground of his view of the Yarra River, with the river in the foreground, looking west from the Botanic Gardens, and the city in the background (124). Freedman's view is a utopian vision of a techno-pastoral ideal in which the city and the river are shown working in unison, but the river has been subsumed (literally and figuratively) by the city.[14]

After the completion of the Westgate Bridge in 1978, with its disastrous history, this bridge became the dominant built landmark of Melbourne. It supplanted Princes Bridge as a monument of modernity and as an object of painterly representation, becoming an icon of hypermodernity. Rick Amor, in his 2001 painting *Lorimer Street*, depicts Westgate Bridge in stark silhouette against the murky sky and reflected in puddles in the foreground (150). Cars and trucks (and their human occupants) crossing the bridge are subsumed in the grungy greyness of the depressing scene and the dismal place.

Similar in mood, Amor's *The Silent River*, also of 2001 (Coote 2012: 151, detail), depicts a dead stream with rotting timber boats and a single hunched monstrous figure beneath the towering columns of the bridge. The sharp, stark lines of the bridge's columns in Amor's paintings contrast with the fluid, amorphous shapes of the bodies of water – whether they be puddles in an industrial wasteland or the muddy and slimy banks of the river – and with the skeletal remains of the rotting boats. *The Silent River* is a kind of postmodern, dystopian allegory of modern alienation and environmental destruction. The river is silent because it no longer burbles over the falls of Queen Street and because it is no longer a working river with the creak of timbers, the slap of canvas and the shouts of workers, and because most Melburnians don't listen to it or don't hear it.

The Yarra, for Davison, 'for much of its course, […] is a secret river, unseen and ignored by the millions of Melburnians who follow and cross it' (2016: 267). For one of the central characters in Birch's (2015: 70) *Ghost River*, 'it's a secret river, almost', as the Yarra is a river of stories that tells its secrets to those prepared to listen and hear. For instance, 'mighty ghost gums growing along the banks of the river' (11) are dotted along its present course. They are visible expressions of the river and telling reminders of the old, invisible mother river that lies beneath the present river that nurtures all Melburnians.

NOTES

1. See also: Victorian Government, 'Landmark legislation to protect the Yarra River', http://www.premier.vic.gov.au/landmark-legislation-to-protect-the-yarra-river/. Accessed 24 June 2017.

2. Two days later, a court in India, citing the New Zealand case and verdict as a precedent, did the same with two Indian rivers. See Safi and agencies (2017).

3. As noted previously, 'the mouth' and 'headwaters' of a river are at opposite ends of a catchment, whereas in human anatomy the mouth is in the head.

4. Individual chapters are devoted to each of these cities in Giblett (2016).

5. Coote (2012: 44) makes these remarks somewhat belatedly and tangentially (almost as an afterthought) in relation to Nash's painting. In her earlier, introductory discussion in *The Art of Being Melbourne* of 'A Sense of Place', which is 'about place' and 'creating Melbourne', Coote (2012: 12–14) does not mention Melbourne's wetlands. Surely, appreciating a sense of the place in which Melbourne was created should include at least some acknowledgement of Melbourne's wetlands. Coote seems to suffer to some extent from Melbournians' wetland amnesia (as also noted previously in *The Melbourne Book* [2013]), but then she is not alone. She does not forget the Yarra River in both books.

6. Becker's painting is reproduced in Coote (2012: 50–51) and discussed later.

7. For the cultures of nature, see Giblett (2011: 21–38).

8. Trollope's description of the Yarra River as 'a torturous, rapid little river' is misquoted by McLaren (2013: 39) as 'a tortuous, narrow little river'.

9. For a reading of Ballard's *Drowned World*, see Giblett (1996: 83–96, 2019b: 112–18).

10. See Otto for 'a rough biblical roll call of those streams that begat the Yarra' (2005: 50–53); see also Cunningham (2011: 226–29).

11. For other World War I writers on mud and slime and their smell, see Giblett (2016: 78–79, 2009: 59–68).

12. For slimy monsters in the sewers of Chicago and New York, see Giblett (2016: 156–60).

13. For the pastoro-technical idyll, see Giblett (2008b: 22).

14. For the techno-pastoral ideal, see Giblett (2008b: 22).

Modes of Transportation and Communication

Various means and modes of transportation and communication – modern and premodern; mechanical, electrical and electronic – helped to make Melbourne what it is today: a modern metropolis with an enviable, though patchy, public transport system containing some black holes. Without them, Melbourne was not, and is not, possible. In the beginning of the city and its history, ships and shipping made Melbourne. Melbourne was a port before it was a city. Melbourne was first and foremost a port city, a maritime metropolis; and a swamp city, a marsh metropolis, before it became a City of Literature, culture and modernity. Melbourne was founded and started to develop in the age of wind-powered, wooden-hulled ships. It continued to develop in the age of steam-powered, steel-hulled ships, when it became the busiest port in the southern hemisphere. The age of steam-power coincided with the development of Melbourne as a modern metropolis initially with steam-powered trains and cable-pulled trams. Melbourne continued to develop later in the age of electric-powered trains and trams.

Trams, initially pulled by cables and later powered by electricity, as with trains, contributed to Melbourne's development. Electrical forms of communication via the telegraph and later the telephone also contributed to the development of Melbourne as a modern city, as did the car, radio and television. Melbourne became a city with one of the largest electric train and tram networks in the world. These amenities contributed, and contribute, to making Melbourne one of the most liveable cities, if not the most liveable city, in the world.

This chapter traces Melbourne's adoption and uptake of these technologies and places them in the larger context of modernity and its technologies, in particular what I call 'sublime communication technologies', including transportation technologies.[1] Steam-powered technologies sublimated the base solid matter of coal into vaporous and gaseous steam to power ships, trains and generators. In turn, generators produced electricity to power the next generation of trains and trams, as well as to enable the communication technologies of the telegraph, telephone and radio. These transportation technologies and communication technologies, such as the telegraph, also sublimated the traditional concepts, experiences and limitations of local time and space in a particular place into the speed and place-lessness of modern life.

Melbourne participated in, and contributed to, these shifts as it was well-positioned to do so by virtue of both its geography and geology. Melbourne's unique geography, located at the head of a bay in the delta of two rivers and at the bottom of the state of Victoria with its unique geology of gold-bearing depos-its, fertile soils and congenial climate with adequate rainfall, contributed to the stellar development of the city as a modern metropolis. The wealth and flows of produce from country Victoria trickled down to Melbourne like a river flowing to the sea. Melbourne was the entrepôt at the point of exchange for imports into the state and exports out of it. This chapter plots the intertwining of the culture of technologies and the nature of geology and geography in Melbourne's develop-ment and use of modern mechanical modes of transportation and communication. Melbourne depended on both.

Ships and shipping

The city of Melbourne eventually outgrew the capacity and capability of the port of Melbourne. Although the location of Melbourne at the 'mouth' of the Yarra River in the sheltered waters of Port Phillip Bay with fresh water readily available upstream provided many amenities for a port, the shallow waters and serpentine course of the river, as well as the adjacent marshes of Fishermens Bend, initially presented limitations for the development of the port and the city (as we have seen in Chapter Three).

Melbourne is situated within the larger context of the continent of Australia and its maritime and colonial history. Australia, as John puts it in his classic *Maritime History of Australia* (1976), is 'a creature of maritime enterprise for it was discovered, explored, settled and sustained by European, mainly British, sea-power' (2, see also 7). By and large this sweeping conclusion applies to Melbourne too. Melbourne is certainly a creature of maritime enterprise for it was discovered and explored by British sea-power beginning in 1802 (as Bach [1976: 30–31] relates and as we have seen in Chapter Two). Yet British power did not go on immediately to settle and sustain a colony at Port Phillip as it was first settled permanently over three decades later by private sea-power instigated by pastoralist squatters (as Bach [1976: 31] also relates and as we have seen in Chapter Two). Here, as elsewhere in Australia, the new settlers' 'first successful economic enterprises were dependent on the sea', Bach (1976: 3) goes on to state, and Port Phillip was no exception. Bach concludes that 'the Europeans came by sea and were supported by sea' (1976: 24). The first Europeans in Australia – explorers and settlers alike – were boat people who came by boats and were dependent on boats for goods and trade. Unlike later boat people, there were no legal restrictions on their movements onshore.

Melbourne is both a port city and a capital city, like London and Toronto (the capital of the Province of Ontario and initially the capital of 'Upper Canada'). Melbourne for a time was also both a state capital and the national capital. It was like all the other state capital cities in Australia in also being a port city. Melbourne is what Bach calls 'the great capital-city port' of Australia (1976: 413). All of Australia's 'administrative establishments save one [the landlocked national capital city of Canberra] are also her major ports', as Bach (1976: 24) puts it, though upriver Perth is the capital city of Western Australia and a river port, while downriver coastal Fremantle is a separate seaport city. All of 'the great Australian coastal cities', as Bach puts it, 'were founded with an eye to their accessibility by sea' (1976: 188). They were also founded with an eye to their accessibility to their hinterlands for the export and import of commodities. Some, such as Melbourne and Perth, were also founded with colonial considerations in mind of pre-empting possible French interest. Like London, Hamburg, Toronto, New York and New Orleans, Melbourne is a maritime marsh metropolis located upstream from the 'mouth' of a river on its marshy banks. Like these port cities, Melbourne is not only a seaport, but it is 'also a river port', as Sanay Yarnasan (1974: 7) puts it.

Perhaps Melbourne does not possess a very good port, and certainly not one blessed with the natural features of some other port cities. Melbourne, as Yarna-san points out, 'is not situated in a natural harbor like Sydney or Hobart' (1974: 9). Nor was choosing a suitable harbour the prime consideration in selecting the site for the settlement that grew into a city. The site for the city, as Yarnasan goes on to point out, 'was not selected with consideration of future port requirements so the limitations of the waterfront became apparent only as the settlement grew and prospered' (1974: 5). One of these limitations was the sinuous course of the Yarra River downstream from the settlement, as the river wound its way around what Sir John Coode (Grant and Serle 1957: 133), 'an eminent British engineer', called 'the great detour' (excerpted in Grant and Serle 1957: 148) of the old Fishermen's Bend.

This limitation was overcome with the construction of Coode's Canal that had devastating impacts on the wetlands of Fishermen's Bend and West Melbourne Swamp (or Batman's Swamp) (as we have seen previously). These 'improvements', as James Grant and Geoffrey Serle (1957: 133) call them in keeping with the deficit model of 'nature' and with the improvers' model of civil engineering, were not only designed to supply nature's deficiencies and overcome nature's imperfections but also, as they go on to argue, 'to shorten and deepen the course of the river and to excavate a dock near the [then] railway terminus' of Spencer Street/Batman's Hill, now Southern Cross, Station. The result 'secured for Melbourne most of the advantages of a natural harbour', as Grant and Serle (1957: 133) put it. As well as providing a secure harbour, the Canal supplied the deficiencies that the swamp presented as obviously unsuitable for a port. The excavation of a dock 'near the railway terminus' was also more precisely on 'the unclaimed area at the east end' of West Melbourne Swamp (or Batman's Swamp), as Coode himself says in 'The Tasks of the Harbor Trust' (excerpted in Grant and Serle 1957: 147–48).

These 'improvements' made Melbourne into what Bach (1976: 129) calls 'a most modern and efficient port'.[2] Melbourne became what Yarnasan (1974: 1) also calls 'Australia's largest general cargo port (in terms of tonnage)'.[3] With the introduction of shipping containers in the 1960s, Melbourne also became 'the largest container port in the southern hemisphere' (Otto 2005: 125) and 'by 1974 among the six top container ports in the world' (Bach 1976: 413). Containers, their ships and routes, are the largely unseen vessels, vectors and vehicles of the import of goods in globalized consumption. Bulk carriers are also the largely unseen vessels, vectors and vehicles of the export of raw materials in globalized production. Without container ships and bulk carriers and their ports, international, globalized trade would not be possible.

Trains, railways and stations

The port and city of Melbourne later developed in step with the introduction of railways and in proximity to each other. Railways are an iconic technology of modernity and a crude conqueror of nature, not least over the premodern nature of wetlands.[4] Railways in Melbourne were no exception.[5] For Frantz Fanon ([1965] 1967: 201), the pioneer theorist of decolonization, 'railways across the bush, the draining of swamps and a native population which is non-existent politically and economically are in fact one and the same thing'. In Melbourne, railways went not only across the bush, but also through drained swamps. In a different register and along similar lines to Fanon, Henry Lawson (cited in Giblett 2008b: 32) described in the 1890s how 'the mighty bush with iron rails / Is tethered to the world'. In Melbourne, railways went not only across the bush and tethered it to the wider world, but also through the drained West Melbourne Swamp and the swampy shores, or the bucolic 'grassy banks of the Yarra River', as Bill Newnham (1985: 132) calls them, home to many Aboriginal people. The major railway stations of Flinders Street Station and Spencer Street/Southern Cross Station were also located in drained swamps. Similarly, in Perth, the central railway station is located in a drained swamp. Railways, drained swamps and 'a native population which is non-existent politically and economically', as Frantz Fanon ([1965] 1967: 201) put it, can be seen occurring together historically and geographically with the locating of railway stations in both Perth and Melbourne in a drained swamp.

Colonization was its most visible and destructive in the construction of hard railway lines of steel through the soft bodies of water in the swamps. Modernity was its most triumphant in the deployment of modern railways against premodern wetlands, the kind of war that modernity likes to fight because short-term victory is readily achievable. Wetlands are at their most invisible beneath railway lines and stations leaving hardly a trace. Decolonization of Melbourne wetlands will be at its most visible when interpretation of the history of Melbourne includes images and stories in public places of its lost wetlands.

In Australia, Melbourne was at the forefront of the colonial development of railways through the bush and swamps, as Australia's first locomotive was completed in 1854 and its first railway line was opened four days later in Melbourne (Newnham 1985: 128, 27, 53; Grant and Serle 1957: 75, see also excerpts from *The Argus* [Grant and Serle 1957: 102]). Asa Briggs sums up that in Melbourne in the decade 'between 1850 and 1860 a number of suburban railways were built' and 'the first, the oldest in Australia, ran from Flinders Street to Port Melbourne' (1963: 289), or to Sandridge as it was called at the time (Grant and Serle 1957: 75; see also excerpts from *The Argus* [Grant and Serle 1957: 102–03]; see also Fiddian 2003: 5). The line was later discontinued and the railway system was redesigned. The railway bridge over the Yarra that ran the Sandridge line still survives as a pedestrian bridge over the river and may be 'upgraded'. The Sandridge line at its terminus in Flinders Street Station has been converted into the riverside 'Arbory' Bar, which must be one of the longest and narrowest drinking establishments in the world. In 1865, Princes Bridge Station was connected by subway beneath Swanston Street to Flinders Street Station, and its number one platform was extended to 2232 feet (nearly 700 metres), one of the longest in the world, according to Newnham (1985: 131), and part of 'one of the world's largest [railway] terminals', also according to Newnham ([1967] 1977: 60).

The current Flinders Street Station was designed in 1899 in a typical Melburnian mishmash of styles, or perhaps more precisely it was designed in different styles according to different historians and commentators.[6] Flinders Street Station, according to Newnham (1977: 60, 1985: 130–32) was built in French Renaissance style. By contrast, the station, according to Marc Fiddian, is 'baroque in style', but he also notes a 'striking resemblance between Flinders Street Station and [the] Taj Mahal' (2003: 11). French Renaissance and European baroque meet Indian Mughal in a typical Melbourne mishmash of architectural styles in a colonialist conquest of time, space, culture and nature (as we will see in Chapter Eleven with other iconic buildings in Melbourne, such as the Royal Exhibition Building).

Construction of Flinders Street Station commenced in 1900 and was completed in 1911 (Coote 2012: 78). The new building, for Fiddian (2003: 17), was 'an opulent one and stood proudly in the cavalcade of grand terminals being built around the world'. Until the construction of the new Southern Cross Station to replace the old Batman's Hill/Spencer Street (now Southern Cross) Station (Newnham 1985: 132–36), Flinders Street Station was 'the largest station in the southern hemisphere' (Anon. cited in Grant and Serle 1957: 202). In 1926, the railway telephone exchange housed at Flinders Street Station was 'the busiest in the world', according to Kristin Otto (2009: 331) and Desmond Fennessy writing in 1952 (excerpted in Grant and Serle 1957: 299). But the railways did not terminate there in the sense of ending definitively. This rail terminal is the centre of a network for the toing and froing of trains.

In his chapter on Melbourne as a Victorian city (in the sense of being built in the age of the reign of Queen Victoria), Briggs remarks that 'the growth of a centralized railway system [in Victoria] favoured Melbourne economically' (1963: 295). This system also contributed to the considerable economic growth and power of the city. The geography of Victoria and the layout of the centralized rail network worked hand in hand with the economic development of Melbourne. For Serle, 'Victoria's was the one Australian railway system which grossly favoured the capital city: "Railways are the rivers of Australia, and all the Victorian rivers have but one mouth," Francis Adam remarked' (1971: 78). In Victoria, the rivers of railways flow down to the 'mouth' in Melbourne. Like the Yarra River, the 'mouth' is the lower endpoint of the system (whether it be rivers or railways), and not the upper starting point. In 1929, the city, for Cunningham, was considered to have 'one of the best railway systems in the world. The lines dictated the shape Melbourne took' (2011: 221). Living within walking distance of this system (and of the tram system) is commodifiable as it makes such locations very desirable, drives up property prices and largely does away with the need for a car, for those fortunate and privileged enough to live in such prime locations and not in the public transport black holes or the outer suburbs.

Disused railway lines also 'still snake through the suburbs [...] many of [which] have become walking tracks and bike paths', as Cunningham (2011: 221) goes on to relate. The terminus of the disused Sandridge railway line at Flinders Street Station and the Sandridge line bridge over the Yarra have now become the Arbory bar and a pedestrian bridge. This bar and pedestrian bridge, and these tracks and paths, are ghost train lines and ghost rivers of transportation, like the serpentine ghost river of the Yarra and the ghost swamps of Melbourne. They contribute to Melbourne's network of walking tracks and bike paths, and to the attractions of

Melbourne for bicycling. Melbourne, for Cunningham, is 'a great place to ride, not least because it's flat' (2011: 247).

Steam-powered engines on suburban railway lines were replaced in the early twentieth century with electric-powered trains with overhead power lines. Electrification of the Melbourne suburban railway system was sanctioned in 1912 and completed about 1922 (Grant and Serle 1957: 263). For Otto, 'the suburban electric train system did become the largest in the world' (2009: 329). The system is not without its drawbacks though. In 1985, Newnham wrote that 'today, level crossings are still one of the problems of the city' (1985: 130). They still are a problem, though one that is gradually being resolved by raising roads or lowering railway lines but not without massive disruption to traffic, services and local residents.

Trams and tramways

Think Melbourne, think trams. Trams are synonymous with Melbourne. 'Trams r us'. Melbourne is the only Australian city with a large tram network and one of only a few around the world. Melbourne, as Roland Wilson and Dale Budd point out in their book on Melbourne trams, 'is alone among Australian cities in retaining a large tram network [...] in one of the world's most liveable cities' (2014: 4). The liveability of the city is in no doubt due in large part to its trams, as they are 'accessible and reliable', by and large, and 'a vital public transport service'. They are also much more than this for they are 'a symbol of the city', as Wilson and Budd (2014: 4) also put it, though the city has not always had them, certainly not for the first fifty years of its life.

The first cable trams were introduced in Melbourne in 1885 (Newnham 1985: 31; Cunningham 2011: 224; Serle 1971: 82). The cable-tram system, Wilson and Budd relate, was 'designed and built essentially as a single entity between 1885 and 1891' and 'comprised nearly 75 kilometres of track serving 17 routes' (2014: 5).[7] Cable trams, for Serle, were 'Melbourne's pride and joy – delightful toys' (1971: 274). Big toy 'trams r us' indeed. Nat Gould, a contemporary observer of trams and Melbourne in their heyday, exclaimed in 1896 that

> Melbourne is the best-laid-out city in Australia. Its streets are wide and long, and the cable-tram system is perfect [...] it would be difficult to find two finer streets than Collins and Bourke Streets [...] Wide and even, and beautifully clean, with the cable-tram running up and down the centre of each, Collins and Bourke Streets excite the admiration of all.
>
> (Gould 1896: 116–19)

Serle relates how 'by 1890 Melbourne was superbly equipped with a suburban transportation system of trains and trams' (1971: 82). Wilson and Budd also relate how 'the last cable tram ran in 1940' (2014: 5), while 'Melbourne's first electric tram ran in 1889' (10) in a short-lived operation that ceased in 1896, while a decade later 'the first successful electric tramway' (68) opened in 1906.

The whole city was being electrified in one way or the other in the late nineteenth and early twentieth centuries. Serle relates that 'it was not until the [eighteen] nineties that electricity was widely adopted for street lighting' (1971: 83). In fact, it was in 1894 (Grant and Serle 1957: 213). Construction of electric tramways began in earnest a decade and a half later in 1909 (Grant and Serle 1957: 263; Wilson and Budd 2014: 10). Wilson and Budd describe how 'today, trams run over 250 kilometres of route, extending more than 20 kilometres from the city centre' (2014: 14).[8] The 'City Circle' tram route girdles Robert Hoddle's grid of the Central Business District (CBD) (Wilson and Budd 2014: 15) and ties it to the northern shore of the Yarra River in a rigid rectangle of perimeter tram tracks mapped over the lost and invisible West Melbourne Swamp (or Batman's Swamp) and over the swampy shores of the river once lining it on the south side of Flinders Street.

Trams provide city dwellers and their city with a human pace of locomotion. Trams, for Maree Coote, provide 'the ideal rate of human progress' (2013: 108). They are faster than walking and slower than a car or train. The tram traveller is a kind of *flâneur* on wheels ambulating along the city streets, who surveys the passing scene through the framing device and protective screen of tram windows. Trams, for Coote (2013: 108), 'pump the blood of bustle around the city'. They are vehicles and vessels for the circulation of the cultural and individual life-blood of the city. The blood vessels of the body of the city are also the pipes conveying life-giving drinking water. The body of the modern city communicates via the nervous system of the wires employed in telegraphy and telephony, and now wirelessly via the electromagnetosphere. Conversely, for Lewis Mumford, in the human body 'the nerves are a telegraph system with a central station' (cited in Giblett 2008a: 19).[9] The body of the modern city is the body electric. The modern city sings the body electric in a Whitmanesque celebratory poem of the glories of modern technology.

Telegraphy

Melbourne began its love affair with telegraphy in 1872 when 'the first overseas telegraph message was received in Melbourne' and 'vanquish[ed] time and space', as Grant and Serle (1957: 133) put it. With the uptake of telegraphy, the expression of similar sentiments was widespread around the world and was a cliché of nineteenth-century technophilia. The 'annihilation of space and time' was borrowed from one of Alexander Pope's relatively obscure poems. It is a stock phrase that appears more often than any other in what Leo Marx calls 'the entire lexicon of progress', as 'the extravagance of this sentiment apparently is felt to match the sublimity of technological progress' (cited in Giblett 2008b: 50).

Yet the phrase not only matches rhetorically the sublimity of technological progress, but it also describes it physically, and chemically. Annihilating anything, making something into nothing, is a process of sublimation counter to the process of creation, creating something out of nothing (*ex nihilo*). By creating sublime railways and telegraphs, 'men' were not being the divine creator who created something out of nothing. They were creating something out of something else, transforming existing matter into other matter. By sublimating solid matter into gaseous steam and electrical impulses, transforming something into airy nothing, they were in fact countering the divine fiat and creation *ex nihilo*. God does not sublimate, only 'men' do.

For one hundred years, from the steam sublime of the railway through the electrical sublime of the telegraph and radio to the electronic sublime of computers and the Internet, the boosters and rhetoricians of transportation and communication technologies have been in the business of proclaiming this annihilation. Of course, space and time will never be annihilated, but the triumph of time over space may have been completed. Indeed, Paul Virilio argues that 'the depth of real time wins out over the depth of the real space of territories' (cited in Giblett 2008b: 51). The capitalist modern sublime strives for the infinite spatiality of global time, or near instantaneity, or 'real time', which overcomes the infinite temporality, or eternity, of local time.[10]

The same rhetoric and practice reached the far-flung corner of the British empire in Melbourne during the 1890s, when telegraphy and telephony boomed (Davison 1978: 132–33). Telegraphy unlocked the coupling and coordination of local space and time and reduced the sense of distance between places by reducing drastically the time taken to communicate between them. Radio, television, telephones, satellites and the Internet have only extended and heightened this process. By freeing communication from the constraints of geography, telegraphy was part of the technological sublime that characterizes modernity. The sublime (including the sublime communication technologies of railways and telegraphy) transcends local place and physical body.[11]

The car

As does the car. Melbourne, for Cunningham, 'like most cities in the last century, began its love affair with the car' in 1915 with the introduction of the Model-T

Ford (2011: 222; see Davison 2004; Otto 2009: 280–81). The car, for Otto, is 'speed wrapped around the human body' (2009: 281). There is a long line of similar critical thinking about the car. The car, for Raymond Williams, is what he calls 'the conditioned atmosphere and internal music of this windowed shell' (cited in Giblett 2008b: 93). Cars, for Walter Benjamin, are 'as beautiful as armour from the age of chivalry' (cited in Giblett 2008b: 94). They are also as aggressive and warlike as armour. Cars are war on humans and nature. The car, for Marshall McLuhan , 'has become the carapace, the protective and aggressive shell, of urban and suburban man'(cited in Giblett 2008b: 95). Instead of finding himself transformed into an organic beetle (like Gregor Samsa in Franz Kafka's story 'Metamorphosis' [1915]), the car-driving urban and suburban dweller is transformed into a mechanical beetle (and not just into a Volkswagen).

All these writers seem to be making a critique of the Italian Futurists whose *First Futurist Manifesto* of 1909 was a hymn to 'the beauty of speed' encapsulated in 'a racing car whose hood is adorned by great pipes, like serpents of explosive breath' (cited in Giblett 2008b: 95). Similar sentiments, albeit in a critical register, were voiced the year before by Pierre Veber in relation to a steam locomotive when 'it emerged from a tunnel, roaring and blowing fire and smoke from its long neck' as if it were 'the legendary dragon-serpent bursting forth from the entrails of the earth' ([1908] 2016: 176). In 1906, the Japanese novelist Natsume Soseki, preceding both the Futurists and Veber, described how a locomotive, 'with a roar, the serpent of civilization comes slowly writhing along the glittering tracks, belching black smoke from its jaws' ([1906] 2008: 145). Whereas Soseki and Veber compare the odious, indeed horrific, locomotive to the dragon-serpent, the Futurists celebrated glowingly the comparison between the dragon-serpent and the car. Whereas the Fairy of Veber's tale is 'the last Fairy', as some of the other fairies were 'killed off by progress' ([1908] 2016: 173), the car for the Futurists is the bearer and bringer of progress.

When the Fairy of Veber's tale sees a car, she remarks that 'it must be enchanted: a hellish smell is trailing that magic carriage!' ([1908] 2016: 178). The car for her, like the locomotive, is a creature of the underworld, of black magic, whereas the car for the Futurists encapsulates literally the Italian Futurist Filippo Tommaso Marinetti's wish-fulfilling fantasy of 'the intoxication of great speed in cars [which] is nothing but the joy of feeling oneself fused with the only *divinity*', the divinity of speed (cited in Giblett 2008b: 105, original emphasis). The car is a divine vehicle of speed for the Futurists, whereas for the Fairy the car is a devilish vehicle of destruction, including of fairies. Veber's fairy tale concludes that 'mankind has succeeded in conquering supreme magic; [...] there is no longer a place for fairies in the modern world' ([1908] 2016: 182). A freeway is no place for fairies, or for the faint of heart.

In 1909, the same year as the *First Futurist Manifesto*, Emile Bergerat ([1909] 2016b) published a fairy tale called 'The 28-Kilometer Boots', in which the car is the boots, a prosthesis for traversing longer distances and at greater speed than humans can with walking. The first-person narrator goes to buy a car and tells 'the genial automaker' (227) that he needs it to be vertiginous. The car is vertiginous because it is 'limitless, death-defying' (230). It is a creation of science 'that can reduce distance to a hypothesis!' (229). Bergerat also wrote a fairy tale in 1909 called 'Cinderella Arrives by Automobile', in which the car of the title is called 'Vertiginous', 'the latest word in earthly location [...] this lightning flash on wheels' ([1909] 2016a: 236). The telegraph was lightning come down to earth, electricity tamed and domesticated; while the car was lightning on wheels across the earth, speed encapsulated and the human body encased within it.

If the telegraph separated time from space by enabling communication to proceed faster than transportation, as a number of commentators on this communication technology have argued (see Giblett 2008b: 38), the car rejoined them. The driver travels through space at the same speed, in the same time, as the car. The car has power over space and time, yet its power is paradoxical. The car liberates and captivates at the same time; the car liberates the driver from the private sphere of the home, office or factory into the public sphere of the street, road or off-road, at the same time as it captivates the driver in the car's private sphere of mobile indoor space. The car encapsulates the paradox of modernity: mastery of space and time, and slavery to space and time too. Free-flowing traffic and traffic jams on the Monash or Tullamarine Freeways show both.[12]

Radio

In the 1920s, Melbourne was beginning its love affair with the radio. Melbourne, as Otto puts it, was 'being electrified, the whole town. The ethereal realm of radio waves and electrical currents was becoming real' (2009: 294). The 1920s, according to Toby Miller writing about the uptake and use of radio in Australia, was the era of 'faith in the "ether", a semi-metaphysical concept that was used to describe the air through which radio waves passed' (cited in Giblett 2008b: 111). Yet the medium through which radio waves pass is not only, or just, air in the strict sense of a mixture of oxygen and nitrogen. The medium is the electromagnetosphere, not limited or restricted to the atmosphere, but also including the ionosphere. The atmosphere and the electromagnetosphere are not co-extensive; the electromagnetosphere is more extensive than the atmosphere, though both are terrestrial phenomena. The ether transcends the earthly into the extraterrestrial, but it is also a terrestrial product of the earth's electromagnetism.

The ether not only had a spatial location above and beyond earthly space but it also had a temporal presence in and through earthly time. The ether is a space–time matrix and a medium of and for communication. It transcends local time and place and enables communication in real time through space. This is applicable not only to modern radio but also to hypermodern telecommunications. By transcending time and space, and the earth below and the below-earth, the ether is also sublime. By utilizing the ether to communicate, radio is a sublime communication technology.[13]

Cinema

Cinema is a curious and symptomatic absence from most of the general histories of Melbourne, certainly the ones cited previously in this chapter.[14] This absence is even more curious in light of the fact that Melbourne was the first place in the world to produce and screen a feature film, when *The Story of the Kelly Gang* was filmed and screened in Melbourne in 1906 (as we saw in Chapter One). Cinema is a sublime communication technology, as it deals with creative, large-scale events and transforms them into soaring and transcending walls of light, into virtual walls, or onto real walls.[15] 'White Night', held in Melbourne each year when the facades of buildings become projection screens for animated light displays, is a form of outdoor cinema.

Television

Television arose out of radio and film: television is simply radio with pictures.

Melbourne, as Coote points out, was 'always the true engine of Australian-made television' (2013: 262) from its beginnings in the 1950s. And probably still is. By arising out of radio, television began life as a broadcast communication technology. On the other hand, by addressing the sense of sight it had more to do with cinema than radio, yet like radio it was received within the private domestic sphere of the home. Television brought cinema home; it brought the power of seeing that cinema enabled into the lounge room. Like cinema and the car, it was associated with a powerful shift in the logistics of perception.

Like cinema and the car, television was also associated with a powerful shift in the logistics of locomotion, or the lack of it. Television is a vehicle for seated passengers that transports us, or at least our gaze, to distant places while confining us in front of the TV set. Television empowers the eye but disempowers the rest of the body, reducing it to an immobile passenger seeing everything, but going nowhere. Television is both mobilizing and immobilizing at the same time: television enables the gaze of the viewer to travel virtually to many places while the body of the viewer is positioned in frozen, immobile space, in one place, in the leisure-discipline of industrial capitalism, within an apartment or other living cell of a hypermodern city such as Melbourne.[16]

Melbourne is a modern metropolis with its rapid uptake and use of modern communication and transportation technologies. Many of these technologies were, and still are, tied to the city's fascination with sport, both transportation to and from sporting venues, and free-to-air broadcast and paid narrow-cast communication about sport, the topic of the next chapter.

NOTES

1. For transportation *as* communication and communication *as* transportation of messages, following in the footsteps of Raymond Williams and others, and for sublime communication technologies, see Giblett (2008b: 1–18).

2. For the history of the development of the port of Melbourne within the colonial and national context of the maritime history of Australia, see Bach (1976: 128–29, 267–71, 345, 413–14). For the international context of the maritime history of 'the world', albeit without referring to Bach and Melbourne, see Paine (2015).

3. Similarly, Bach (1976: 414) says that Melbourne is 'Australia's leading general-cargo port'.

4. For further discussion of railways (including as a sublime communication technology triumphing over slimy wetlands), see Giblett (2008b: 19–36).

5. For a general history of railways in Melbourne, see Newnham (1985: 128–30). For a general history of trams and railways in Melbourne, see Davison (1978: 156–71).

6. For the history of the design of Flinders Street Station, see Otto (2009: 332–33).

7. For these cable tram routes, see the map on page 8 of Wilson and Budd (2014).

8. For the electric tram routes, see the map on page 23 of Wilson and Budd (2014). For the various 'classes' of electric trams (including line drawings), see pages 31–34 of Wilson and Budd (2014), provided for the avid 'tram spotter' to identify them.

9. *The Body of Nature and Culture* (Giblett 2008a) presents on a chapter-by-chapter basis an extensive discussion and history of the tropes (technological, political, organic, etc.) that have been used as figures for the human body, for instance, the body as machine, etc.

10. For further discussion of telegraphy (including as a sublime communication technology), see Giblett (2008b: 37–55).

11. For further discussion of the electrical and technological sublime, see Giblett (2008b: especially 45–55).

12. For further discussion of the car (including as a sublime communication technology), drawing on the work of Walter Benjamin, Paul Virilio, Raymond Williams and others, including Kenneth Grahame's *The Wind in the Willows* (1908), see Giblett (2008b: 92–109).

13. For further discussion of the ether and radio (including as a sublime communication technology), see Giblett (2008b: 110–27).

14. The exception (and one not cited previously in this chapter) for films (and television) set in and about Melbourne is Sinclair (2015: 154–65).

15. For further discussion of cinema (including as a sublime communication technology), see Giblett (2008b: 74–91).

16. For further discussion of television (especially as a panorama and panopticon), see Giblett (2008b: 128–45).

Sport and Its Homes

Sport plays a leading role in the life of Melbourne. Sporting places are prominent sites in the landscape of Melbourne. Some sporting places in Melbourne, such as the Melbourne Cricket Ground (MCG) and Flemington Racecourse are, or were, home to many iconic sporting events in Melbourne, such as the 1956 Olympics, the Boxing Day cricket Test match, the Australian Football League (AFL) Grand Final (usually held on the last Saturday in September) and the Melbourne Cup horse race (always held on the first Tuesday in November). Both places are hallowed turf for athletes, players, riders, supporters and fans. These events and the places in which they are held show how nature and culture are intertwined in the life of Melbourne and in the human body. The location and number of cricket pitches, football fields and racecourses in Melbourne highlight the cultural and environmental politics of the city, especially the privileged position given to sport. This chapter is an environmental and cultural history and study of sporting fields, buildings and bodies.

The central place and pivotal role of sport in the life of the city of Melbourne and for its people has been central to its and their identity for over a century. In the nineteenth century, Richard Twopeny 'with Melbourne in mind, called Australia "the most sporting country in the world"' (cited in Briggs 1963: 309). One wonders whether he was referring to Australia as a country of participants in sport or spectators of sport or both? The same question could be asked of James Grant and Geoffrey Serle, who claim that after World War II 'Melbourne had become the most sport-minded metropolis in Australia' (1957: 254). Sport is arguably war by other means, or sublimated war (see Giblett 2008a: 131–32). Asa Briggs notes that in the nineteenth century, 'the city [of Melbourne] was called "a city of spectators"' (1963: 310). But it was also a city of participants in sport. Geoffrey Serle argues that 'by the late [eighteen] eighties, organized sport – both as pastime and spectacle – had become a distinguishing feature of Australian urban life' (1971: 291), including Melbourne, and it still is.

Melbourne is, or was, also a city of wetlands (as we have seen in Chapters Two to Four), or what Alf Batchelder (2005: 1), in his history of the Melbourne Cricket Club (MCC) and the MCG, rather disparagingly calls 'endless quagmires' of 'the swampy lands bordering the Yarra' (22) on both the north and south sides of the river. One of these wetlands was the venue for the settle-ment's first major sporting events. In 1838, Batman's Swamp (or West Melbourne Swamp) was the site of both Melbourne's first cricket match and Melbourne's first formal race meeting. In similar terms to George Gordon McCrae's elegy, penned in 1912, for this swamp as it was in the 1840s (as we saw in Chapter Two and as cited in Batchelder [2005: 16]), in 1888 Garryowen (Edmund Finn) recalled how in 1840,

> the grassy flat that surrounded it [Batman's Hill] on all but the Yarra side and stretched away into the swamp, then swarming with native wild fowl, was if formed by Nature's hand for a racecourse, unless when inundated by floods. Here, where the Spencer Street [now Southern Cross] Railway Station now stands, was marked out with a few stakes, saplings, and broad palings, Melbourne's first racing ground.
>
> (Garryowen excerpted in Grant and Serle 1957: 30)

'Nature', in Garryowen's eyes, created the ideal place for a horse racing ground – the grassy, flat, horizontal extension of Batman's Swamp – provided it did not flood. However, the swamp was flood-prone. The indigenous grasses and periodic inundation did not make the site ideal for a cricket ground (as we will see later in this chapter).

Horse racing

The first formal horse race was held here in March 1838 (Batchelder 2005: 2). Horse racing, as Serle puts it, had 'both a fashionable and a mass following' (1963: 364). And still does. Serle reiterated later that '[horse] racing was the great popu-lar sport where the classes and the masses mingled' (1971: 292), and still do at the racecourse. Horse racing is not only 'the sport of kings', as Robyn Annear (2014: 210) says, but also the sport of commoners. The Melbourne Cup is not only the pinnacle of horse racing in Australia, 'Australia's richest horse race', as Coote (2013: 236) says, but also an occasion when the classes and masses mingle, as they did at the MCG before it became corporatized.

The Flemington Racecourse was inaugurated in 1840, and 'in 1861 the first Melbourne Cup was raced over two miles, a distance that has never been altered' (Newnham 1985: 193–94; see also Briggs 1963: 310; Coote 2013: 236; Serle 1963: 364). Mark Twain called the Melbourne Cup race day 'the Australian National Day', surpassing Australia Day on 26 January and 'the great annual day of sacrifice' (cited in Briggs 1963: 310; see also Coote 2013: 242).

Who or what was being sacrificed to what or whom is not clear. Perhaps it was horses or morality that were being sacrificed. In 1896, Nat Gould said that 'at Cup time Melbourne is not the most moral city on the face of the globe' (1896: 127). And still is not. Graeme Davison describes the Melbourne Cup as 'that favourite rite' (1978: 209). For many teenagers coming of age at 18, the legal drinking age, going to Flemington Racecourse for the Melbourne Cup is a rite of passage to adulthood. For many women, it is a rite of dressing up in fashionable costumes, wearing a fascinator, having a flutter (millions of dollars are bet on the outcome of the race) and drinking a flute of champers or a few. The Melbourne Cup, for Coote, is 'a nationally-sanctioned intoxicated obsession' (2013: 236). It is also a nationally sanctioned nationalist obsession: 'nowhere else in the world does a nation stop for a single horse race', as Kristin Otto (2009: 128) puts it. In the State of Victoria, a public holiday is gazetted for the first Tuesday of every November. The Monday before it is the national sickie day. Elsewhere around the country many Australians are glued to the radio or television at home or at work awaiting the outcome of the race and the success or otherwise of the bet they may have placed in the office sweepstake or through a betting agency. Similarly, the AFL Grand Final is traditionally played on the last Saturday in September with a gazetted public holiday the day before when a street parade of the two teams is held through the CBD. In a break with tradition, the Grand Final was held on the first Saturday in October in 2015 and 2016, only to revert to tradition on the last Saturday in September in 2017, 2018 and 2019.

Cricket

In 1838, the same year as the first horse race was run, and on the site of the present-day Southern Cross Station on Spencer Street, the first cricket club was established and the first cricket match was played (Annear 2014: 211; Batch-elder 2005: 3; Grant and Serle 1957: 31; Dunstan 2000: 2, 7). This site gradually became unsuitable because, in the words of the report into the architectural heritage of the MCG, it was 'immediately downstream from the township, [so it] proved intolerable due to pollution from the nearby Yarra' (Levenspiel 2006: 15). Or more precisely, it proved intolerable due to the polluted Yarra, as the Yarra was not the polluting agent but the carrier of the pollution produced by, as Batchelder puts it, the 'boiling-down operations [of livestock] in the swamp below Batman's Hill' (2005: 19). The bio-chemical agent of these operations, beginning in 1843, produced not only foul waste that flowed into the Yarra River and polluted its waters, but also 'terrible odours that the prevailing westerlies carried into the city' and polluted its air, as Batchelder (2005: 19) goes on to relate. Batchelder calls the pollution of Batman's Swamp an 'environmental tragedy' (2005: 20). The pollution of Melbourne's air and the pollution of the Yarra River were also environmental tragedies.

Air and water pollution were major motivators in the next shift for the MCC. In 1848, the MCC moved from the polluted Batman's Swamp on the north bank of the polluted Yarra, to South Melbourne and 'the flood prone south bank of the Yarra' (Levenspiel 2006: 15; Batchelder 2005: 20–22). Rather than the physical drawbacks of the site, it was the prospect that the first railway line in Australia might go right through the cricket ground that prompted the MCC to look for another site, as Batchelder (2005: 31–34) points out.

The present-day site of

> the Melbourne Cricket Ground was established in 1853 when 10 acres of land at Yarra Park in Jolimont was set aside [by Governor La Trobe in a 'Deed of Grant'] for the use of the Melbourne Cricket Club [...] [in order] 'to promote the recreation and amusement of the people'.
>
> (Levenspiel 2006: 10)

This area was previously known and used as the 'Police Paddock' for training and drilling horses and men. Keith Dunstan, in his monumental book about the MCG, describes the site as 'a lovely place, full of wattle, wildflowers and heath' (2000: 16).[1] This was Aboriginal country and part of the greatest estate on earth, to use Bill Gammage's (2012) term. Batchelder, in his two-volume history of the MCG, movingly acknowledges that

> [f]or centuries, it had been a special place. On the northern side of the Yarra, from the source to its junction with Maribyrnong River, lived the Wurundjeri-willam clan. To these speakers of the Woi-wurrung dialect, the region was, like all of the land, a source that sustained them in both body and soul. Each year, social and spiritual needs took the hunter-gatherers [and farmers of fish, eels and vegetables in a sustenance and sustainable culture] into specific areas at particular times.
>
> (Batchelder 2005: 35)

The site of the MCG is a site of social and spiritual significance for Aboriginal people.

Edward La Trobe Bateman depicted the place as a wetland or flooded paddock in his drawing *Jolimont, From the Hill beyond the Yarra Yarra* (1854).[2] Unlike Dunstan, and as with the two previous homes of the MCC, Bateman also depicts the area as partially flooded. 'Eunice' (cited in Batchelder 2005: 35) recalled in 1853 that 'at the lower end of the paddock' there was 'a very pretty, shallow lagoon'. This lagoon could revert to a swamp during a game of Australian rules football, as occurred in 1859 and as Batchelder (2005: 56) describes. This Aboriginal place with its pretty lagoon and beautiful botanic objects all had to make way for the greater good and glory of what Dunstan (2000: 17) calls the 'picturesque ground' and 'the finest cricket ground in the colonies'.

Yet, unlike 'Nature's' provision of 'a grassy flat' suitable for horse racing at Batman's Swamp, in Australia, 'the peculiarity of climate and indigenous grasses are both opposed to the natural formation of a suitable turf' for cricket, as Batchelder (2005: 38) puts it. English rye grass was sown in 1872 and spread thickly. In the words of one early observer (cited in Batchelder 2005: 122), the result of 'the beautiful fresh green appearance of the sward is delightful to the eye of the cricketer'. From beautiful botanic place to the beautiful sward of the MCC ground marks the practical subsuming of Aboriginal country and Aboriginal horticultural practices of 'fire-stick farming', to European landscape aesthetics and European horticultural practices of landscape architecture and gardening in creating the pleasing prospect of the gentleman's park estate.

A landscape engraving of 1864 depicts the MCG in picturesque mode in a pastoral setting, with framing trees whose branches provide impromptu, elevated points of view for daring spectators (Troedel 1863–64). A pretty lagoon and a beautiful botanic place had to make way for a picturesque cricket ground. The site was transformed in the terms of European cultural and aesthetic categories. In similar terms to Dunstan (2000), Brian Matthews describes how the MCG 'as a broad, open, parklike expanse in the 1860s' was gradually transformed in the early 1900s into the beginnings 'of its later incarnation as a true "stadium"' (2005: 154). A pretty lagoon and a beautiful botanic place (part of 'the greatest estate on earth') had to make way for a picturesque cricket ground, and then in turn for a monumental and sublime sports stadium. The site and ground were transformed in terms of European cultural, aesthetic and architectural categories. Aboriginal country and Aboriginal cultural and spiritual categories were subsumed literally and figuratively beneath the MCG in terms of European aesthetics and architecture.

The MCG is first and foremost a cricket ground, as its name indicates. A report into the architectural history and heritage values of the MCG states that

> the MCG is [...] of historical and social significance for its association with the Melbourne Cricket Club, the oldest club in Victoria and a major force in the development of cricket and other sports in Victoria from the nineteenth century.
>
> (Levenspiel 2006: 10)

The site of the MCG is also of social and spiritual significance due to its association with the local Aboriginal people, though they are not mentioned in this report and are written out of the history and heritage of the MCG as a consequence. Serle relates how 'cricket boomed in the late fifties after inter-colonial games had begun' (1963: 364). In 1862, the first cricket match against an English team was played at the MCG (Newnham 1985: 185) and 'the first-ever Test match at the MCG [was played between Australia and England] in March 1877' (Matthews 2005: 45). In a precisely clockwork repetition of history, the Centenary Test in March 1977 had the same winning margin for the host side.

Australian rules football

Like the playing of cricket in Melbourne, Australian rules football dates from the late 1850s. Serle relates how 'organized football began in Melbourne in 1858' (1963: 364–65 note; see also Grant and Serle 1957: 112). It was more the game of the people than cricket, though it was developed as the off-season game to keep cricketers fit. For Matthews, 'the Australian code [of football was and still is] a game of the people. *Populi ludos populo* was its early motto – the game of the people for the people' (2005: 29). It is also a game played by the people on 'the people's ground' of the MCG (Dunstan 2000). Or at least it began by being played nearby. Matthews describes how in 1858 'the first match of what was recognizably the new code of Australian Rules Football took place [...] adjacent to the MCG' (2005: 31). The consultants' report into the architectural history and heritage values of the MCG states that 'the MCG is also of historical and social significance for its egalitarian image as the "people's ground" and its long tradition of serving the people of Victoria' (Levenspiel 2006: 10).

Australian rules football has Aboriginal origins in their game of 'Marn grook' (see Otto 2005: 155; Coote 2013: 205).[3] The game's indigenous origins are incontrovertible. Jenny Hocking and Neil Reidy (2016) assemble an impressive body of evidence to counter those who deny the game's Aboriginal origins, which they see as symptomatic of a denial of indigenous history in general. '*Marn grook* – "game ball"', for Matthews, is 'a game as much about air as about earth' (2005: 30). It is a game played in the air, with the ball and players in the air much of the time, rather than with the ball and players on the ground like rugby and 'soccer' most of the time. It is a game played in the element of least resistance to ball and bodies, hence its spectacular airborne displays of dexterity in the 'screamer' (a group of players leap off the ground, and one of them, often gaining additional elevation from the back or shoulders of another player,

169

catches the ball overhead or on the chest, or 'takes a mark'). Sometimes with the addition of water, the game gets bogged down in the muddy earth (though with well-drained grounds this is less likely nowadays). It is a game trying to transcend the vagaries of earth and water, of drought and flooding rain in Australia (and it is well-suited to doing so), through the air, the clear and crystalline element. Cricket is also a game of the elements of 'earth, air, fire and water', as Matthews (2005: 66 and 70) argues. Wetlands are the places of the play of these four elements too, so the playing of Australian rules football at the MCG in wet weather is reverting the MCG to its swampy origins (for the four elements, see Giblett [1996: 156–62]).

Australian rules football undoubtedly has major indigenous origins, but dispute over its settler paternity still rages. The 'Father of the Game', according to Serle (1963: 364, 364–65 note), was H. C. A. Harrison. Dunstan (2000) captions a portrait of Harrison as 'The Father of Australian Rules Football'. Others lay claim to paternity rights for Thomas Wentworth Wills.[4] Coote (2013: 205) thinks so; Batchelder (2005: 52) thinks not. Dunstan ducks and dives on this issue, like a wingman dodging and weaving around all comers on the flank in an Aussie rules football game. Dunstan wonders whether 'perhaps he [Wills] started it' (2000: 19). Dunstan later says,

> with his cousin, Tommy Wills, H. C. A. Harrison was responsible for the start of Australian Rules Football. In 1858, when they were only 20 [years old], they arranged the first game of football and later drafted a code which they felt would be more suitable to our conditions.
>
> (Dunstan 2000: 146)

Even later, Dunstan says that Wills was 'the prime inventor' (2000: 245). Dunstan (2000: 297–98) also points out that Wills and others (but not Harrison) signed the 1859 Rules of the Melbourne Football Club. Finally, Tom Wills, for Dunstan, was 'the man who virtually founded our game of football' (2000: 316). Wills left for his father's property in Queensland in 1860 and returned four years later. According to Dunstan (2000: 363), during this period Harrison took over the administration of the game.

Martin Flanagan asks,

> [W]hose game is it, you ask? The blackfellas say it's theirs. The Irish claim they invented it and poor old H. C. Harrison went to the grave swearing it was British. If you want my opinion, it's a bastard of a game – swift, bold and beautiful – for a bastard of a people.
>
> (Flanagan cited in Coote 2013: 205)

In other words, it is the illegitimate offspring born out of wedlock between an Aboriginal and either an English pastoralist or an Irish servant. It is what we call today by the empty euphemism 'multicultural'. It is emblematic of Australia's hybrid heritage rooted in the land and dispossessed Aboriginal people, and settled by the Irish and English, who were dispossessors, appropriators or reconciliators.

The Australian game has attracted diametrically opposed opinions. For Richard Twopeny in 1883, 'the Victorian game is by far the most scientific, the most amusing both to players and onlookers, and altogether the best' (excerpted Flannery 2002: 296). A century later Bill Newnham concurred with Twopeny, relating how 'enthusiasts of the game argue that the spectacular high marking, long-distance kicking, short hand- and foot-passing and the robust non-stop play makes the Australian game the most exciting and fastest football [game] in the world' (1985: 188, see also 188–91). These are still features of the game that attract fans from around the world.

Other features of the game are not so attractive. For John Stanley James, writing under the nom de plume of 'A Vagabond' in *The Argus* in 1876, it is a brutal, bruising and cruel game:

> *Mens sana in corpore sano* [a sound mind in a sound body – the motto of the Carlton Football Club] I believe to be generally true, but the principle may be carried to excess, and a healthy mind certainly does not exist where cruel and brutal sports are indulged in. Football as now carried on here is not only often rough and brutal between the combatants, but seems to me to have a decided moral lowering and brutalising effect upon the spectators. The records of the past season show that several promising young men have been crippled for life in this 'manly sport;' others have received serious temporary injuries, and laid the foundations of future ill-health, the luckiest getting off with scars which they will bear with them to their graves [...] If an intelligent foreigner had been present, watching these young men clad in party-coloured garments running after an inflated piece of leather, kicking it and wrestling for it, receiving and giving hard blows and falls, he must have thought it the amusement of madmen. The spectators, who howled and shrieked and applauded, he would have thought equally mad. It is true that as a spectacle of bodily activity and endurance the show was a fine one, but the cruelty and brutality intermixed with it, and which the crowd loudly applauded, and appeared to consider the principal attraction, was anything but a promising evidence of a high civilization. I was told by several that it would be a pretty rough game, and they gloated in the fact.

> (James excerpted in Flannery 2002: 292–94)

This is probably the most accurate description of a game of Australian rules football ever penned. It is still pertinent 140 years later. Nothing much has changed.

In order to situate sport and ascertain its role in the life of Melbourne, various writers and commentators have made comparisons with other activities in which Melburnians have been either spectators or participants. The comparison with religion is tried and true. Coote, for instance, claims that 'in Melbourne sport is certainly a religion' (2013: 209). For Sophie Cunningham, 'religion and sport are never far apart' (2011: 70), and in Melbourne they are bedfellows, as she relates.[5] J. H. Barrows decried 'the jumbo worship of football' (cited in Davison 1978: 234).

Religion is, or was, the opiate of the masses, as Marx and Engels said in the nineteenth century in *The Communist Manifesto* (1848). Sport is arguably the opiate of the masses in the twentieth and twenty-first centuries. With the decline in church attendance, sport has taken the place of religion. Both are united, though, in the love of music. Music, for Peter Sloterdijk, is 'the real religion of the modern age' ([2014] 2017: 11) and 'the opium of the masses' (34). The biggest crowd recorded at the MCG is not for a sporting event but for a musical religious one, when 143,750 people came to hear the preacher Billy Graham, his choir and soloists, and to participate in hymn singing in March 1959. They also came to be converted to Christianity (Matthews 2005: 173–75).[6] This 'one-off' event, and subsequent secular concerts at the MCG, though, do not seriously imperil sport's ongoing importance and presence in the life of Melbourne as evidenced by the number of venues devoted to cricket and football. Coote relates how 'in greater Melbourne there are more footy ovals and cricket pitches [...] than there are churches or schools. Which is not ideal' (2013: 209). Yet many sporting clubs do more than play sport. They have taken over many of the social support and charitable functions of church and state, such as the provision of food and shelter for the homeless and for victims of domestic violence.

The MCG

Just as the Christian religion has its sacred sites, cathedrals, shrines and temples, so does sport. 'The Outer at Princes Park [in Carlton] was like a sacred site' for actor and critic Graeme Blundell (cited in Cunningham 2011: 66). The MCG has been called a cathedral, shrine and temple. The MCG, for Matthews, is 'the temple down the road' (2005: n.pag.) and 'the cathedral-like stadium' (32), 'that great cathedral-like space' (67) with its 'broad, oval, green nave' (67). The 'G' for him is also 'Melbourne's great secular cathedral' (93), one of three cathedrals in Melbourne to go along with the sacred cathedrals of St Patrick's Catholic and St Paul's Anglican Cathedrals (55, see also 53–57, 84, 108–09, 153–54, 203, 217).

He does not rate the Royal Exhibition Building as a cathedral, though it is modelled on a cathedral with two naves and a transept. It is a secular cathedral to industry (as we will see in the following chapter). Thus, Melbourne has two Christian and two secular, or post-Christian, cathedrals, all of which are sacred places at one time or another, for someone or other.

The MCG is St Peter's post-Christian cathedral for following and believing in the religion of sport. Like its biblical counterpart in the disciple St Peter, it is the rock on which Melbourne is built. St Peter is also the voice of Satan that Jesus commanded to 'get behind me Satan' when St Peter tempted him away from his sacred mission of painful self-sacrifice for a higher good. The MCG displays the pain and suffering of the sportsperson as a salvific spectacle for the sports fan. The sports player suffers instead of the sports fan, just like Jesus suffered for the believer's sins, and saves him or her from damnation. The mass or communion ritually re-enacts Jesus' salvific self-sacrifice. For Matthews, 'the [football] Grand Final is the high mass of the MCG cathedral' (2005: 101). Just like the mass or communion, in which the bread and wine are symbols of, or are transubstantiated into, the body and blood of Jesus, so the sporting cathedral stages a secular mass in which the body and blood of the sports person are transformed into spectacular display. Just like the mass or communion with its bread and wine, the pie and sauce and beer consumed by the spectator are transubstantiated into the blood and flesh of the spectator's body. Nature and culture are intertwined in the human body of the spectator and player (see Giblett 2008a).

The 'G', for Matthews (2005: 125), is also the temple from which it is unlikely the Pharisees will ever be chucked out, unlike the young Jesus who threw the moneychangers out of the temple in Jerusalem. Young players are leading, like the Pied Piper, older spectators into the cavernous MCG. Money changing hands is installed front and centre in the functions of the sporting temple. Like the temple in Jerusalem, going to 'G' for a big game for Matthews is making 'a pilgrimage to a holy shrine' (2005: 60). It requires the purchase of indulgences in the form of a ticket of admission and of sacred relics in the form of team paraphernalia and sporting memorabilia. The pilgrimage can mean descending into the slough of despond when one's team is beaten, or ascending into the celestial heights of ecstasy when one's team wins, especially if they win the premiership, the grand final in footy.

Ultimately the MCG serves social functions of solidarity and cohesion above and beyond its spiritual and sporting purposes. The MCG, for Matthews, 'like all great cathedrals in great cities, it is central to more than the spiritual, or sporting, like of the people. The 'G' is, for example, a good place to, well, just meet' (2005: 206). But not just to meet, but to stand in a queue, to shuffle forward through a turnstile, to get into the game, to sit or stand with a mate or partner, to share a drink and juggle a pie, to barrack for one's team, to dissect the game, to analyse the moves and the tactics, to cheer dexterity or a win, and to boo the other side or the umpire or both.

For Gideon Haigh, 'being in a crowd' at the MCG means enjoying 'a perfect balance of solitude and companionship' (2003: n.pag.). Being in the sports stadium is the ideal modern urban experience of being in a crowd and partly of the crowd. Sports-goers in the stadium are united in the communion of a common belief and pursuit, and in solitary devotion to, and reflection on, the spectacle of sport. They are united and divided by their different allegiances to one team or player or another, or their appreciation or knowledge of different aspects of the game. By contrast, the usual modern urban experience of walking in the 'busy thorough-fares' of 'big cities', as Haigh (2003: n.pag.) puts it, is of being *in* and *of* a crowd with no solitude, totally superficial companionship and little communion. The driver in their car on the 'busy thoroughfares' of 'big cities' is neither in, nor of the crowd. They are in solitude when they are on their own, in possible companion-ship sometimes with passengers, have little or no communion with other drivers, and may or not be in communion with the commodity of the car.

Just as religion was social cement, so is sport today. Mark Holsworth relates how 'the MCG is frequently described as a "shrine to footy," showing the deep, religious significance of football to Melbourne' (2015: 37–43). The MCG, for Otto, is 'still the game's [Australian rules football] spiritual centre' (2005: 154). Similarly, for Sinclair, 'the MCG is our spiritual home' (2015: 68) and, for Haigh, 'it is our MCG' (2003: n.pag.). To whom does 'our' refer? For Megan Ponsford, the MCG is 'home ground' (2003: n.pag.). Whose home ground? Whose ground is it home to? For whom is the ground home? For Dunstan the MCG is 'the people's ground' (2000). But again, which people? The site was still a Kulin camping ground in 1844, as Sinclair (2015: 68–69) relates, but the ground was not home for the Kulin from the 1850s. The site became sporting ground for white fellas, so it ceased to be a Kulin camping home ground. They were excluded from 'the people' and the plural possessive pronoun of solidarity 'our'. They were re-included later inso-far as they participated in playing or watching football. Today, the MCG is a site of inclusiveness across the indigenous–non-indigenous divide as many Austral-ian rules football teams have indigenous players (though few prominent cricket teams do). The indigenous origins of the site are acknowledged these days in 'the welcome to country' given at the beginning of major sporting events at the MCG, such as the Boxing Day Test or the AFL Grand Final. How many spectators at the MCG or viewers at home know about the environmental and cultural history of the site more than that it is Wurundjeri country is another matter.

A recent report into the architectural history and heritage values of the MCG answers the question of *how* the MCG is significant by suggesting that 'the MCG in its entirety is of historical, social/spiritual and aesthetic significances to the State of Victoria and at a national and international level' (Levenspiel 2006: 10). The report goes on to answer the question of *why* the MCG is significant by suggesting that

> the MCG is of historical and social/spiritual significance as one of the oldest and largest capacity contained sporting venues in the world and one of the best-known of international cricket grounds, and as the pre-eminent venue for top level cricket in Australia since the mid to late nineteenth century. Since the late nineteenth century it has also been the main venue and symbolic home of Australian Rules Football in Melbourne, making it of great historical and social/spiritual significance in a state and metropolitan context, and – following the expansion of the Australian Football League to include interstate clubs – in a national context. The MCG is also significant as the main venue and ceremonial focus for the 1956 Melbourne Olympic Games, and for its associations with numerous other sports and events.
>
> (Levenspiel 2006: 10)

The site of the MCG is also of social and spiritual significance for its association with the local Aboriginal people. It is hardly surprising that a sporting venue should be so significant to the history and life of the city of Melbourne and the State of Victoria given that sport is so central to them too.

Sports stadiums

Sport has a wider cultural and historical pertinence and broader social functions than charitable works and the spectacular display of physical prowess and endurance, or the inflicting or suffering of pain, and the pleasure of watching it. Holsworth notes that 'body culture and muscular nationalism have racist and totalitarian overtones' (2015: 43; for 'body culture' see Giblett 2008a: 14). Mateship involves solidarity with other mates of one's own 'tribe' or team against another 'tribe' or team. Mateship, including mateship in sport, is implicitly racist and sadistic (see Giblett 2011: 117–34). It involves discrimination against the other (team or tribe) on the basis of the colour of their skin, or guernsey, and inflicting pain on them physically or psychologically with the pleasure of winning and watching them lose.

Politics is war by other means, and so is sport. Yet, whereas war is conducted on the battlefield and politics is played out in the halls of power and in the media, sport is played in arenas and stadiums, such as the MCG. In *Foams*, the third and final volume of his immense and wide-ranging *Spheres* trilogy, Sloterdijk calls arenas and amphitheatres 'large containers for the passive-jubilatory agglomeration of subjects' ([2004] 2016: 574). The MCG is no exception. Sloterdijk traces the evolution and genealogy of 'modern "mass" culture as the staging of events' that makes 'the connection between audience, spectacle and assembly container' ([2004] 2016: 578). In the assembly container of the modern sporting stadium, the sporting event is staged and the player and spectator are engaged in the event. Their bodies cease to perform actions but engage in the event for the spectator in the stadium or for the audience at home in front of the TV.

One vehicle and vector for the spectator's engagement in, and performance of, the sporting event, for Sloterdijk, is what he calls 'the autopoiesis [self-making] of noise' : 'The quasi-nation assembled in the circus stadium experiences itself in an acoustic plebiscite whose direct result, the jubilatory noise over the heads of all, erupts from the gathered like an eruption before returning to the ears of each individual'([2004] 2016: 579). In this echo chamber of making and hearing noise, each individual participates in the ritual of the mass in two senses.

In what Sloterdijk goes on to call 'political hymnody', 'the transformation of the crowd into a choir' ([2004] 2016: 580) occurs, often quite literally, at football games, or at evangelical mass gatherings of the Billy Graham crusades with a choir that leads the crowd in hymn singing or entertains it with soloists and a backing choir. 'Open-air mass gatherings', as Sloterdijk ([2004] 2016: 580) calls them, such as the crowds at sporting events or evangelical rallies of the Billy Graham type, occur in 'the "mass" containers [of] the amphitheater, the arena and the circus'. The circus is a closed-air mass gathering under the 'big top' and held in its lighted interior. Increasingly, sporting events are held under retractable roofs with artificial lighting in order to ignore the disruptions of the weather (rain or shine, hot or cold) and to stage events at night.

The open-air stadium of the MCG lit up at night for a game becomes a glowing orb that illuminates and colonizes the vertical space above the ground in a cathedral-like soaring space. The space above the surface of the ground on which sport is being played is lit for players and spectators, while the space above the ground of the sporting arena is lit like an orb that can be seen from miles away and is an attractor that attracts spectators like moths to light. In 1879, a football match was played at night under electric light at the MCG (Newnham 1985: 31; Dunstan 2000: 50, 345). Night football and night cricket at the MCG have become regular sporting fixtures.

The stadium is not merely a modern cathedral but more specifically a post-Christian cathedral. For Sloterdijk, '[t]he fascinogenic ritual and the collective autohypnosis made operative combine to form the stuff the cathedrals of the post-Christian commune are made of' ([2004] 2016: 585). The MCG is a post-Christian cathedral. Melbourne's St Paul's and St Patrick's are Christian cathedrals that are monuments to a bygone age, whereas the post-Christian cathedrals of the sporting stadium, such as the MCG, are monuments of and to the current age. Or were. With the televising of major events and declining attendances at some long-form sporting events (such as at the Boxing Day Test), especially those that are televised live, sporting stadiums with large attendances are also becoming monuments of a bygone age in some instances. They are becoming empty containers, mere stages for the performance of sport for the cameras and commentators, and not for the spectators but for the audience at home in front of the TV in the cellular space of their living room, often in an apartment (see Giblett 2008b: 128–45). The transformation of cricket from five-day test cricket into shorter formats, such as one-day cricket, still means massive attendances, even when the game is televised live.

Referring to Walter Benjamin's ([1982] 1999a) work on the arcades, the arcade, for Sloterdijk, 'no longer has a key function for understanding the space-creating processes in contemporary society' ([2004] 2016: 586). Rather than the arcade, for Sloterdijk, 'the abstract constellations of stadiums and apartments is more significant than anything else' ([2004] 2016: 586) and 'the apartment and sports stadium are the key architectural icons of the twentieth century' (Sloterdijk [2014] 2017: 152). Yet arcades live on, either in their original form preserved in the central city, such as in Melbourne, or transformed into shopping centres in the inner and outer suburbs. Sloterdijk sees them as two distinct architectural forms when he argues that 'the arcades were separated from the shopping centres on the edges of urban complexes' ([2004] 2016: 586). Central city arcades are certainly separated spatially in terms of distance from shopping centres on the suburban fringes, but they are not separated spatially from them in terms of their spatial design (both architectural and interior), nor are they separated functionally in terms of their centrality to commodity capitalism.

The suburban shopping centre took the arcade's spatial configuration of the interior commercial passageway and its cellular shops and made it into a shopping mall. Ingress to and egress from the supermarkets and department stores of the suburban shopping centre is via an arcade or passageway of smaller, specialty shops. Not everyone in modern western or westernized cities lives in an apartment, or goes to a stadium, but every consumer goes to an arcade of some sort in one form or another. They are inescapable. Arcades, stadiums and apartments have a triadic key function for understanding the space-creating processes in consumer capitalism and contemporary society, with the inner-city dweller circulating from one to the other in the morphologies of modern space in which each is a transformation of the other with elements of the other. This is not to mention the inner-city dweller's place of work, the bars and restaurants they frequent, where they congregate, commune and consume, all those survivors of a bygone era constantly getting a new lease of life in the perpetual self-reinvention of consumer capitalism. Within this matrix of space-creating processes, the contemporary inner-city dweller lives and moves and has his or her being.

Arcades, stadiums and apartments are all cellular constructions of space, or bubbles of foam within the spheres of globes, as Sloterdijk might say in the terms of his *Spheres* trilogy, *Bubbles* ([1998] 2011), *Globes* ([1999] 2014) and *Foams* ([2004] 2016). The stadium is more specifically a bowl or vessel that creates and nurtures communal dreams and spectacles within its enclosing and protecting space. The stadium, or at least the corporate box, is an artificial womb or matrix pampering, to use a favourite word of Sloterdijk (see [2004] 2016: 327–800, [2005] 2013: 211–22), the spectator in the lap of luxury, to use another favourite word of Sloterdijk (see [2004] 2016: 327–800, especially 657–58, [2005] 2013: 228–29).

Stadiums and arcades are not mutually exclusive building types as they have some features in common. Stadiums have arcades outside the perimeter seating with cellular spaces for the selling of team merchandise, drinks and eats, and for ablutions. Stadiums also have interior passages, ramps, stairways and service corridors for spectators to gain ingress and egress to stadiums, as well as for those serving the spectators and for the commodities, such as merchandise, food and drink. Arcades have windows and doors facing into their passageways, whereas apartments and corporate boxes in stadiums have windows facing out from their interiors and doors only facing into their passageways. Arcades are similar to the panopticon in that they have 'door-windows', as Paul Virilio (1988: 187–97) calls them, facing into their passageways, which allow bodies and light to pass through. Unlike arcades, though, the panopticon also has windows in the opposite, outside wall that allow light in to backlight the occupant.[7]

Prison cells in the panopticon, shops in arcades, corporate boxes in stadium and apartment rooms, have various spatial configurations of doors and windows that all construct their cellular spaces for the passage of both bodies and light. The screens of the car windscreen, the cinema, the television, the computer monitor, Windows®, the smartphone and the tablet are what Virilio calls 'the third window' (1988: 187–97) that allows light, but not bodies, to pass through. After the cell of the panopticon and its static, frozen, immobile space comes the static, frozen, immobile body of the screen jockey gazing fixedly at the screen monitor wherever his or her body happens to be at the time. The construction of cellular spaces for the passage of bodies and light, and of passageways that link these spaces, are the essential condition of modern architectural and interior design that has its roots in the cells of medieval monasteries and classical stadiums and amphitheatres.

The archetypal stadium of the Colosseum in Rome built in the first century of the common era had 'passages', as one of its historians observed (cited in Trumpbour 2007: 11), and 'corridors and cells', as the recent consultants' report into the architectural history and heritage values of the MCG describes the Colosseum (Levenspiel 2006: 169). The MCG followed suit for, as the report goes on to relate, it

> gradually developed toward the form of its ancient Roman prototype [...] [Since the construction of the Southern Stand in 1937,] the 'stadium' model has been the typological approach adopted by all subsequent redevelopment at the MCG [...] The completion of the New Northern Stand in 2006 has more or less completed the logical path of this trajectory, fully enclosing the ground as a compound of two large elliptical stands in the manner of a Roman auditorium.
>
> (Levenspiel 2006: 171)

Contemporary stadiums, such as the MCG, also have elevated cellular corporate boxes that are like high-rise apartments with windows and balconies for viewing the game from above and overlooking the spectacle below in the manner of both the Greek and Roman amphitheatre and stadium. Calling the MCG a Colosseum is a commonplace of television sports commentators.

Corporate boxes in stadiums are also like boxes at the theatre. The twenty-first century stadium has 'an increasing level of spectator stratification' in 'the new luxury skyboxes', as Robert Trumpbour (2007: 4) calls them. These boxes are like 'royal suites', as Frank Deford (cited in Trumpbour 2007: 4) also calls them. The twenty-first century stadium for Deford is a departure from the 'twentieth century village green where we could all come together in common excitement' (cited in Trumpbour 2007: 4). The MCG in the nineteenth century was a village green. It later became a stadium as the twentieth-century equivalent to, simulacrum of, or pale replica of, a village green. The twenty-first century stadium is a theatre where we can all come together in common to watch the game, but our levels of excitement and our experiences (food, comfort, view of the game, interactions with fellow spectators, etc.) are different depending on whether we are in corporate boxes or in blocks and rows of plastic seating.

The stadium is a modern, post-Christian cathedral not only because of the mass rituals that are performed inside it, but also because of its architectural form and function in the cities in which it resides. For Trumpbour, 'in recent times, the stadium has supplanted the ancient cathedral as the most visible and recognizable structure in many communities' (2007: 2). The MCG is no exception, considering that the recent report into the architectural history and heritage values of the MCG describes it as 'a landmark on the edge of the [central] city, a vast stadium which retains its traditional parklike setting' (Levenspiel 2006: 10), but it does not retain its ancient, living, functioning wetland with its beautiful botany, nor its early colonial picturesque cricket ground.

179

The modern city dweller traversing arcades, stadiums and apartments has as much idea about the architectural and engineering design and workings (and their history) of these structures and spaces as did the medieval devotee of the Gothic cathedral. Roland Barthes called the car 'the Gothic cathedral of modern times [...] the supreme creation of an era, conceived with passion by unknown artists, and consumed in image if not in usage by a whole population which appropriates them as a purely magical object' (1973: 88). The same could be said about the sporting stadium as the modern cathedral.

The car and the sports stadium are the modern equivalents of a Gothic cathedral, not only because they are consumed by users who have little idea of how they are built or how they work, but also because they are a transcendent, magical object. For Barthes,

> [i]t is obvious that the new Citroën has fallen from the sky inasmuch as it appears at first sight as a superlative *object*. We must not forget that an object is the best messenger of a world *above* that of nature: one can easily see in an object at once a perfection and an absence of origin, a closure and a brilliance, *a transformation of life into matter* (matter is much more magical than life), in a word a *silence* which belongs to the realm of fairy-tales.
>
> (Barthes 1973: 88, emphases added)

The same process of sublimation could be said to occur with the superlative object of the modern cathedrals of sports stadiums. The life and body of the athlete or other sportsperson are transformed magically into the fairy tale of good versus evil that is staged, told and played out in the sports stadium.

The stadium may have statues of living and deceased sporting heroes erected outside it (as is the case with the MCG), but the focus and function of the stadium is the display of the living bodies performing inside it and the comfort and pleasure of the spectator watching, consuming and being pampered. According to the report into the architecture of the MCG, 'rather than being a monument, the MCG is significant as a living icon' (Levenspiel 2006: 10). The stadium is an icon that lives with living sports players and spectators, rather than having dead icons in stained glass and monuments or statues to the deceased as in the Christian cathedral. The MCG is nevertheless monumental in its dimensions and scale. It is also an ongoing monument to live sport played in the present, rather than a dead monument to past lives.

The 'stadium typology', as the recent report into the architectural history and heritage values of the MCG (Levenspiel 2006) describes and traces it, derives from ancient Greek and Roman templates: Greek, in that 'from the beginning the pattern of settlement of the MCG followed an ancient Greek pattern, where natural contours, particularly hollows, are used as the basis for [amphi]theatre and stadium construction' (5, see also 171); and Roman, in that the Colosseum was not only an 'edifice of spectacle' (9), but it was also built in a locale that was 'marshy, damp and unsteady' in the words of Trumpbour (2007: 10). In other words, like the MCG, the Colosseum was built in the quaking zone of a wetland where the earth trembles.

The MCG also followed suit as an edifice of spectacle. The soaring verticality of the external elevation and the sweeping horizontality of the forecourt of the sublime stadium greet the spectator on their arrival from every point of the compass and at every entrance.[8] The monumentality of this edifice puts the spectator into his or her place and makes him or her feel small by comparison before the immense scale of the sublime stadium, but it also makes the spectator feel privileged to be a participant in its mastery of nature by architecture and engineering. In terms of Kant's distinction between the dynamic and mathematic sublime (see Giblett 1996: 35), the stadium is designed by architects and engineers following the precepts of reason in the realm above nature, while the spectator feels mastery over nature in the form of the original site below and before it and him or her.

The site of the MCG, also like the location of the Colosseum, was marshy, damp and probably unsteady as a result. The Police Paddock was a flood-prone hollow that lent itself initially in the nineteenth century to the development of the MCG as an in-ground amphitheatre or stadium of the Greek type. The MCG was later developed in the twentieth century into an aboveground amphitheatre or stadium of the Roman type. This development also marks a shift in emphasis and use from the sacred to the secular. Trumpbour (2007: 9) contrasts 'the religious basis of the original Greek *stadion*' exemplified in the ancient Olympic Games, with 'Roman athletics [which] was a more secular experience' and in which 'a higher priority was ascribed to entertainment and spectatorship', as with the modern Olympic Games.

The Greek stadium was the venue for running foot races during the ancient Olympic Games. The Olympic Games and stadiums go together; one is not possible without the other, as the modern revival of the Olympic Games demonstrates. The report into the architecture of the MCG relates how 'the first major revival in the development of the stadium type was prompted by the revival of neo-Olympian ideals in the late nineteenth century' (Levenspiel 2006: 169). The development of the modern Olympic Games in the late nineteenth century, for Sloterdijk, was 'a globalized renaissance of athletes and stadiums' ([2004] 2016: 589) that superseded the Renaissance in the arts and learning of the fifteenth century in Europe. The Olympics became what Sloterdijk goes on to call

> a psycho-political machine whose primary function is to produce victories
> and victors and to make spectators witness to the distinction taking place in

181

real time: that between the first and the rest [as] the central sacrament of the modern event cult.

(Sloterdijk [2004] 2016: 592)

This sacrament is celebrated in the modern sporting stadium, and the Olympic Games are its ritual apotheosis.

The MCG is significant for being the main stadium for the 1956 Olympic Games. In his history of Melbourne for the City of Melbourne, Miles Lewis argues that 'the holding of the XVIth Olympiad was perhaps the first event in Australia of international significance, and certainly of enormous importance to Melbourne' (1995: 108). In making 'the case for Melbourne' to host the Olympic Games, the *Argus* newspaper in 1948 argued that

> Melbourne's claim to hold the Games is not based on whims of parochial ambi-
> tion. Australia is the only one of four nations which have competed at every
> Olympiad of the modern era not to hold the Games. Furthermore, the Games
> have never been held in a British Dominion and have never been held in the
> Southern Hemisphere.
>
> (Grant and Serle 1957: 295)

Consequently, the Olympic Games held in Melbourne in 1956 was the first time that the games had been held in the southern hemisphere and the first time that the games had been held in a commonwealth country besides the United Kingdom.

The MCG as the main Olympic stadium participated in the cult rituals of the modern Olympics. Olympic stadiums (and the MCG is no exception), in Sloterdi-jk's terms, 'establish themselves as the preferred cult locations of the modern bio-re-ligion – sites of the vicarious suffering of athletes for the popular dream of trans-forming the trivial body into the superhumanly capable statue' ([2004] 2016: 592). Or, in other words, of transforming what Benjamin called 'the tiny, fragile human body' into the hard, statuesque Fascist body of the war machine (see Giblett 2008a: 90–107). At the Berlin Olympics of 1936, Sloterdijk argues that 'the tendencies towards neoheroic-monumental and narco-narcissistic mass spectacle that had been obvious since [the] Los Angeles 1932 [Olympics] were taken to their logical conclusion' ([2004] 2016: 593). These tendencies were, in a word, Fascist, irre-spective of the type of political regime in power at the time in the nation of the city hosting the Olympics. The Olympic stadium and the sporting body have Fascist overtones despite the nature of the political regime (democratic, dictatorial, total-itarian or monarchical in name or fact) of the nation of the hosting city.

These overtones and tendencies certainly lived on and were played out in the 1956 Melbourne Olympics, if the story of Herb Elliott is anything to go on. This

Western Australian-born and -raised runner had travelled as an 18-year-old spectator to the 1956 Olympics in Melbourne. Four years later he won the Gold Medal in the 1960 Rome Olympics for winning the 1500 metres running final. Of all his memories of the 1956 Olympic Games, which were held primarily at the MCG, 'the one that burns deepest', he said, is of a Russian long-distance runner who was obviously tired 'and yet tortured himself by continual bursts of sprinting' (cited in Trengrove 1961: 30). This heroism of self-inflicted torture became the ideal to which Elliott aspired. He found the same quality in his coach, Percy Cerutty, who 'courageously whipped himself to perform almost frightening athletic feats. I reckoned that if I didn't try to punish my young, strong body as he did his older body I'd despise myself' (cited in Trengrove 1961: 36). Punishing his body became the means of not despising his self. Body and self are separate and antagonistic entities, not two parts of one whole. The sporting self is disembodied. Self and body are dualistic entities, just as the soul and body are for Socrates and the mind and body are for Descartes. The sporting body suffers (from) body-self dualism.

The sporting body is 'a body built on pain', to use the title of one of the chapters of the story of Elliott (Trengrove 1961: 48).[9] Torturing and punishing the body as a means to subdue the flesh and purify the soul (or self, or mind) has a long history in ascetic religions. Modern athletics and sport are the inheritor and reproducer of this doctrine. Sport is a post-Christian religion. The choice, as Cerutty sums it up in the title of one of his books, is to 'be fit, or be damned' (1967). Fitness equals salvation through pain, whereas unfitness means damnation through a lack of self-discipline and an inability to inflict pain on oneself and endure it. The alternative to fitness is damnation, not unhealthiness. Fitness is moralized in Christian terms as salvation. The alternative is stark, with no other option than to be either fit for heaven or damned to hell. A far more fitting (pardon the pun) and affirmative title would have been, 'be fit and be healthy', or at least, be healthier.

Sport is a post-Christian religion in which fans assemble in the hypermodern cathedrals of sports stadiums to participate in rituals, hymns, scriptures and mass or communion in which the body and blood of sportsmen and women are transubstantiated into the glorious spectacle of skill, dexterity, scoring and winning for one team and its fans. This ritual is broadcast live via television in media events to enable viewers in their own homes to participate in the mass-at-home. Suffering and spectacle in 'sports mad' countries such as Australia are arguably a displacement of the suffering and treatment of indigenous people, ethnic migrant minorities and asylum seekers. Instead of acknowledging and confronting the dispossession and oppression of these people by the white hegemony, the suffering of the former is displaced and sublimated into spectacles of suffering in sport for the latter. Rather than confronting and dealing with the suffering of others, sports-mad countries would rather deflect attention away from it and inflict suffering upon themselves in a massive act of displacement and disavowal. It is as if they are saying to their indigenous peoples, ethnic migrants and asylum seekers: 'you have suffered, but we suffer too – look at our sport'. But the latter is self-inflicted and masochistic (pleasure gained from pain inflicted on oneself), whereas the former is inflected by oppressive regimes and sadistic (pleasure gained from pain inflicted on others).

NOTES

1. Dunstan (2000) may have had in mind something like 'Eunice's' extensive description of the flora of the site and her botanic species list when he came to this conclusion; cited in Batchelder (2005: 34–35).

2. http://digital.slv.vic.gov.au/view/action/nmets.do?DOCCHOICE=480946.xml&d-vs=1484512807746~591&locale=en_US&search_terms=&adjacency=&VIEWER_URL=/view/action/nmets.do?&DELIVERY_RULE_ID=4&divType=&usePid1=true&use-Pid2=true. Accessed 1 September 2016.

3. See also Flanagan (2016: 41) and the documentary film about Wills screened on broadcast television the following day and now available online at: https://tenplay.com.au/channel-ten/documentaries/2016/8/tom-wills--s1-ep-1. Accessed 1 September 2016.

4. For Wills's biography and sporting career, see also Batchelder (2005: 47–53).

5. For Cunningham's (2011) discussion of Aussie Rules 'footy', see 59–70, and of an AFL Grand Final, see 189–96.

6. The record for the biggest attendance for an Australian rules football game is the Grand Final of 1970 with 121,696 (Matthews 2005: 176). The official attendance at the Billy Graham crusade was approximately 130,000 (Dunstan 2000: 216–17).

7. See Foucault (1977: especially 200) and Foucault (1980: 146–65, especially 147).

8. See the photo of the Cleveland Stadium on the cover of Trumpbour (2007), http://www.syracuseuniversitypress.syr.edu/fall-2006/new-cathedrals.html. Accessed 1 September 2016. The similarities between the external facade and sweeping forecourt of this stadium and the MCG are plain to see.

9. See Giblett (2008a: 125–39) for further discussion of the sporting body imprisoned in the time-machine of the stop-watch and clock, as well as of the role of sport in sports-mad settler societies such as Australia.

Culture on Display

Melbourne has all the characteristic cultural institutions of the age of high modernity of the late nineteenth and early twentieth centuries, including exhibition buildings, botanic and zoological gardens, public parks, art galleries, public libraries, theatres, museums, memorials and monuments. Melbourne has them all in a visible display of its modernity and as the Australian capital of modernity. These institutions establish modernity in relation to time and space, to place and to the past, present and future. Preserving and presenting a moment in time in the recent or distant past through its artefacts or mementos was a compelling commemorative contemporary drive, as was connecting the local and the global through imported specimens of plants and animals, as well as artefacts and books. Other buildings and structures displayed Melbourne's modernity, such as shopping arcades, department stores, railway stations, market halls, sports stadiums and bridges traversing rivers (as we have seen in previous chapters).

This chapter considers the momentous events, and the memorials and monuments – including buildings – to those events and the mainly men who reacted to or shaped them, and which established Melbourne as 'Marvellous Melbourne'. The discovery of gold in country Victoria, the ensuing gold rush and later exhibitions, were characteristic, momentous events of the high modern age of the mid-nineteenth century. Melbourne's versions of these events and institutions put it at the forefront of modernity – both in Australia and the world. This chapter considers Melbourne's cultural events, buildings and institutions, in which culture is put on display, often in similar ways to how nature is put on display. As with previous chapters, by no means is this an exhaustive survey, but only the tip of an iceberg.

Gold and the gold rush

The discovery of gold in 1851 in Victoria and the ensuing gold rush was a momentous event with far-reaching ramifications and consequences that altered the shape and tone of society and culture in Melbourne, as well as the major regional towns of Ballarat, Ararat, Bendigo and Maldon, among others in Victoria. The Victorian gold rush changed Melbourne in the second half of the nineteenth century from a sleepy provincial British town in a rural backwater into a dynamic, cosmopolitan metropolis powering ahead in a global headwater. As a result, Melbourne was transformed in its urban form and fabric. Bill Newnham relates how 'until 1851[,] Melbourne was the principal town of a large pastoral and agricultural district, but the discovery of gold completely changed its character' (1985: 26). Contemporary observers such as Richard Twopeny, writing in 1883, described how 'the gold-diggings transformed Melbourne from a village into a city almost by magic' ([1883] 1986: 113). A century later, Miles Lewis relates how 'Melbourne was catapulted to city status' by the gold rush (1995: 41). He goes on to relate how Melbourne 'consolidated' and took advantage of its 'good fortune' (41) by developing as a port and railway centre. Melbourne became 'the gateway city to the golden crescent' (44). Lewis concludes that 'the legacy of gold was the transformation of Melbourne into an instant metropolis' (59).

Gold also transformed Melbourne into an international metropolis. It put Melbourne on the international stage and thrust it into the limelight as a, if not the, capital city of the leading colony in the British empire. Geoffrey Serle relates how 'in ten years gold had transformed Victoria from a minor pastoral settlement to the most celebrated British colony' (1963: 369). It certainly outranked its northern neighbour of New South Wales as the 'scale of business activity [in Victoria] was twice as great as that of New South Wales', as Serle (1963: 369) goes on to state.

Gold transformed Melbourne in its urban character and class structure. Serle relates how 'the ruling class' was 'alarmed and shocked' by the behaviour of the 'diggers', 'the new class of conspicuous consumers' (1963: 29). As Ben Wilson notes (and as we have seen in Chapter One), the 'swaggering, bearded diggers' were dubbed 'the hairystocracy', for they 'seemed to rule Melbourne' (2016: 38).[1] Serle states that 'society was indeed being overturned' (1963: 30). The ruled were becoming the rulers, a fact noted with some alarm, if not exaggeration, by at least one contemporary observer, such as the Anglican clergyman in Melbourne who said 'we have here the French Revolution without the guillotine' (cited in Serle 1963: 30). His neck was safe, for, as Serle puts it, 'in social relations, though not in politics, a "French Revolution" had indeed occurred' (1963: 30). The ruling class may no longer have ruled financially in terms of accumulation of wealth and conspicuous displays of consumption, but they continued to rule politically and economically.

Gold had an impact on popular cultural activity, rather than on high cultural activity. For Serle, 'any cultural activity during the early [eighteen] fifties was spasmodic and largely ephemeral. The values of a gold-society were inimical to such activity' (1963: 353). The values of a gold-society were not inimical to popular cultural activity, such as sport and horse racing (as we have seen in the previous chapter); quite the contrary because they flourished in this period. Gold had its most visible and long-lasting effects on the development of institutions, and their architecture and buildings. Serle describes how in the mid-1850s 'the cultural habits and institutions of Britain were transplanted, and a worthy replica of the cultural life of an English provincial city was formed' (1963: 353). Such institutions included the Public Library (now State Library) and the University of Melbourne, in the foundation of both of which Sir Redmond Barry was instrumental. A statue of him outside the State Library commemorates his role.

Statues

Memorials and monuments in the form of statues of prominent figures were representative features of the age, and Melbourne followed suit beginning with what Lucy Sussex calls 'the 1865 Burke and Wills memorial statue, the first public monument in Melbourne, [...] translocated slightly downhill [in Collins Street], at the corner of [...] Swanston Street' in City Square (2015: 3), now in storage during the extension of the underground rail tunnel. For Newnham, 'the Burke and Wills Memorial is one of the best-known in Victoria' (1985: 59), and Burke and Wills are 'two of Australia's best-known explorers' (257). Newnham related in the 1980s how

> the forty-ton statue of Burke and Wills [...] dominates the ornamental foun-
> tains and quiet pools [of City Square] – an ironic touch remembering that the
> explorers' tragic journey across the continent was made hazardous by heavy
> rain, and not by the expected blistering heat.
>
> (Newnham 1985: 59)

Perhaps the fountain and pools commemorated the fact that Burke and Wills' poorly planned and executed journey (despite being 'the largest and probably the best-equipped exploration ever to set out in Australia', as Newnham [1985: 167] goes on to relate) was also made hazardous by water, not least by the swamps at the southern end of the Gulf of Carpentaria.

Burke and Wills may be two of Australia's best-known explorers for Melbur-nians, though perhaps for the wrong reasons because their 'ill-fated expedition across the continent' in 1860 was 'incompetently managed', as Lewis (1995: 63) puts it. Neither man survived and the monument is a testament to their failure, not their success. Lewis relates how 'the romance of the tragedy captivated Melbourne' and 'the funeral was a major event in Melbourne' (1995: 63). Newnham seems to have been caught up in the romance of the tragedy that had already endured for a century, as he gives an extensive account of the Burke and Wills expedition, which seems strange in a book devoted to the 'biography' of Melbourne (1985: 257–62). Part of the fascination that the expedition and the statue exerted in Melbourne may be attributable to the fact that the sculptor, Charles Summers, modelled Burke's head on 'Michelangelo's Moses, another leader in the desert', as Mark Holsworth (2015: 53) puts it.[2] It was as if Burke were leading God's chosen people through the desert to the promised land. This implies that Melburnians were enslaved in a foreign land on the coast and that the interior promised better. The mythology surrounding the expedition and statue is hardly clear and consistent.

For Serle,

> [t]he interest, enthusiasm and emotional involvement which Victorians of the time displayed [towards the Burke and Wills expedition] is staggering in retrospect and not readily explicable. Part of the answer lies in the challenge presented by the 'ghastly blank' in geographical knowledge of the north and centre of the continent. Moreover, Victoria had made no contribution to exploration [of the continent beyond its borders]. Men of scientific interests were fascinated and irritated by the unsolved question of the northern interior, and saw its solution as the most pressing issue of their generation.
>
> (Serle 1963: 367)

Sitting at the bottom of the continent, Melbourne had a tenuous toehold in Victoria, which it wanted to secure by claiming some imperial hold over the interior. The Burke and Wills expedition represented an attempt to assuage that anxiety and advance those ambitions. The Burke and Wills memorial statue was perhaps a way for Melbourne to have its cake and eat it too: a way to commemorate the failure of the well-funded expedition and to ostentatiously display its newfound wealth and power, garnered from the gold rush, to the other Australian colonies and the world.

Public buildings and Christian churches

The wealth and power derived from the gold rush was also displayed in public buildings. The gold rush, for Wilson, 'bequeathed [to] Melbourne some of the finest public buildings of the Victorian period, including the State Library, the University and [the State] Parliament House, among others' (2016: 49). The university had its less than auspicious beginnings on what Newnham calls '100 acres of rough swampy land' ([1967] 1977: 58). Not only the city of Melbourne, but also the

University of Melbourne had its beginnings in a swamp. For Richard Twopeny, 'there is certainly no city in England which can boast of nearly as many fine buildings, or as large ones, proportionately to its size, as Melbourne' ([1883] 1986: 116). Serle relates how the

> architecture of the period [of the mid-1850s after the gold rush] was characterized by a remarkable confusion of revivalist styles. Churches tended to be Gothic, public buildings of Roman inspiration. There was little distinctiveness other than the occasional local bluestone and massiveness of scale which reflected wealthy pretensions.
>
> (Serle 1963: 361)

Melbourne's St Paul's Cathedral for Newnham is a 'fine example of post-Gothic revivalist architecture' ([1967] 1977: 26). Its central spire, according to him, is 'the second highest Anglican spire in the world'. Melbourne's St Patrick's Catholic Cathedral, for Newnham is 'now regarded as one of the finest examples in Australia of the Gothic Revival Style' ([1967] 1977: 30). Its tallest spire is 26 feet taller than St Paul's in a game of one-upmanship.

The architecture of the post-gold era helped to give Melbourne the moniker of 'Marvellous Melbourne'. Marvellous Melbourne's architecture, for Graeme Davison, 'bespoke a preoccupation with metropolitan and even imperial aspirations, shamelessly aping the classical modes of Greece, Rome and Renaissance Italy' (1978: 233). Melbourne looked back to the past to legitimate its place in the present and its prospects for the future, which were supposed to be bright. The title of Davison's *The Rise and Fall of Marvellous Melbourne* (1978) echoes both Edward Gibbon's *The History of the Decline and Fall of the Roman Empire* (1776–89) and William Shirer's *The Rise and Fall of the Third Reich* (1960). Melbourne's ambitions to found an empire were overblown. Not only Melbourne's architecture, but also, as Davison argues,

> a rich blend of ingredients – cultural, social, economic and political – [...] make up the story of 'Marvellous Melbourne' [...] 'Marvellous Melbourne', like any authentic myth, interpreted the past, illuminated the present and offered a clue to the future.
>
> (Davison 1978: 15)

Rome on the Yarra never reached the same heights or depths, or spatial reach and influence, as the Roman empire, either in its ancient manifestation or as the later 'Holy Roman Empire'. Berlin on the Yarra never had the same reach as the unholy Nazi empire, though it certainly had a genocidal impact on indigenous peoples like the Nazi's genocide of ethnic minorities and marginalized people. Like its German counterpart, Melbourne was born among wetlands at the junction of two rivers. Berlin, for Otto Friedrich (cited in Giblett 2016: 97), was 'born [...] in the mud and swamps at the junction of the Spree and Havel rivers'. Melbourne is not only 'the Paris of the south', but also the Berlin of the south as it was born in the mud and swamps at the junction of the Maribyrnong and Yarra rivers (for Berlin, 'a dingy city in a marsh', see Giblett 2016: 97–113).

In devising the title 'Marvellous Melbourne', George Augustus Sala, for Davison (1978: 229), 'celebrated the gold rush as the beginning of Melbourne's greatness', though it had its roots much earlier in pastoralism and urbanism. Davison calls Sala 'the old lion of journalism', who

> had hit upon a phrase with just the sweep and crude euphony to captivate real estate promoters, guide-book writers and other city 'boosters.' 'Marvellous Melbourne' hinted at several themes: the city's material progress, the lively temper of its commercial and social life, its precedence among the Australian capitals.
>
> (Davison 1978: 230–31)

Moreover, for Davison, 'Marvellous Melbourne' was 'the ideal of a city ruled by the market' (1978: 137), and 'Marvellous Melbourne' was 'an unashamed plutocracy' (190). Money rules, okay? Marvellous Melbourne was a capitalist's paradise.

Marvellous Melbourne did not disturb what Davison calls the commonplace that 'the entire nineteenth-century metropolis was but a concrete expression of the capitalist order' (1978: 131). The growth of the nineteenth-century city was fuelled by commodities from the country (in Melbourne's case, gold, agricultural produce and pastoral products), supplied by manufacturing in the city and it was an outgrowth of industrial capitalism. The nineteenth-century city was industrial capitalism writ large. Davison relates how 'Marvellous Melbourne' was

> literally built of iron, wood and clay and, fed by the city's seemingly insatiable demand for iron girders, corrugated iron, railway lines, water and gas pipes, wrought iron balustrades, nails and screws, the metals industry entered upon a phase of breakneck expansion.
>
> (Davison 1978: 48)

'Marvellous Melbourne' was metallic Melbourne and monstrous Melbourne, a metal mechanical monster, with a greedy appetite for iron products.

Architecture was the visible expression of money, and lots of it, in 'Marvellous Melbourne'. During this period, Serle relates how

[t]he most prominent architect now [1850s] and until the nineties, was [...] Joseph Reed. In the [eighteen] fifties he assisted in the plans for Parliament House, designed the Public Library [...] and was later responsible for the Town Hall [...] (361), Scots' and Independent Churches[and] the [Royal] Exhibition building.

(Serle 1963: 361–62)

Looking back over Reed's career, Serle sums up how, 'during a practice of forty years, Joseph Reed designed most of Melbourne's public buildings in any and every historic style' (1971: 276).

According to the anonymous authors of a 'Footpath Guide' devoted to the work of Joseph Reed for their series of 'Melbourne Architectural Walking Tours', these styles included: French Renaissance (Flinders Street Station) (Anon. 2015: 11); Gothic Transitional (St Paul's Cathedral) (12); French Second Empire (Town Hall) (27); Classical Roman (Baptist Church) (35); English Decorated Gothic (Scots Church) (37); Lombardic Romanesque (Independent Church) (43); Neoclassical (State Parliament and Treasury Building) (44); English Gothic Revival (Wesley Church [47] and Ormond College [71]); Academic Classical (Royal Society Building) (51); Italian Florentine and German Rundbogenstil (Royal Exhibition Building) (55); Roman Revival (State Library) (65); Renaissance Revival (originally the Bank of New South Wales's facade, now Melbourne University School of Architecture, Building and Planning's west facade) (73); and Picturesque Gothic (Melbourne University Gatekeeper's Cottage) (75).[3] Joseph Reed's mishmash of architectural styles colonizes space and time, history and geography. His styles taken from elsewhere (and 'else-when') in the European colonial centre and transported to the Australian colonized periphery make a mark in place and inscribe a moment in time from the past in the present. They obliterate the local, indigenous place and time in the colonial periphery and link them back to the centre in the imperial network.

Reed's Parliament House, for Newnham, is 'one of the handsomest classical buildings in Australia with its colonnade of nine Doric columns' ([1967] 1977: 14) and 'Melbourne's most distinguished building' (1985: 206). For Asa Briggs, it is 'one of the finest examples in the world of Victorian architecture' (1963: 292–93). Victorian (referring to the period, though it also applies to the Australian state) architecture, certainly in the case of Joseph Reed, was an eclectic amalgam of disparate styles that reached across history, even back to the classical times of ancient Rome. Parliament House, for Maree Coote, is 'the finest example of classical architecture in Australia' (2013: 67). Newnham goes on to relate how 'in 1901 the first Federal Parliament of Australia took over the State Parliament House. In 1927, when Federal Parliament was opened in its [first] permanent house in Canberra, the State Government moved back to its rightful home' (1985: 208), as he calls it. One of the most distinguished facets of the Parliament is the library. For Kristin Otto, 'this jewel of a library – still one of the most beautiful spaces in the city, if not nation – was a significant factor leading to Melbourne becoming for nearly thirty years the [national] capital of Australia' (2009: 18). This library and the State Library both contributed to Melbourne being the cultural capital of Australia and the Australian capital of modernity.

Joseph Reed also designed the original Public Library, now incorporated into the State Library of Victoria. The Public Library was, for Newnham, 'almost immediately one of the most successful institutions in the city' (1985: 225). Part of its success can be attributed to the fact that the modern library employs the same means of display as the arcade, that representative architectural expression of the age (for Walter Benjamin [(1982) 1999a], as we have seen in Chapter Six). 'The stacks of large libraries', for Johann Geist, 'employ the arcade's method of spatial access' (1983: 33). The connoisseur of knowledge and the consumer of commodities are both avatars of the arcade. Benjamin and Tim Flannery, as *flâneurs* of libraries, are following in the footsteps of the *flâneurs* of arcades.

Like the arcades and the State Parliament Library, the Public Library employed a variety of architectural styles, including the classical style. In 1883, Richard Twopeny described the Public Library's 'classical simplicity' ([1883] 1986: 115). In 1870, 'the imposing portico', with what Newnham calls 'its fine Doric columns', was added ([1967] 1977: 62). In 1872, J. H. Kerr described the Public Library as 'a noble building of Corinthian architecture' (excerpted in Grant and Serle 1957: 128; see also Lewis 1995: 74). Of course, the two styles are different. Extensions to the rear of Reed's original building included a modern innovation: the construction of 'the largest reinforced concrete dome in the world', designed by John Monash (later Australia's most famous and successful military general) (Otto 2009: 109, see also 131–33). Opened in 1913, 'the Domed Reading Room' – to give it its original grandiose title (now the La Trobe Library of Victorian History) – is, for Otto, 'one of the most beautiful and solemn spaces in Melbourne' (2009: 133), certainly on a par with its nearby State Parliament counterpart. For Otto, it 'elevated the [...] Library [...] architecturally to stand with the great libraries of the world' (2009: 133). Serle has also said that it is 'one of the great libraries of the world' (1971: 275).

Statues of Joan of Arc, the patron saint of France, and Saint George, the patron saint of England, killing a dragon, now flank the entry to the library.[4] Sir Jacob Edgar Boehm's sculpture of *St George and the Dragon* (1876) signifies, for Serle, 'the triumph of good over evil' (1971: 287; see Ridley 1996: 97–99). More to the point, this foundation myth of the nation of England signifies the triumph of Christianity (or 'sanctuarism') over 'paganism' (or 'sacrality') (and patriarchy over matriarchy) at home and abroad in the British empire, beginning with Ireland and continuing with Australia. The dragon is a monster who lives in 'a plague-ridden lake' in one version of the story. In Boehm's statue, St George plunges his long lance vigorously into the writhing dragon whose jaws clamp around it, trying to stop it or pull it out, and whose forked tongue, like a serpent's, wraps around it, a signifier of evil. The myth functions along similar lines to the Old English poem *Beowulf*, which also signifies the triumph of sanctuarism over sacrality, represented by Beowulf killing two marsh monsters, Grendel and his mother.[5] This statue in this location can be read as an allegory of British colonialism conquering Melbourne's monstrous maternal marshes. Perhaps St George is a fitting patron saint for Melbourne, too, as the city triumphed over the wetlands. It is a memorial to the destruction of those wetlands, not to their life and loss.[6]

A much more edifying statue in Melbourne is the modest, unassuming and much overlooked 'Free Speech' memorial erected in the 1930s outside the Brunswick Mechanics Institute on the corner of Sydney and Glenlyon Roads in Brunswick, not far from where I live. It is not a monument (though it is sometimes described as such), but a memorial to, and a memento of, political free speech, a right not enshrined in the Australian constitution, unlike the first amendment to the American constitution. The memorial of and to 'Free Speech' has a small cast dove of peace with open wings atop a draped base of a fluted and draped Greco-Roman column. The memorial suggests that peace overcomes war, free speech trumps hate speech, good triumphs over evil and resistance wins over empire.

As well as Parliament House and the Library, Joseph Reed also designed a number of cathedrals both sacred and secular. Lewis describes how

> the chapel which Joseph Reed designed for the Methodists in Lonsdale Street was truly Gothic, though with an interior still designed like an auditorium [...] It was described as a 'cathedral of Methodism' and some thought it the finest Methodist church anywhere.
>
> (Lewis 1995: 57)

Reed also designed Scots Presbyterian Church. David Mitchell, Dame Nellie Melba's father, built it. Sussex says it was 'the tallest structure in the city during the last decades of the nineteenth century' (2015: 2). It was the pinnacle of the grand old dame of the city. Serle calls it 'the "Cathedral" church of Presbyterianism' (1971: 134). Methodists and Presbyterians dissented from Anglican and Roman Catholic theology, but when it came to church architecture the preference for Gothic-style cathedrals transcended theological differences culminating in a common architectural language, which tends to nullify differences.

Joseph Reed, for Robin Boyd in his study of Australian ugliness, was 'the supreme eclectic, the master Featurist',[7] in and of the city of Melbourne, and Melbourne, in turn, is 'the featurist capital' of Australia, to which Boyd devotes a chapter ([1960] 2010: 55). What William Guilfoyle was to the landscape architecture of the Botanic Gardens by designing and constructing land and water features, Reed was to the built architecture of Melbourne by designing and building buildings with a range of architectural features drawn from a variety of different periods and styles, such as 'several variations of Gothic [...], Italian Renaissance, Romanesque, "French picturesque chateau styles", and so on', as Boyd ([1960] 2010: 55) puts it dismissively.

The Royal Exhibition Building

The Royal Exhibition Building, for Boyd (1960] 2010: 56), was Reed's 'and Melbourne's most spectacular building'. In her guide to the building, Elizabeth Willis relates how 'at the time it was built, the Great Hall was the largest building in Australia and taller than any spire in the city' (2004: 5). The Royal Exhibition Building out-spired the cathedral and churches of the city and showed who ruled: the secular over the sacred. With new buildings and annexes built for the Centennial Exhibition of 1888–89, Willis concludes that 'Melbourne now had the largest building in the world under one roof' (2004: n.pag.).

What Serle calls Reed's 'hybrid Florentine-French' Royal Exhibition Building of the late 1870s encouraged what he also calls 'an orgy of decoration and display in the business palaces and suburban mansions of the boom years' (1971: 276). In the monumental, 500-page celebration of the building published in 1996 by the Exhibition Trustees, in which the history of the building and the exhibitions held in it, and seemingly every detail of both, are exhaustively discussed by a huge cast of contributors, Davison describes how 'Joseph Reed's design for the Melbourne Exhibition of 1880 combined Gothic and classical elements in a manner consistent with his main aim – to create a building that was at once useful and ceremonial, secular and sacred' (1996: 14). The Royal Exhibition Building was a cathedral to the sacred secular sublime. Rather than being, as Alan Willingham puts it, 'more a temple than a palace to industry' (1996: 52),[8] it was both a palace *of* industry and temple *to* industry, as it displayed industry in a luxurious and sumptuous setting, and invited adoration and worship of industry by devotees of the new religion of industrial capitalism and its technologies.

Nearly twenty years earlier, and perhaps not constrained by the same requirement to write a triumphalist 'corporate history', and enjoying the critical freedom presented in the writing of a Ph.D. thesis, Davison was less flattering about the Royal Exhibition Building, as he said that it was designed in the 'Italian Gothic' style, which gave 'the completed building a kind of bloated grandeur' (1978: 2). The Royal Exhibition Building does look like a beached white whale, the monstrous terrestrial or architectural equivalent of Herman Melville's marine mammalian albino cetacean 'Moby Dick', of his novel of the same title (1851). Along similar lines, Newnham describes how some 'architects contemptuously described the exhibition, as it is usually called, as a monstrosity of Italian and French styles and the public criticized it as a "white elephant"' ([1967] 1977: 66). It was more of a white whale.

The Royal Exhibition Building had a variety of distinguishing features, including a 'large dome similar to [the] Crystal Palace [in] London and higher than St Paul's' Cathedral in London, according to Newnham ([1967] 1977: 66 and 1985: 219). The dome, for Boyd ([1960] 2010: 57), 'was claimed to be not only the biggest but also the most beautiful [...] in the world'.[9] The Crystal Palace exhibition building in London is an icon of modernity (as we will see later in this chapter). The Royal Exhibition Building in Melbourne followed in its footsteps as a place for the display of the products of industrialized nature and culture. The Royal Exhibition Building outdid St Paul's Cathedral by soaring higher. The Royal Exhibition Building was, and still is, a monument to modernity. It was a secular cathedral because, for James Smith, it 'correspond[ed] in magnitude, as well as in its cruciform design, with a huge cathedral' (1904 excerpted in Grant and Serle 1957: 222). Along similar lines, for Michael Cannon, 'the great Melbourne Exhibition of 1880 set the theme for the boom decade. The building [...] was by far the largest structure in Australia [...] and had [...] two naves'([1966] 1976: 12) and 'soared skywards' (15). As the Gothic church was the sacred sublime, so the modern Royal Exhibition Building was the secular sublime.

Construction was 'completed in twenty months', according to Briggs (1963: 306–07). David Mitchell, the father of Dame Nellie Melba, built the Royal Exhibition Building (Otto 2009: 35; see also Willingham 1996: 53–55). Perhaps the Royal Exhibition Building is the Dame Nellie Melba of buildings – a diva attracting and gaining attention with an outlandish performance, a celebrity or star larger than life, a monument international in style, size and status. Perhaps it is a bachelor machine, the brainchild of Reed, who gave birth to it assisted by Mitchell, the midwife. Sophie Cunningham relates that 'in 2004 this beautiful building and its gardens became the first urban site in Australia to be given World Heritage status' (2011: 44). Patrick Greene, the then Chief Executive Officer (CEO) of Museum Victoria, of whose precinct the Royal Exhibition Building is a part, claims that 'one building epitomizes' the 'spirit and history' of 'most great cities' (2004: n.pag.). He concludes that 'it may be a cathedral, a palace, a town hall or a parliament. In [the case of] Melbourne it is undoubtedly the Royal Exhibition Building' (2004: n.pag.). This conclusion is self-serving boosterism. Many Melburnians would disagree and insist that the Melbourne Cricket Ground (MCG) and its cavalcade of buildings and events over the past 150 years epitomizes the spirit and history of the great city of Melbourne. For Brian Matthews, for instance, the MCG is 'one of Melbourne's most dramatic and talismanic monuments' (2005: 32). The MCG is a cathedral of sport, a shrine to footy and cricket, and the spiritual home of many Melburnian sports fans (as we saw in the previous chapter). The Royal Exhibition Building is a cathedral of industry, a palace of industry, and the venue for the opening of Federal Parliament in 1901. It also housed the State Parliament from 1901 to 1926, while the national capital of Canberra and its Federal Parliament building were being developed.

The Royal Exhibition Building has thus been other things and served other purposes. After the depression of the 1890s, the Royal Exhibition Building came to new prominence in 1901 when, as Newnham puts it, 'the most important ceremony in the history of a nation – the opening of its first Parliament' took place (1985: 34–35). 'The tiny village [of Melbourne] had become the capital of Australia [...] It was to remain so for the next 26 years' (220) until Federal Parliament moved to its permanent home in Canberra.[10] The Royal Exhibition Building was ideal for displaying the car as an icon of modernity. In 1912, it was 'the setting for the first Motor Show' (Otto 2009: 124) in Australia and for the second in 1923 (281). In 1919, the Royal Exhibition Building became 'a fever hospital' for Spanish flu and 'its basement a temporary mortuary' (246). In 1922, the Royal Exhibition Building became the Australian War Memorial until a permanent one was built in Canberra (276).

Exhibitions

Despite its myriad later uses, the Royal Exhibition Building, as the name suggests, was built primarily and especially to house exhibitions. The second half of the nineteenth century was the age of exhibitions par excellence, and Melbourne in this period was no exception; indeed, it was a leader in Australia, if not in the world. The nineteenth-century World Exhibitions, for Davison, 'extended the scientific principles of classification and comparison from the world of nature to the built environment' (1996: 12). And to manufactured commodities. In other words, the nineteenth-century World Exhibitions took taxonomy, that had its birthplace in natural history and the scientific botanic garden (in both of which nature was put on display), and extended it to the sphere of industrial commodities and the built environment in which culture was put on display – both in the Exhibition and in the Royal Exhibition Building itself. International Exhibitions, for Willis, 'served as showcases for the natural resources of the colonial world, and for the ingenuity and technological achievements of the machine age' (2004: 1). In other words, they served as showcases for the manufactured cultural commodities and resources of the colonizing, industrial world, derived from the natural resources of the colonized world.

Like botanic gardens, Exhibitions privileged the sense of sight and the pedagogy of learning by looking. They comprised what Jürgen Osterhammel calls 'the most salient combination of panoramic gaze with encyclopedic documentation' (2014: 14). Exhibitions, for Davison, were

> a straightforward application of the principle of learning by looking [...] The [English] Victorians perfected the science of learning by looking. They invented the most characteristic cultural institutions of the period – the museum, the art gallery, the diorama and the cyclorama.
>
> (Davison 1996: 12)

The public library and the public park were other cultural institutions characteristic of the nineteenth century, while the scientific botanic garden, the panorama and the panopticon were invented in the late eighteenth century. All these cultural institutions practised the pedagogy of learning by looking, and hence privileged the sense of sight over the other senses. The Australian Victorians followed suit. The State Library, public art galleries and museum in Melbourne were characteristic cultural institutions of Victorian Melbourne, and are still prominent institutions in Melbourne today.

Exhibition Buildings, beginning with Joseph Paxton's Crystal Palace of 1851, became both the chief exhibit and the pre-eminent mechanism of exhibition in the Exhibitions that they housed. The exterior and interior of Paxton's Crystal Palace exhibited itself and its contents for the external and internal viewer. The Crystal Palace inverted Jeremy Bentham's panopticon, initially a design for a prison and made famous by Michel Foucault (1977), who described the way in which the inmates of an institution were placed under the surveillance of the gaze of a single unseen supervisor, and so were placed ideally under internalized self-surveillance, or that was the plan in theory anyway. Unlike the institutionalized inmate of the panopticon who 'sees, but does not see', as Foucault (1977: 200) puts it,[11] the visitor to the Exhibition not only sees, but is also seen, as a perceptive Melbourne journalist remarked in 1888, by other visitors in a mutually regarding gaze or in competition for wearing the most fashionable clothes (cited in Davison 1996: 18).

Bentham's panopticon and Robert Barker's panorama were contemporaneous. Yet the connection between Bentham's panopticon and Barker's panorama may be more than mere coincidental contemporaneity. In a note to his famous discussion of the panopticon, Foucault wonders whether

> Bentham [was] aware of the panoramas that Barker was constructing at exactly the same period (the first seems to have dated from 1787) and in which the visitors, occupying the central place, saw unfolding around them a landscape, a city or a battle. The visitors occupied exactly the place of the sovereign gaze.
>
> (Foucault 1977: 317, note 4)[12]

This 'place' was found in the central observation tower of the panopticon. The panoramas positioned viewers to gaze upon and master the monumental.

The Crystal Palace

The Crystal Palace and the other Exhibition Buildings positioned the sovereign gaze in a similar way. The Crystal Palace, as Davison puts it,

> allowed the eyes of the multitude to range over a vast assemblage of glamorous commodities. With its walls of glass it created the illusion of unlimited space and flooded its interior with white light [...] [I]n his famous engravings of the Crystal Palace Joseph Nash exaggerated the interior spaces by lengthening the perspective and dwarfing the human figures – a technique that Australian exhibition illustrators were later to emulate.
>
> (Davison 1996: 13)

Including in Melbourne with the Royal Exhibition Building. The awesome grandeur, overwhelming dimensions and sublime power of the Crystal Palace dwarfed the 'tiny, fragile human body', as Benjamin says in the context of the destructive forces unleashed during World War I, the first full-scale industrial war ([1982] 1999b: 732). The Crystal Palace displayed the creative forces of modern industry in a palace of light that presaged the walls of light of the cinema screen, the Nuremberg Rally, the searchlights of World War II and 'White Night' in Melbourne, in an enduring modern urban fascination with the sublime power of vertical displays of light.

The Great Exhibition of 1851 in London was 'the world's first trade fair', according to Briggs (1979: 179). It heralded the worldwide rise of the Exhibition in the second half of the nineteenth century, of which Melbourne was an early adopter beginning in 1854. The World Exhibitions for Osterhammel were 'another novelty of the nineteenth century' (2014: 14) to rank alongside museums. Both the museum and the Exhibition required suitably monumental buildings to mark the occasion, attract attention and display their contents. For Osterhammel, 'it all started with the Great Exhibition [...] in London [...] whose spectacular crystal palace, a glass and iron hall 600 meters long, [which burnt down in 1936] has remained in the collective memory' (2014: 14). The Crystal Palace has also remained in the individual memory and cultural unconscious, and has been manifested in the work of writers and commentators on the city, including Fyodor Dostoevsky, Walter Benjamin, Marshall Berman and Peter Sloterdijk. Sloterdijk ([2005] 2013 and [2014] 2017) works from Dostoevsky's account, while Berman (1988) works from Dostoevsky and Lothar Bucher's, and Benjamin reads Joseph Nash's illustrations of Joseph Paxton's design.

The Crystal Palace for Fyodor Dostoevsky's 'underground man' represents a place where suffering is unthinkable and doubt is impossible as 'suffering is doubt, negation – what kind of crystal palace would it be if one could doubt in it?' ([1864] 2009: 32). The crystal palace is a place of no suffering and no doubt partly because, for Dostoevsky's underground man, 'the crystal edifice [...] is forever indestructible' ([1864] 2009: 33). Crystal is hard, adamantine and reflective, a symbol of certitude, the sublime and sublimation.

Following on from Dostoevsky, the Crystal Palace, for Berman is both 'fact and symbol' (1988: 235) and 'the most visionary and adventurous building of the whole nineteenth century. Only the Brooklyn Bridge and the Eiffel Tower, a generation later, will match its lyrical expression of the potentialities of an industrial age' (237). Yet, rather than Dostoevsky, for Berman 'the most interesting and penetrating [contemporary] account of the Crystal Palace – the real one, that is, was written by [...] Lothar Bucher', whose account concludes with a rapturous hymn to 'the transept which dissolves into a distant background where all materiality is blended into the atmosphere' (cited in Berman 1988: 239–40). In other words, and in a word, all materiality is sublimated. The Crystal Palace is a secular cathedral to, and of, modernity and industry, as is the Royal Exhibition Building in Melbourne (Wilson 2016: 4). 'The point of the event', as Wilson puts it of the Great Exhibition and the Crystal Palace, was 'to revel in modernity' (2016: 5). It was also to relish its power, to savour its wares, to bask in its glory. The Crystal Palace was, as Wilson goes on to say, 'a physical monument to modern-mass production and a wonder of the age' of high modernity (2016: 6).

Berman notes that Bucher managed 'to appropriate one of Marx's [and Engels's] richest images and ideas: "all that is solid melts into air". Like Marx, Bucher sees the tendency of solid material to decompose and melt as the basic fact of modern life' (1988: 240). Yet this image and idea is precisely about the sublime, both as that in which solid matter is transformed into a gas and as the basic fact of modern life. Decomposition occurs when solid matter breaks down into its constituent parts and when it is blended into the atmosphere. Melting occurs when a frozen liquid that has become solid thaws back into its liquid state, not when solid matter is transformed into a gas. The sublime is the basic fact of modern life in which the solidities of traditional ways of life, cultures and modes of production and consumption, etc., are transformed into thin air, or etherealized.

Around the name of the sublime, as Jean-François Lyotard says, 'modernity triumphed' (1989: 199), not least over wetlands (see Giblett 1996). The slime of swamps, in which the solid earth is desublimated into liquid water, is the counter to the sublime of the city in which the solid earth is sublimated into gaseous air. The sublime city, like London or Melbourne, fills or drains the slimy swamp so as to create solid earth that it then sublimates into the gaseous heights of its ethereal structures, like the Crystal Palace and the Royal Exhibition Building. The slimy swamp precedes and resists the sublime city. The sublime city reverts to feral slimy swamp in major floods, such as New Orleans in the aftermath of Hurricane Katrina.

The Crystal Palace, for Benjamin, writing in the 1930s, was 'the edifice built expressly for London's industrial exhibition [...], the first world exhibition and the first monumental structure in glass and iron!' ([1982] 1999a: 176). The Crystal Palace was an industrially produced monument to modern industry and industrial capitalism. It appropriated the architectural style of the glass-house for its monumental edifice. As for the interior, Benjamin relates how he saw 'with amazement' – from looking at the series of watercolours painted of the Crystal Palace by Joseph Nash – 'how the exhibitors took pains to decorate the colossal interior in an oriental fairy-tale style, and how – alongside the assortment of goods that filled the arcaded walks – bronze monuments, marble statues, and bubbling fountains populated the giant halls' ([1982] 1999a: 176–77). The interior of the Crystal Palace was an orientalist phantasy and a ginormous arcade rolled into one.

Along similar lines to Benjamin, Davison describes how 'many displays took the form of pyramids and obelisks – shapes which conveniently suggested both bulk and height, achievement and aspiration' (1996: 13). They also suggested exotic orientalism and the triumph of the occident over the orient. For one wry wit, the Crystal Palace was 'neither crystal nor a palace. It was a bazaar'. For the novelist William Thackeray, it was 'a palace as for [sic] fairy Prince' (cited in Briggs 1979: 165). The World Exhibition in the Crystal Palace was imperialism, industrial capitalism, orientalist phantasy, colonialism and commodity fetishism rolled into one and writ large, a covered market hall and arcade combined into one. Monumental metal, adamantine glass and lifeless commodities dominated the interior and the exterior.

'World exhibitions', for Benjamin,

> are places of pilgrimage to the commodity fetish [...] World exhibitions glorify the exchange value of the commodity. They create a framework in which its use value recedes into the background. They open a phantasmagoria in which a person enters in order to be distracted.
>
> (Benjamin ([1982] 1999a: 7 and 17–18)

Writing on phantasmagoria, Margaret Cohen describes how, 'in nineteenth century usage[,] this term designated both a form of magic lantern show and a psychological experience when the distinction between subject and object breaks down' (1993: 219, see illustration on 216). As a result of this breakdown, the subject becomes object in the alienated, reified relationship between the worker and work, consumer and commodity. Cohen goes on to argue that in 'the magic [...] of commodity fetishism [...] social relations [...] take on the phantasmagorical form of relations between things' (1993: 222). For Benjamin, 'reifying representations [...] enter the universe of a phantasmagoria' (1999a [1982]: 14), in which the consumer is placed under what he calls 'the phony spell of a commodity' (1973: 233).

Benjamin was developing what Karl Marx called 'the fetishism of commodities', in which made material things were imbued with quasi-religious or spiritual significance. The fetishism of commodities was, for Davison, 'nowhere better illustrated than in the great exhibition' (1996: 13), except that at the Exhibition the viewer could not buy and consume any of the products that were on display as none of them were on sale, unlike in the department stores that were developing in the same era in which, as Briggs puts it, 'the bazaar would become permanent [...] It was not until after the Great Exhibition that the department store emerged as a distinct kind of enterprise: Aristide Boucicault started his Bon Marché [department store] one year later in 1852' (1979: 174).

The phantasmagoria, for Benjamin ([1982] 1999a), has its representative human figures and manifest expressions. For him, 'the *flâneur* abandons himself to the phantasmagoria of the marketplace', and Baron Georges Eugène Haussmann is 'the champion' of 'the phantasmagoria of civilization', whose 'manifest expression' is 'his transformation of Paris', when he blasted boulevards through what he saw as potentially seditious neighbourhoods ([1982] 1999a: 14–15). A later expression of phantasmagoria is the transformation of Melbourne. In the case of both cities, an abject wetland is transformed into a phantasmagorical city in which the subject is objectified by commodity capitalism in modernity. For Benjamin, 'modernity' is 'the world dominated by its phantasmagorias' ([1982] 1999a: 26), which he saw exemplified in the arcades and the *flâneur*. This is no less so than in the founding and building of the cities of modernity, such as Melbourne, the Australian capital of modernity, and Paris, 'the capital of modernity' as Harvey (2006) calls it, both built in premodern and abject swamps and marshes. Here the distinction between subject and object has not yet been constituted; here the phantasmagoria of commodity capitalism has not yet broken down the distinction between subject and object in the reification of subject into object under the phony spell of a commodity; here the magic of the marsh and swamps casts its binding spell before the city drains and fills them and creates its phantasmagorias, not least of itself, including in 'World Exhibitions', of which Melbourne was a serial proponent and expert exponent.

More recently, the Crystal Palace, for Sloterdijk ([2005] 2013: 169), is an architectural archetype, or archetypal architecture, for modernity. Indeed, for Sloterdijk ([2005] 2013: 170, 173–76) it is a more fitting and apt archetype of modernity than the arcades as propounded by Benjamin ([1982] 1999a), though Sloterdijk later suggests that 'it was not so much the arcades as the greenhouses that offered the key to the principle of the interior, of which Benjamin rightly stated that modernity could not be understood without it' ([2004] 2016: 323). Sloterdijk calls Paxton 'the English greenhouse architect' ([2004] 2016: 321). Paxton used what Sloterdijk describes as 'the new cast iron technology with monumentalist intentions' ([2004] 2016: 321). Or more precisely, monumentalist pretensions given the dimensions of the Crystal Palace (enumerated by Sloterdijk [2004] 2016: 321, see also [2005] 2013: 169–70) that made it 'by far the largest enclosed space in the world' (Sloterdijk [2004] 2016: 321) and given its borrowing in length, breadth and height from cathedrals.

After Sloterdijk thinks of Dostoevsky's 'reference to Western civilization as a "crystal palace"' ([2005] 2013: 169), he goes on to argue that

> with its construction, the principle of the interior overstepped a critical bound-ary [as] it began to endow the outside world as a whole with a magical imma-nence transfigured by luxury and cosmopolitanism. Once it [the world] had been converted into a large hothouse and an imperial culture museum, it revealed the timely tendency to make both culture and nature indoor affairs.
>
> (Sloterdijk [2005] 2013: 170)

(And to make the world an indoor affair inside the hothouse of global heating.) The Crystal Palace, for Sloterdijk, is 'the shared house of purchasing power' that 'repre-sents comfort and convenience' and 'self-fulfillment for the consumer' ([2014] 2017: 163). It also represents discomfort, inconvenience and self-diminution for all beings (including the consumer) in the hothouse of 'global heating', with hotter days and hotter bush and forest fires burning more frequently around the world. Hothouse indeed to be contrasted with the greenhouse of the swamp world in which London and Melbourne were founded.

Melbourne's Exhibitions were held first in 1854, then in 1861, again in 1866–67, 1875, 1880 and the Centennial Exhibition in 1888–89 (whose building 'survives today', as we have seen and as Lewis [1995: 61] puts it) 'to celebrate the cente-nary of [British] settlement – which took place in another colony', the colony of New South Wales, 'discovered' by Captain James Cook. Just as Cook had never landed in Victoria (and was not the first European explorer to 'discover' Australia [only the east coast]), so the house of his parents (in which he may have never set foot according to Lewis [1995: 110]) was relocated stone-by-stone to Fitzroy Gardens in 1933–34. Melbourne was not averse to appropriating and arrogating to itself the British history of Australia, and putting it, and itself, on display. Briggs argues that 'a huge International Exhibition, which was held in 1880 and 1881, put Melbourne "on the map"' (1963: 294–95), as it were, as an international modern city, with the 'opening day' procession attracting 20,000 people lining the streets. The Centennial Exhibition of 1888 had over 2 million people attending, according to Briggs (1963: 307). For Davison, 'the international exhibitions heralded the age of great mass events' (1996: 18). The Melbourne 'Centennial International Exhibition' of 1888–89 was probably the culmination of the rise of 'Marvellous Melbourne'.[13] It also marked the beginning of its fall into the depression of the 1890s.

The Shrine of Remembrance

Melbourne was a monument to industrial capitalism and had its own monuments to it, besides the Royal Exhibition Building. Later monuments commemorated later events and activities. For Newnham,

> one of the most striking features of Melbourne from the air is a huge white cross set in acres of green lawn in front of a massive square building – the Shrine of Remembrance – Victoria's monument to men and women who served in the two world wars.
>
> (Newnham 1985: 242)

And the following wars. One of the most striking features of Melbourne from the air is also the Yarra River and Port Phillip Bay. The wetlands no longer feature. Newnham (1985: 242–47) goes on to give an extensive discussion of the Shrine, which does not seem strange on this occasion as he is not giving a potted history of World War I but providing a useful historical context for the design that would be unknown to most Melburnians.[14] Newnham describes how 'the Shrine is modeled partly on the design of the monument erected in 353BC[E] at Halicarnassos by Queen Artemisia in memory of her husband, King Mausolus, which was considered one of the seven wonders of the ancient world' (1985: 242–43; see also Carroll [1974] 1977: 76).

Rather than a monument, Queen Artemisia erected a mausoleum, whose name enshrines the memory of her husband, King Mausolus, just as much as the mausoleum at Halicarnassos enshrines his mortal remains. Unlike the mausoleum at Halicarnassos, the Shrine of Remembrance in Melbourne is a memorial monument to participants in warfare and houses no mortal remains. Also unlike the mausoleum at Halicarnassos, 'one of the seven wonders of the ancient world', the Shrine of Remembrance in Melbourne is not a wonder of the modern world. It is a wonder of modern Melbourne, not least because it, as Newnham puts it, is in 'a direct line [and a direct line of sight] with the centre of the city's most important thoroughfare, Swanston Street' (1985: 243). Looking the other way from Princes Bridge straight down St Kilda Road, the Shrine of Remembrance looms large directly in the distance like a sentinel. These aligned features function as the spine of the city, the central column to which all its organs attach. As St Kilda Road is a boulevard, the Shrine of Remembrance is a bit like the Arc de Triomphe in Paris at the top end of the Champs-Élysées, arguably the most impressive thoroughfare of the city. The Shrine of Remembrance is a constant, though distant, reminder of war across from the centre of the city. And perhaps it is also a reminder of the centrality of war to the foundation of the city, and of the wars that cities have fought against wetlands. The Shrine of Remembrance is a prominent Melbourne landmark.

The city and the body of the earth

The Yarra River and Port Phillip Bay are also prominent Melbourne landmarks. They are vital parts of Melbourne, organs of the body of the city and the body of the earth. Rivers and streams are arteries and veins of the body ecologic, the earthly body. Roads and streets are arteries and veins of the body politic, the urban body. The streets of the city have, as Davison points out, been 'likened to the arteries and veins of the human body' (2016: 159). Figuring the city in terms of the body in this way is often employed as a naturalizing trope in order to legitimate the cultural in terms of the natural. Figuring the earthly in terms of the bodily has traditionally been a way of interconnecting the human body and the earth (see Giblett 2008a). Rivers and streams have been likened to the lifeblood of the land, to the arteries and veins of the body of the earth. I propose figuring the urban and the earthly in terms of the bodily as a way of interconnecting city dwellers with their bioregional home.

Wetlands have also been likened to the womb, placenta and kidney as organs of the body of the city and the body of the earth (see Giblett 1996: 135–38). Wetlands are also the heart or lungs or kidneys. For Cunningham, 'the broad wetlands that sustained the Wurundjeri clans [...] sit in the heart of Melbourne and I like to think that [this] heart still beats, albeit weakly, creating a gentle pulse' (2011: 25). The wetland heart of Melbourne pumps lifeblood through the body of the earth. 'Melbourne's rivers, creeks, swamps and billabongs', for Cunningham, 'actually look like arteries, veins and capillaries' in an aerial photo (2011: 138).

Along similar lines, perhaps with similar images in mind, Tony Birch acknowledges the Yarra River and 'her heartbeat' (2015: n.pag.). Davison describes how
the Yarra, 'Melbourne's ancient river', 'often regarded with contempt', 'was, and
remains, the city's lifeblood' (2016: 266–67), (though he also regards it with some
contempt himself when he describes it earlier in condescending aesthetic terms as
'a fine stretch of water *in its way*' [1, emphases added]). Rather than the river and
the wetlands, the managers of Federation Square (cited in Davison 2016: 263)
describe it as 'the heartbeat' of Melbourne. However, the residents of Melbourne
could live without Fed Square, but they (we) could not live without the life-giving
waters of the Yarra River catchment, the lifeblood of the city. Fed Square beats
to the rhythm of a different drummer from the wetlands and the waterways of
Melbourne, and drowns them out. Ideally, they should beat together in unison.

The 'green belt' surrounding Melbourne, 'comprised of forests, grasslands and
wetlands', is, for Cunningham, 'the lungs of Melbourne' (2011: 272). Along similar lines, though in terms that figure the belt as an item of female underclothing and
the city as the body of a woman, Davison refers to Melbourne's 'consoling girdle
of parks and gardens' (2016: 179). Girdle implies containing, constraining and
flattening out the contours of the feminized body of the earth to make its shape
conform to masculine ideals of beauty. Davison is like 'the leaders of the modern
movement' in Melbourne, whom he later refers to as 'presenting Melbourne as a
woman' (2016: 181–82). They were following in the footsteps of those modern
writers and thinkers who figured Paris as a woman. Melbourne, for Jenny Sinclair,
has a feminine heart and masculine head with 'the offices of Parliament and the
public service [banks and corporations] as its head, the transport systems as its
flowing blood, the different communities and specialist buildings as organs of the
body, each supporting the other' (2015: 87).

The city is a body, but it is not necessarily a healthy body. Indeed, the city has
operated surgically on the earth. Roads and streets have been inscribed onto the
surface of the earth leaving external scarring; rivers have been rerouted into canals
and canals have been cut across wetlands leaving internal scarring in the depths of
the earth. The city ends up looking like a collection of cicatrices that crisscross the
earth's surface and penetrate its depths. Jan Senberg's painting *Melbourne* (1999),
for Coote , is 'visceral and organic, the city is a living thing', but it is not a healthy
body, as 'Melbourne is all grafts and transplants, patches and scars' (2012: 144).
For Coote, there is an 'increasing tension between [...] Melbourne's vital organs
[of] the Grid and the Gardens' (2012: 152), referring specifically to the Royal
Botanic Gardens, though this observation also applies to other gardens and parks.
In Senberg's *Melbourne*, the 'Gardens' are the only green space among the grafts
and transplants, the patches and scars of the 'Grid', not only the Central Business
District (CBD), but also its outgrowths on Southbank and into the suburbs. The

'Grid', the 'Gardens', the 'Green Belt' and the 'River', as well as the billabongs and wetlands, are all vital for the life of Melbourne. Thinking and figuring all of these aspects of Melbourne as part of the body of the city together with the body of the earth is a way of acknowledging the role they all play in sustaining Melbourne. For Melbourne to be in any way vaguely sustainable economically and environmentally, it needs to nurture symbiosis between all of these organs.

Melbourne would thus cease to be parasitic and become symbiotic. In the late nineteenth century, 'the pastoral and mercantile communities' saw Melbourne as what Davison calls 'a noisome excrescence on a sustaining rural economy' (1978: 6). A noisome excrescence is, in a word, a wen. For some early-nineteenth-century writers, such as William Cobbett, London is 'a great wen' and a 'putrid sore' (Cobbett cited in Davison 2016: 77), or more elaborately 'a swelling sore that simultaneously drained and corrupted the surrounding countryside' (Davison 1983: 366). A wen, in other words, is a grotesque excrescence on the surface of the body politic. A wen is a parasite on the body politic and ecologic. For one rural writer in 1879, 'the abnormal growth of Melbourne and Sydney [...] bid fair to become "the great wens of Australia"' (cited in Davison 1978: 235). For Francis Adams in the late 1880s, 'Melbourne is the phenomenal city of Australia' and 'everything drains into Melbourne' (like a cesspit?) at the bottom of the state, as a river and sea port city (cited in Anon. 1984: 3).

In this respect, Melbourne is akin to another wetland and river city, viz. New Orleans. Writing of New Orleans, Rebecca Solnit and Rebecca Snedeker relate how

> way down where all the effluvia of the continent drains out, all the toxins and manure and muck of a great river system flowing through agricultural and industrial lands, way down there underneath in the softness of the alluvial soil, is the cloaca or pudendum of the continent [...] 'Pudendum' a word for the female genitalia, comes from a Latin word for shame.
>
> (Solnit and Snedeker 2013: 82)

Melbourne on the Yarra River in Victoria is not the cloaca of a great river system and continent like New Orleans in Louisiana on the Mississippi River that flows through several states of North America, but it is the cloaca of a vital river system and state, and it is a port city like New Orleans. Like New Orleans, Melbourne also produced and accumulated locally its own 'toxins and manure and muck' (Solnit and Snedeker 2013: 82). As an anonymous writer put it, 'before underground sewerage, Melbourne was a city that literally wallowed in its own filth' (Anon. 1984: 10). In other words, Melbourne was like a pig, or was a pig of a city.

'Wen' is an archaic term not in common usage these days. Its equivalent term today is the term 'sprawl', which functions like wen once did as a pejorative term for the protean and parasitic growth of cities, especially of their suburbs. 'Sprawl' is a persistent term in the lexicon of discussion about town planning if, for instance, the subtitle of Anthony Flint's book, *The Battle over Sprawl and the Future of America* (2006), is anything to go by. Sprawl, for Flint in this book, is implicitly a threat to the future of America, or at least sprawl makes the future of America look bleak. The same rhetoric that is often applied to the battle against cancer, or drugs, or obesity, or terrorism, is applied to the battle over sprawl with the same threat to the future of the nation. 'Sprawl' means, literally, as Davison points out, 'an awkward or clumsy spreading of the limbs' (2016: 95), like a gawky teenager spread-eagled on the family room floor, not a trim, taut and toned body. In 1948, sprawling Melbourne, for Boyd, meant that 'the city is putting on weight without muscle' (cited in Davison 2016: 98). In other words, sprawl is to fast food as proper growth is to slow food. Sprawl has the same result as eating fast food. Sprawl, as Davison remarks, is 'to the body politic what obesity was to the human body' (2016: 98).

The imminent danger and moral panic are that sprawl will kill the obese city, but for many prospective first homebuyers, the sprawling outer suburbs of cities, such as Melbourne, can be the only viable financial option. They also provide sufficiently large lots to fulfil the Australian dream of the detached house with a garage and swimming pool. The challenge for all 'sprawling' cities is to provide employment opportunities and services, such as public transport, in the new, outlying suburbs, and so to incorporate them into the body politic and the body urban. Davison concludes that 'over the century since it was first coined, the concept of "sprawl" had metamorphosed from an aesthetic, to an economic, and finally to an ecological concept, while never losing its strong negative charge' (2016: 102). Figuring the city as a body with a variety of ills and illnesses, and with functioning organs, such as a grid; parks and wetlands; and arteries, such as rivers and roads, may be a way of living 'sustainability' or symbiotically with the earth in what Glenn Albrecht (2019: 102–06) calls the Symbiocene, the hoped-for-age superseding the Anthropocene (as discussed in the first chapter of *Modern Melbourne*; see also Giblett 2019e: 108–11).

The city as body with parks as lungs was a nineteenth-century cliché of the city. I propose seeing the city as body with twentieth-century skyscrapers as head and brain; the water supply and sewerage systems as oesophagus and intestines; the rivers as arteries; the wetlands as kidneys, liver and placenta; the 'mouth' and the estuary of the river as anus and bowels; slums as a sore to be treated and cared for, not bled or lanced in the gentrification of slum clearance; and so on. Rather than figuring slums as swamps in pejorative terms as places of disease and horror, I propose seeing them as artificial wetlands whose liveability for their residents could be improved by improving their ecological functionality as kidneys, liver and placenta, as places of hope and new life. Figuring both the urban and the earthly in terms of the bodily can be a way of interconnecting city dwellers with their bioregional site and of living in the Symbiocene, as well as in the Anthropocene.

The bioregion of the Yarra and Maribyrnong River catchments is the home for the body/city of Melbourne. The people of Melbourne cannot live without the watershed, air-shed, food bowl, climate and lands (wet or dry) of this home. The people and the city of Melbourne are a product of their past lands (wet or dry) and they have destroyed or inherited their resources. To be sustainable into the future, the people of Melbourne need to look after their home place of the bioregion in the globalized world. Or more precisely and elaborately, they need to live bio- and psycho-symbiotic livelihoods in their bioregional home habitat of the living earth.[15]

NOTES

1. As also noted in Chapter One, Wilson (2016: 30–52) calls his chapter on the Victorian gold rush and Melbourne of the period, 'The Hairystocracy'.

2. Holsworth (2015: 50–55) devotes several pages to discussing this sculpture and includes several photos of it; see also Ridley (1996: 37–40).

3. I am grateful to Sandra Giblett for her gift of this guide for the serious tourist and built-heritage buff.

4. For photos of both statues, see Holsworth (2015: 63, 65).

5. For environmentally and animal friendly discussions of the legend of St George and the Dragon and of the stories of Beowulf, Grendel the marsh monster and his mother, and Beowulf and the Dragon, see Giblett (1996: 182–83, 2015: 132–43, 2018b: 21–36, 2019b: 125–27, 2019d: 111–62); see also Collins (2012: 91).

6. For environmentally and animal friendly retellings of the legend of St George and the Dragon and of the story of Beowulf and the Dragon, see Giblett (2018a [with a photo of Boehm's statue on the cover], 2018c and 2019a, c, d).

7. Boyd ([1960] 2010: 53–57) devotes several pages to discussing Reed's (ugly Australian?) architecture.

8. Willingham (1996: 51–66) gives an extensive account of Reed's life and architectural career, and of the designing and building of the Royal Exhibition Building.

9. See the illustration in Cannon ([1966] 1976: 13).

10. See also Otto (2009: 7–29); Grant and Serle (1957: 221–24).

11. See also Foucault (1977: 195–228) for his discussion of 'Panopticism'.

12. On the panopticon and panorama, see also Giblett (2008b: 131–41).

13. See Davison (1978: 1–5); Serle (1971: 285–87).

14. For photographs of the 'Shrine Reserve' and its monuments and memorials, see Freeman and Pukk (2015: 50–54); see also Ridley (1996: 152–57) and Holsworth (2015: 10–11, 26–33, 78).

15. For further discussion of these terms and the development of the argument for them, see Giblett (2011, especially 211–58).

References

Ainge Roy, Eleanor (2017), 'New Zealand river granted same legal rights as human being [*sic*]', *The Guardian*, 24 March, p. 12, https://www.theguardian.com/world/2017/mar/16/new-zealand-river-granted-same-legal-rights-as-human-being. Accessed 24 March 2017.

Albrecht, Glenn (2019), *Earth Emotions: New Words for a New World*, Ithaca, NY: Cornell University Press.

Annear, Robyn (2014), *Bearbrass: Imagining Early Melbourne*, 2nd ed., Melbourne: Black Inc.

Anon. (1887), 'Fishermen's Bend canal: The formal opening', *The Argus*, 8 July, p. 27.

—— (1914), 'Port Melbourne, Parish of South Melbourne, County of Bourke', map, Melbourne: State Library of Victoria.

—— (1936), 'Transformation of Fishermen's Bend: Momentous day in history of Port Melbourne official opening of General Motors-Holden's huge plant: Prime Minister performs ceremony in presence of 1,500 guests', *Record*, 14 November, p. 4.

—— (1937a), 'Birmingham of Australia: Fishermen's Bend', *The Argus*, 15 April, p. 10.

—— (1937b), 'Factories at Bend no longer "No Man's Land"', *The Argus*, 17 November, p. 4.

—— (ed.) (1984), *Melbourne 1840–1900: 'The Phenomenal City': A Joint Exhibition of the State Library of Victoria and the Melbourne City Council… 18 July–7 October 1984*, exhibition catalogue.

—— (2002), 'Swamp became home to Melbourne Cup', *Illawarra Mercury*, 4 November, http://ezproxy.ecu.edu.au/login?url=http://search.proquest.com/docview/364305255?accountid=10675. Accessed 1 May 2015.

—— (2015), *Melbourne Joseph Reed 1850–1890*, Melbourne: Footpath Guides.

—— (2016), 'The world's most liveable cities', *The Economist*, 18 August, https://www.economist.com/blogs/graphicdetail/2016/08/daily-chart-14. Accessed 1 May 2017.

—— (n.d.), 'History of the company', Austin Memories, http://www.austinmemories.com/styled-4/index.html. Accessed 1 May 2015

Arnold, John (1983), *The Imagined City: Melbourne in the Mind of Its Writers*, Sydney: George Allen and Unwin.

Bach, John (1976), *A Maritime History of Australia*, West Melbourne, Victoria: Nelson.

Backouche, Isabelle (2008), 'From Parisian river to national waterway: The social function of the Seine, 1750–1850', in C. Mauch and T. Zeller (eds), *Rivers in History: Perspectives on Waterways in Europe and North America*, Pittsburgh: University of Pittsburgh Press, pp. 26–40.

Barlow, Elizabeth (1971a), *The Forests and Wetlands of New York*, Boston: Little Brown.

—— (1971b), *Frederick Law Olmsted's New York*, New York: Praeger.

Barthes, Roland (1973), *Mythologies* (trans. A. Lavers), London: Granada.

Batchelder, Alf (2005), *Pavilions in the Park: A History of the Melbourne Cricket Club and Its Ground*, Melbourne: Australian Scholarly Publishing.

Benjamin, Walter ([1950] 2006), *Berlin Childhood around 1900* (trans. H. Eiland), Cambridge, MA: Belknap Press of Harvard University Press.

—— ([1950] 2015), *Berlin Childhood circa 1900* (trans. C. Skoggard), Catskill, NY: Publication Studio.

—— (1973), *Illuminations* (trans. H. Zohn), London: Fontana.

—— ([1982] 1999a), *The Arcades Project* (trans. H. Eiland), Cambridge, MA: Belknap Press of Harvard University Press.

—— (1999b), *Selected Writings, Volume 2: 1927–1934* (eds M. Jennings, H. Eiland and G. Smith, trans. R. Livingstone and others), Cambridge, MA: Belknap Press of Harvard University Press.

—— (2003), *Selected Writings: Volume 4, 1938–1940* (eds H. Eiland and M. Jennings, trans. E. Jephcott and others), Cambridge, MA: Belknap Press of Harvard University Press.

Bergerat, Emile ([1909] 2016a), 'Cinderella arrives by automobile', in G. Schultz and L. Seifert (eds and trans.), *Fairy Tales for the Disillusioned: Enchanted Stories from the French Decadent Tradition*, Princeton: Princeton University Press, pp. 233–37.

—— ([1909] 2016b), 'The 28-kilometre boots', in G. Schultz and L. Seifert (eds and trans.), *Fairy Tales for the Disillusioned: Enchanted Stories from the French Decadent Tradition*, Princeton: Princeton University Press, pp. 226–31.

Berman, Marshall (1988), *All that Is Solid Melts into Air: The Experience of Modernity*, New York: Penguin.

Billot, C. P. (1979), *John Batman: The Story of John Batman and the Founding of Melbourne*, Melbourne: Hyland House.

Birch, Tony (2015), *Ghost River*, St Lucia: University of Queensland Press.

Blackbourn, David (2008), '"Time is a violent torrent": Constructing and reconstructing rivers in modern German history', in C. Mauch and T. Zeller (eds), *Rivers in History: Perspectives on Waterways in Europe and North America*, Pittsburgh: University of Pittsburgh Press, pp. 11–25.

Blainey, Geoffrey (1963), *The Rush that Never Ended: A History of Australian Mining*, Carlton, Victoria: Melbourne University Press.

Bolitho, Janet (2013a), 'Fishermans Bend – do the maps', Port Melbourne Historical and Preservation Society, http://www.pmhps.org.au/2013/07/fishermans-bend-do-the-maps/. Accessed 1 May 2015.

—— (2013b), 'What's in a name and does it matter?', Port Places, http://www.portplaces.com/whats-in-a-name-and-does-it-matter/. Accessed 1 May 2015.

—— (2015), 'Water filters', Port Places, http://www.portplaces.com/water-filters/. Accessed 1 May 2015.

Boyce, James (2011), *1835: The Founding of Melbourne and the Conquest of Australia*, Melbourne: Black Inc.

Boyd, Robin ([1960] 2010), *The Australian Ugliness*, Melbourne: Text Publishing.

Briggs, Asa (1963), *Victorian Cities*, London: Oldham Press.

—— (1979), *Iron Bridges to Crystal Palace: Impact and Images of the Industrial Revolution*, London: Thames and Hudson.

British Admiralty (1864), *Victoria-Australia, Port Phillip: Hobson Bay and River Yarra Leading to Melbourne Surveyed by H.L. Cox; Assisted by Thos. Bourchier and P.H. McHugh; Engraved by J. and C. Walker*, Melbourne: State Library of Victoria.

Brown-May, Andrew and Swan, Shirlee (eds) (2005), *The Encyclopedia of Melbourne*, Cambridge: Cambridge University Press.

Bryson, Bill (2001), *In a Sunburned Country*, New York: Broadway Books.

Buckrich, Judith Raphael (1999), *George Turner: A Life*, Carlton South, Victoria: Melbourne University Press.

Bunyan, John ([1678] 2008), *The Pilgrim's Progress* (ed. R. Pooley), London: Penguin.

Burrows, Edwin G. and Wallace, Mike (1999), *Gotham: A History of New York City to 1898*, New York: Oxford University Press.

Cannon, Michael ([1966] 1976), *The Land Boomers*, illus. ed., Melbourne: Thomas Nelson.

Carroll, Brian (1972), *Melbourne: An Illustrated History*, Melbourne: Lansdowne Press.

—— ([1974] 1977), 'Marvellous Melbourne', *Historic Melbourne Sketchbook*, Adelaide: Rigby, pp. 70–128.

Carter, Paul (1987), *The Road to Botany Bay: An Essay in Spatial History*, London: Faber and Faber.

—— (2005), *Mythform: The Making of* Nearamnew *at Federation Square*, Carlton, Victoria: Miegunyah Press of Melbourne University Press.

Cerutty, Percy (1967), *Be Fit! Or Be Damned!*, London: Pelham.

Chapman, Heather and Stillman, Judith (2015), *Lost Melbourne*, London: Pavilion.

Christie, F. C. (1853), 'An early and important British Government Surveyor's map of Melbourne', Canberra: National Library of Australia, MAP RM 3473, https://nla.gov.au/nla.obj-232283310/view. Accessed 1 May 2015.

City of Melbourne (n.d.), 'Port Phillip Monument', eMelbourne, http://www.emelbourne.net.au/biogs/EM02136b.htm. Accessed 1 May 2015.

City of Port Phillip (2012), 'Amendment C102 – Fishermans Bend Urban Renewal Area (FBURA)', http://www.portphillip.vic.gov.au/amendment-c102.htm. Accessed 1 May 2015.

Clacy, Ellen (1988), 'A lady's visit to the gold diggings', in D. Spender (ed.), *The Penguin Anthology of Australian Women's Writing*, Ringwood, Victoria: Penguin, pp. 113–42.

Clark, Ian D. and Heydon, Toby (2004), *A Bend in the Yarra: A History of the Merri Creek Protectorate Station and Merri Creek Aboriginal School 1841–1851*, Canberra: Aboriginal Studies Press.

Clarke, Marcus ([1874] 1972), 'The Café Lutetia', in L. T. Hergenham (ed.), *A Colonial City: High and Low Life: Selected Journalism of Marcus Clarke*, St Lucia: University of Queensland Press, pp. 337–42.

Cohen, Margaret (1993), *Profane Illumination: Walter Benjamin and the Paris of Surrealist Revolution*, Berkeley: University of California Press.

Cole, Colin E. (ed.) (1980), *Melbourne Markets 1841–1979: The Story of the Fruit and Vegetable Markets in the City of Melbourne*, Melbourne: Melbourne Wholesale Fruit and Vegetable Market Trust.

Collins, Michael (2012), *St George and the Dragons: The Making of English Identity*, n.p.: CreateSpace.

Collins, Timothy M., Muller, Edward K. and Tarr, Joel A. (2008), 'Pittsburgh's three rivers: From industrial infrastructure to environmental asset', in C. Mauch and T. Zeller (eds), *Rivers in History: Perspectives on Waterways in Europe and North America*, Pittsburgh: University of Pittsburgh Press, pp. 42–62.

Coote, Maree (2012), *The Art of Being Melbourne*, Melbourne: Melbournestyle Books.

——— (2013), *The Melbourne Book: A History of Now*, 4th ed., South Melbourne, Victoria: Melbournestyle Books.

Costello, Mary (2009), 'Creative space', *The Age*, 4 July, p. 8.

Cunningham, Sophie (2011), *Melbourne*, Sydney: New South.

Daley, Charles (1940), *The History of South Melbourne: From the Foundation of Settlement at Port Phillip to the Year 1938*, Melbourne: Robertson and Mullens.

Davison, Graeme (1978), *The Rise and Fall of Marvellous Melbourne*, Carlton, Victoria: Melbourne University Press.

——— (1983), 'The city as a natural system: Theories of urban society in early nineteenth-century Britain', in D. Fraser and A. Sutcliffe (eds), *The Pursuit of Urban History*, London: Edward Arnold, pp. 349–70.

——— (1984) 'Preface', in Anon. (ed.), *Melbourne 1840–1900: 'The Phenomenal City': A Joint Exhibition of the State Library of Victoria and the Melbourne City Council… 18 July–7 October 1984*, exhibition catalogue, p. vii.

——— (1986), 'Goldrush Melbourne', *The Australian City, Unit A: Marvellous Melbourne, a Study of Nineteenth-Century Urban Growth: Reader*, Victoria: Deakin University, pp. 120–25.

——— (1996), 'The culture of the international exhibitions', in D. Dunstan (ed.), *Victorian Icon: The Royal Exhibition Building Melbourne*, Melbourne: Exhibition Trustees in Association with Australian Scholarly Publishing, pp. 11–18.

——— (2004), *Car Wars: How the Car Won Our Hearts and Conquered Our Cities*, Sydney: Allen and Unwin.

——— (2016), *City Dreamers: The Urban Imagination in Australia*, Sydney: NewSouth Publishing.

Davison, Liam (1993), *Soundings*, St Lucia: University of Queensland Press.

De Jean, Joan (2014), *How Paris Became Paris: The Invention of the Modern City*, New York: Bloomsbury.

Dostoevsky, Fyodor ([1864] 2009), *Notes from the Underground* (trans. B. Jakim), Grand Rapids: William B. Eerdmans.

Douglas, Mary (1966), *Purity and Danger: An Analysis of the Concepts of Pollution and Taboo*, London: Routledge.

Dovey, Kim and Jones, Ronald (2018), 'Introduction', in K. Dovey, R. Adams and R. Jones (eds), *Urban Choreography: Central Melbourne 1985–*, Carlton, Victoria: Melbourne University Press, pp. 9–12.

D'Sylva, Adam (2017), 'My city: Melbourne', *Selector*, September/October, pp. 90–92.

Dunstan, Keith (2000), *The People's Ground: The MCG*, 4th ed., Kew, Victoria: Arcadia/ Australian Scholarly Publishing.

Durack, Mary ([1959] 1966), *Kings in Grass Castles*, Moorebank, NSW: Corgi.

Eidelson, Meyer (2014), *Melbourne Dreaming: A Guide to Important Places of the Past and Present*, 2nd ed., Canberra: Aboriginal Studies Press.

Elborough, Travis (2016), *A Walk in the Park: The Life and Times of a People's Institution*, London: Jonathan Cape.

Elden, Stuart (2013), *The Birth of Territory*, Chicago: University of Chicago Press.

Ellul, Jacques (1970), *The Meaning of the City* (trans. D. Pardee), Grand Rapids: William B. Eerdmans.

Engels, Friedrich ([1845] 1987), *The Condition of the Working-Class in England* (ed. V. Kiernan), London: Penguin.

Fairbairn, K. J. (1973), *Melbourne: An Urban Profile*, Sydney: Angus and Robertson.

Fairfield, George (ed.) (1998), *Ashbridge's Bay: An Anthology of Writings by Those Who Knew and Loved Ashbridge's Bay*, Toronto: Toronto Ornithological Club.

Fanon, Frantz ([1965] 1967), *The Wretched of the Earth* (trans. C. Farrington), Harmondsworth: Penguin.

Fiddian, Marc (2003), *Flinders St Station: Melbourne's Taj Mahal*, self-published book.

Flanagan, Martin (2016), 'The life and times of Tom Wills make one hell of a story', *The Age: Football: Sport*, 6 August, p. 41.

Flannery, Tim (ed.) (2002), *The Birth of Melbourne*, Melbourne: Text Publishing.

Flemming, James (ed.) ([1802–03] 1984), *Journal of the Explorations of Charles Grimes*, Carlton, Victoria: Queensberry Hill Press, http://www.livingmuseum.org.au/download%20pdf/Flemings%20Journal.pdf. Accessed 1 May 2015.

Flint, Anthony (2006), *This Land: The Battle over Sprawl and the Future of America*, Baltimore: Johns Hopkins University Press.

F. N. (1935), 'Sandridge: To the editor', *The Age*, 9 February, p. 8.

Forster, Edward M. ([1924] 1936), *A Passage to India*, Harmondsworth: Penguin.

Foucault, Michel (1970), *The Order of Things: An Archaeology of the Human Sciences*, London: Tavistock.

—— (1977), *Discipline and Punish: The Birth of the Prison* (trans. A. Sheridan), Harmondsworth: Penguin.

—— (1980), 'The eye of power', in C. Gordon (ed.), *Power/Knowledge: Selected Interviews and Other Writings 1972–1977*, Brighton: Harvester, pp. 146–65.

Freeman, Kornelia and Pukk, Ulo (2015), *Parks and Gardens of Melbourne*, Melbourne: Melbourne Books.

Gammage, Bill (2012), *The Biggest Estate on Earth: How Aborigines Made Australia*, Sydney: Allen and Unwin.

Garryowen ([1835–52] 1967), *Garryowen's Melbourne: A Selection from the Chronicles of Early Melbourne, 1835 to 1852, by Garryowen* (ed. M. Weidenhofer), Melbourne: Nelson.

Garside, Janet and White, Deborah (1963), 'Arcades of Melbourne', *Architecture in Australia*, 52:2, pp. 80–84.

Geist, Johann Friedrich ([1979] 1983), *Arcades: The History of a Building Type*, Cambridge, MA: Massachusetts Institute of Technology.

Giblett, Rod (1996), *Postmodern Wetlands: Culture, History, Ecology*, Edinburgh: Edinburgh University Press.

—— (2006), *Forrestdale: People and Place*, Bassendean, Western Australia: Access Press.

—— (2008a), *The Body of Nature and Culture*, Basingstoke: Palgrave Macmillan.

—— (2008b), *Sublime Communication Technologies*, Basingstoke: Palgrave Macmillan.

—— (2009), *Landscapes of Culture and Nature*, Basingstoke: Palgrave Macmillan.

—— (2011), *People and Places of Nature and Culture*, Bristol: Intellect.

—— (2012), 'Nature is ordinary too: Raymond Williams as the founder of ecocultural studies', *Cultural Studies*, 26:6, pp. 922–33.

—— (2013a), *Black Swan Lake: Life of a Wetland*, Bristol: Intellect.

—— (2013b), *Traces: Of an Active and Contemplative Life, 1983–2013*, Champaign, IL: Common Ground.

—— (2014), *Canadian Wetlands: Places and People*, Bristol: Intellect.

—— (2015), 'Theology of wetlands: Tolkien and *Beowulf* on marshes and their monsters', *Green Letters: Studies in Ecocriticism*, 19:2, pp. 132–43.

—— (2016), *Cities and Wetlands: The Return of the Repressed in Nature and Culture*, London: Bloomsbury.

—— (2017), 'Walking in the wasteland of the docklands: A *flâneur* crosses the frontier of the un-Paris end of Collins St', *Law, Literature, Humanities Association of Australasia Conference*, La Trobe University Law School, Melbourne, December.

—— (2018a), *The Dragon and Saint George: A Fairy Tale Novella*, Cambridge: Vanguard Press.

—— (2018b), *Environmental Humanities and Theologies: Ecoculture, Literature and the Bible*, London: Routledge.

—— (2018c), *Tales of Two Dragons*, London: Austin Macauley.

—— (2019a), *Black Swan Saga*, Sharjah: Austin Macauley.

—— (2019b), *Environmental Humanities and the Uncanny: Ecoculture, Literature and Religion*, London: Routledge.

—— (2019c), *New Lives of the Saints*, Lanham, MD: Hamilton.

—— (2019d), *The Oxbridge Book of Dragons*, London: Olympia.

—— (2019e), *Psychoanalytic Ecology: The Talking Cure for Environmental Illness and Health*, London: Routledge.

Giblett, Rod and Tolonen, Juha (2012), *Photography and Landscape*, Bristol: Intellect.

Gilpin, William (1794), *Three Essays: On Picturesque Beauty; on Picturesque Travel; and on Sketching Landscape*, 2nd ed., London: A. Blamire.

Gould, Nat (1896), *Town and Bush: Stray Notes on Australia*, London: George Routledge.

Grann, David (2017), *Killers of the Flower Moon: Oil, Money, Murder and the Birth of the FBI*, London: Simon and Schuster.

Grant, James and Serle, Geoffrey (eds) (1957), *The Melbourne Scene 1803–1956*, Carlton, Victoria: Melbourne University Press.

Green, Julian ([1983] 2012), *Paris* (trans. J. A. Underwood), London: Penguin.

Greene, J. Patrick (2004), 'Foreword', in Elizabeth Willis, *The Royal Exhibition Building, Melbourne: A Guide*, Melbourne: Museum Victoria, n.pag.

Grimwade, Stephen (ed.) (2009), *Literary Melbourne: A Celebration of Writing and Ideas*, Prahran, Victoria: Hardie Grant.

Haigh, Gideon (2003), 'Foreword', in Megan Ponsford, *Home Ground: Reflections of the Melbourne Cricket Ground 2001–2002*, South Yarra, Victoria: Hardie Grant Books, n.pag.

Harvey, David (2006), *Paris, the Capital of Modernity*, London: Routledge.

Hazan, Eric (2010), *The Invention of Paris: A History in Footsteps* (trans. D. Fernbach), London: Verso.

Hocking, Jenny and Reidy, Nell (2016), 'Marngrook, Tom Wills and the continuing denial of indigenous history: On the origins of Australian football', *Meanjin*, https://meanjin.com.au/essays/marngrook-tom-wills-and-the-continuing-denial-of-indigenous-history/. Accessed 1 March 2017.

Holsworth, Mark S. (2015), *Sculptures of Melbourne*, Melbourne: Melbourne Books.

Homberger, Eric (2002), *New York: A Cultural and Literary Companion*, Northampton, MA: Interlink.

Horne, Alistair (2002), *Seven Ages of Paris*, New York: Random House.

Howard, Ebenezer (1902), *Garden Cities of Tomorrow*, 2nd ed., London: S. Sonnenschein.

Hume, Fergus ([1886] 1999), *The Mystery of a Hansom Cab*, Melbourne: Text Publishing.

Hussey, Andrew (2006), *Paris: The Secret History*, New York: Bloomsbury.

Jillett, Neil (1982), 'We were *all* wrong, Ava', *The Age*, 14 January, p. 11.

Jones, Colin (2002), *Paris: Biography of a City*, London: Penguin.

Jones, Ronald (2018), 'Melbourne, sung as it were a new song', in K. Dovey, R. Adams and R. Jones (eds), *Urban Choreography: Central Melbourne 1985–*, Carlton, Victoria: Melbourne University Press, pp. 85–142.

Just, Karl and French, Garry (2010), 'Vegetation management and hydrological restoration of Bolin Billabong, Victoria', *Australasian Plant Conservation*, 18:4, pp. 11–12.

Kristeva, Julia (1982), *Powers of Horror: An Essay on Abjection* (trans. L. Roudiez), New York: Columbia University Press.

Lacey, Geoff (2004), *Still Glides the Stream: The Natural History of the Yarra from Heidelberg to Yarra Bend*, Melbourne: Australian Scholarly Publishing.

Lahey, John (1994), 'When Coode Island was a paradise for birds, boats and boys', *The Age*, 15 March, p. 7.

La Nauze, Robert D. (2011), *Engineer to Marvellous Melbourne: The Life and Times of William Thwaites*, North Melbourne, Victoria: Australian Scholarly Publishing.

Landy, John (2004), 'Foreword', in Geoff Lacey, *Still Glides the Stream: The Natural History of the Yarra from Heidelberg to Yarra Bend*, Melbourne: Australian Scholarly Publishing, pp. vii–viii.

Latour, Bruno (2017), *Facing Gaia: Eight Lectures on the New Climate Regime*, Cambridge: Polity.

———— (2018), *Down to Earth: Politics in the New Climatic Regime*, Cambridge: Polity.

Lefebvre, Henri (1991), *The Production of Space* (trans. D. Nicholson-Smith), Oxford: Blackwell.

Levenspiel, Gina (2006), *Architecture at the MCG: The History of Building the Melbourne Cricket Ground*, Melbourne: Lovell Chen Architects and Heritage Consultants.

Lewis, Miles (1995), *Melbourne: The City's History and Development*, 2nd ed., Melbourne: City of Melbourne.

Lyotard, Jean-François (1989), 'The sublime and the avant-garde', in A. Benjamin (ed.), *The Lyotard Reader*, Oxford: Basil Blackwell, pp. 196–211.

Maltezos, Peter (n.d.), 'The incredible Cole's Book Arcade', Urban Melbourne, https://urban.melbourne/culture/2013/05/29/the-incredible-coles-book-arcade. Accessed 1 May 2015.

Marks, Robert B. (2015), *The Origins of the Modern World: A Global and Environmental Narrative from the Fifteenth to the Twenty-First Century*, 3rd ed., Lanham, MD: Rowman & Littlefield.

Matthews, Brian (2005), *The Temple Down the Road: The Life and Times of the MCG*, Camberwell, Victoria: Viking/Penguin.

Mauch, Christof and Zeller, Thomas (2008), 'Rivers in history and historiography: An introduction', in C. Mauch and T. Zeller (eds), *Rivers in History: Perspectives on Waterways in Europe and North America*, Pittsburgh: University of Pittsburgh Press, pp. 1–10.

Meadows, Josh (2018), 'Realising the dream of Birrarung', *Habitat Australia*, 46:1, pp. 13–15.

McComb, A. J. and Lake, P. S. (1990), *Australian Wetlands*, Sydney: Angus and Roberston.

McCrae, George Gordon (1912), 'Some recollections of Melbourne in the "forties"', *The Victorian Historical Magazine*, 7, pp. 114–36.

McLaren, John (2013), *Melbourne: City of Words*, North Melbourne, Victoria: Australian Scholarly Publishing.

Meiers, Allan (2006), *Fisher Folk of Fishermans Bend*, Port Melbourne, Victoria: Port Melbourne Historical and Preservation Society.

Missac, Pierre ([1987] 1995), *Walter Benjamin's Passages* (trans. S. Weber Nicholson), Cambridge, MA: MIT Press.

Morrison, Crosbie (1957), *Melbourne's Garden: A Descriptive and Pictorial Record of the Botanic Gardens, Melbourne*, 2nd ed., Carlton, Victoria: Melbourne University Press.

Mumford, Lewis (1961), *The City in History: Its Origins, Its Transformations, and Its Prospects*, New York: Harcourt.

Murphy, Aunty Joy and Kelly, Andrew (2019), *Wilam: A Birrarung Story* (illustrations by L. Kennedy), Newtown, NSW: Black Dog Books.

Murray, Brian (1985), 'Foreword', in W. H. Newnham, *Melbourne: The Biography of a City*, 2nd ed., Melbourne: Hill of Content, pp. x–xi.

Murray, Peter R. and Wells, John C. (1980), *From Sand, Swamp and Heath…: A History of Caulfield*, Caulfield, Victoria: City of Caulfield.

Newnham, William H. ([1967] 1977), 'Nineteenth-century Melbourne', *Historic Melbourne Sketchbook*, Adelaide: Rigby, pp. 8–66.

—— (1985), *Melbourne: The Biography of a City*, 2nd ed., Melbourne: Hill of Content.

Osterhammel, Jürgen (2014), *The Transformation of the World: A Global History of the Nineteenth Century* (trans. P. Camiller), Princeton: Princeton University Press.

Otto, Kristin (2005), *Yarra: A Diverting History of Melbourne's Murky River*, Melbourne: Text Publishing.

—— (2009), *Capital: Melbourne When It Was the Capital City of Australia, 1901–1927*, Melbourne: Text Publishing.

Paine, Lincoln (2015), *The Sea and Civilization: A Maritime History of the World*, New York: Vintage.

Pallisco, Mark (2015), 'Car maker gearing up to sell chunks of GMH site', *The Age: Commercial Real Estate*, 18 April, p. 12.

Parks Victoria (2012a), 'Cheetham wetlands', https://parkweb.vic.gov.au/explore/parks/point-cook-coastal-park/things-to-do/cheetham-wetlands. Accessed 1 May 2015.

—— (2012b), 'Cheetham wetlands: Culture and heritage', https://parkweb.vic.gov.au/explore/parks/point-cook-coastal-park/culture-and-heritage Accessed 1 May 2015.

Perry, T. M. (1986), 'The shape of the suburbs', *The Australian City, Unit A: Marvellous Melbourne, a Study of Nineteenth-Century Urban Growth: Reader*, Victoria: Deakin University Press, pp. 131–34.

Pescott, Richard T. M. (1982), *The Royal Botanic Gardens Melbourne: A History from 1845 to 1970*, Melbourne: Oxford University Press.

Platt, Harold L. (2005), *Shock Cities: The Environmental Transformation and Reform of Manchester and Chicago*, Chicago: University of Chicago Press.

Plumwood, Val (2008), 'Shadow places and the politics of dwelling', *Australian Humanities Review: Eco-Humanities Corner*, 44, pp. 1–11.

Ponsford, Megan (2003), *Home Ground: Reflections of the Melbourne Cricket Ground 2001–2002*, South Yarra, Victoria: Hardie Grant Books.

Poore, Gary C. B. and Poore, Lynsey A. (2014), 'Middle Park – low swampy country', in *Middle Park: From Swamp to Suburb*, Middle Park, Victoria: Middle Park History Group, pp. 1–26.

Potter, Emily (2007), 'Reimagining place: The possibilities of Paul Carter's *Nearamnew*', in E. Potter and S. McKenzie (eds), *Fresh Water: New Perspectives on Water in Australia*, Carlton, Victoria: Melbourne University Press, pp. 246–58.

Preiss, Benjamin (2015), 'Sky the limit at Fishermans Bend', *The Age: News*, 18 April, p. 11.

Presland, Gary (1985), *The Land of the Kulin: Discovering the Lost Landscape and the First People of Port Phillip*, Fitzroy, Victoria: McPhee Gribble.

——— (1994), *Aboriginal Melbourne: The Lost Land of the Kulin People*, Ringwood, Victoria: McPhee Gribble.

——— (2008), *The Place for a Village: How Nature Has Shaped the City of Melbourne*, Melbourne: Museum Victoria.

——— (2014), 'A boggy question: Differing views of wetlands in 19th century Melbourne', *The Victorian Naturalist*, 131:4, pp. 96–105.

Priestley, Susan (1995), *South Melbourne: A History*, Carlton, Victoria: Melbourne University Press.

Radway, Janice A (1991), *Reading the Romance: Women, Patriarchy, and Popular Literature*, Chapel Hill, NC: University of North Carolina Press.

Ramsar Convention Bureau (n.d.), 'The importance of wetlands', http://www.ramsar.org/about/the-importance-of-wetlands. Accessed 1 May 2015.

Repton, Humphry ([1803] 1980), *Observations on the Theory and Practice of Landscape Gardening: Including Some Remarks on Grecian and Gothic Architecture, Collected from Various Manuscripts, in the Possession of the Different Noblemen and Gentlemen, for Whose Use They Were Originally Written: The Whole Tending to Establish Fixed Principles in the Respective Arts*, facsimile ed., London: Phaidon.

Ridley, Ronald T. (1996), *Melbourne's Monuments*, Carlton, Victoria: Melbourne University Press.

Roe, Jill (1974), *Marvellous Melbourne: The Emergence of an Australian City*, Sydney: Hicks Smith and Sons.

Royal Botanic Gardens (n.d.a), 'Our story', https://www.rbg.vic.gov.au/about-us/our-story. Accessed 1 May 2015.

——— (n.d.b), 'Victorian conservation seedbank', https://www.rbg.vic.gov.au/science/projects/victorian-conservation-seedbank. Accessed 1 May 2015.

Royal Park (2012), 'Royal Park wetlands', https://www.royalpark.org.au/wetlands. Accessed 1 May 2015.

Russell, Robert (*c*.1837), *Map Shewing the Site of Melbourne: And the Position of the Huts & Buildings Previous to the Foundation of the Township by Sir Richard Bourke in 1837*, London: Day & Haghe, http://nla.gov.au/nla.obj-231448674/view. Accessed 1 May 2015.

Ryan, John Charles, Brady, Danielle and Kueh, Chris (2015), 'Where Fanny Balbuk walked: Re-imagining Perth's wetlands', *MC: A Journal of Media and Culture*, 18:6, http://journal.media-culture.org.au/index.php/mcjournal/article/view/1038. Accessed 1 May 2015.

Safi, Michael and agencies (2017), 'Ganges and Yamuna rivers granted same legal rights as human beings', *The Guardian*, 21 March, https://www.theguardian.com/world/2017/mar/21/ganges-and-yamuna-rivers-granted-same-legal-rights-as-human-beings. Accessed 26 March 2017.

Sanderson, Eric (2009), *Mannahatta: A Natural History of New York City*, New York: Harry N. Abrams.

Schenker, Heath (2009), *Melodramatic Landscapes: Urban Parks in the Nineteenth Century*, Charlottesville, VA: University of Virginia Press.

Sennett, Richard (1994), *Flesh and Stone: The Body and the City in Western Civilization*, New York: W. W. Norton.

Serle, Geoffrey (1963), *The Golden Age: A History of the Colony of Victoria, 1851–1861*, Carlton, Victoria: Melbourne University Press.

—— (1971), *The Rush to be Rich: A History of the Colony of Victoria, 1883–1889*, Carlton, Victoria: Melbourne University Press.

—— (1986), 'The gold generation', *The Australian City, Unit A: Marvellous Melbourne, a Study of Nineteenth-Century Urban Growth: Reader*, Victoria: Deakin University, pp. 126–30.

Shaw, Alan (1989), 'The founding of Melbourne', in P. Statham (ed.), *The Origins of Australia's Capital Cities*, Cambridge: Cambridge University Press, pp. 199–215.

Shillinglaw, J. J. (1984), 'Untitled preface', in James Flemming, *Journal*, Carlton, Victoria: Queensberry Hill Press, n.pag.

Sinclair, Jenny (2010), *When We Think about Melbourne: The Imagination of a City*, Mulgrave, Victoria: Affirm Press.

—— (2015), *Much Ado about Melbourne: From Maps to Movies – the Creativity that Makes a City*, South Melbourne, Victoria: Affirm Press.

Skoggard, Carl (2015a), 'Afterword', in Walter Benjamin, *Berlin Childhood Circa 1900*, Catskill, NY: Publication Studio, pp. 296–316.

—— (2015b), 'Commentary', in Walter Benjamin, *Berlin Childhood Circa 1900*, Catskill, NY: Publication Studio, pp. 159–294.

Sloterdijk, Peter ([1998] 2011), *Spheres: Volume 1: Bubbles Microspherology* (trans. W. Hoban), Los Angeles: Semiotext(e).

—— ([1999] 2014), *Spheres: Volume 2: Globes Macrospherology* (trans. W. Hoban), South Pasadena: Semiotext(e).

—— ([2004] 2016), *Spheres: Volume 3: Foams Plural Spherology* (trans. W. Hoban), South Pasadena: Semiotext(e).

—— ([2005] 2013), *In the World Interior of Capital: For a Philosophical Theory of Globalization* (trans. W. Hoban), Cambridge: Polity.

—— ([2014] 2017), *The Aesthetic Imperative: Writings on Art* (trans. K. Margolis), Cambridge: Polity.

Smith, Alexander Kennedy (1859), 'On the reclamation and cultivation of Batman's Swamp', *Transactions of the Philosophical Society of Victoria*, 3, pp. 9–18.

Solnit, Rebecca and Snedeker, Rebecca (2013), *Unfathomable City: A New Orleans Atlas*, Berkeley: University of California Press.

Soseki, Natsume ([1906] 2008), *Kusamakura* (trans. M. McKinney), London: Penguin.

Sussex, Lucy (2015), *Blockbuster! Fergus Hume and the Mystery of a Hansom Cab*, Melbourne: Text Publishing.

Taleb, Nicholas (2007), *The Black Swan: The Impact of the Highly Improbable*, London: Allen Lane.

Taylor, John (2014), 'Melbourne's Royal Park under threat', *Australian Garden History*, 25:3, pp. 35–36.

Thomas, Keith (1984), *Man and the Natural World: Changing Attitudes in England, 1500–1800*, Harmondsworth: Penguin.

Trengrove, Alan (1961), *The Golden Mile: The Herb Elliott Story as Told to Alan Trengrove*, London: Cassell.

Troedel, Charles (1863–64), *The Melbourne Album*, Melbourne: Charles Troedel, Melbourne Album Office, http://artsearch.nga.gov.au/Detail.cfm?IRN=160617&PICTAUS=TRUE. Accessed 1 May 2015.

Trollope, Anthony (1876), *Australia and New Zealand*, vols I and II, 3rd ed., London: Chapman and Hall.

Trumpbour, Robert C. (2007), *New Cathedrals: Politics and Media in the History of Stadium Construction*, Syracuse, NY: Syracuse University Press.

Tuohy, S. W. (2012), 'An integrated approach to protecting our wetlands in Port Phillip Bay', *Wetlands Australia National Wetlands Update 2012*, 20, https://www.environment.gov.au/water/wetlands/publications/wetlands-australia/national-wetlands-update-february-2012-11. Accessed 1 May 2015.

Turner, George ([1987] 2013), *The Sea and Summer*, London: Victor Gollancz.

Twopeny, Richard E. N. ([1883] 1986), 'A walk round Melbourne', *The Australian City, Unit A: Marvellous Melbourne, a Study of Nineteenth-Century Urban Growth: Reader*, Victoria: Deakin University, pp. 112–19.

U'Ren, Nancy and Turnbull, Noel (1983), *A History of Port Melbourne*, Melbourne: Oxford University Press.

Veber, Pierre ([1908] 2016), 'The last fairy', in G. Schultz and L. Seifert (eds and trans.), *Fairy Tales for the Disillusioned: Enchanted Stories from the French Decadent Tradition*, Princeton: Princeton University Press, pp. 173–82.

Veitch, Michael (2012), 'My secret Melbourne', *The Age: Life and Style*, 17 February, p. 10.

Victoria State Government (n.d.), 'VICNAMES: The register of geographic names', Department of Transport, Planning and Local Infrastructure, LASSI (Land and Survey Spatial Information), http://maps.land.vic.gov.au/lassi/VicnamesUI.jsp?placeId=15591. Accessed 1 May 2015.

Vines, Gary (2013), *Fishermans Bend Heritage Study: Report for Places Victoria*, Melbourne: Biosis.

Vines, Gary and Lane, Brett (1990), *Worth Its Salt: A Survey of the Natural and Cultural Heritage of the Cheetham Saltworks, Laverton*, Maribyrnong, Victoria: Melbourne's Living Museum of the West, Inc.

Virilio, Paul (1988), 'The third window: An interview', in C. Schneider and B. Wallis (eds), *Global Television*, New York: Wedge, pp. 187–97.

———— (2007), *The Original Accident* (trans. J. Rose), Cambridge: Polity.

———— (2010), *The University of Disaster* (trans. J. Rose), Cambridge: Polity.

Virilio, Paul and Lotringer, Sylvere (1983), *Pure War* (trans. M. Polizzotti), New York: Semiotext(e).

Ward, Maya (2011), *The Comfort of Water: A River Pilgrimage*, Yarraville, Victoria: Transit Lounge.

Western Australian Museum (2015), 'Reimagining Perth's lost wetlands', http://museum.wa.gov.au/explore/wetlands. Accessed 1 May 2015.

Wheelwright, Horace (1861), *Bush Wanderings of a Naturalist*, London: Routledge, Warne and Routledge.

Williams, Raymond (1973), *The Country and the City*, London: Chatto and Windus.

———— ([1982] 1989), 'Socialism and ecology', in R. Gable (ed.), *Resources of Hope: Culture, Democracy, Socialism*, London: Verso, pp. 210–26.

———— ([1983] 1985), *Towards 2000*, Harmondsworth: Penguin.

———— ([1984] 1989), 'Between country and city', in R. Gable (ed.), *Resources of Hope: Culture, Democracy, Socialism*, London: Verso, pp. 227–37.

Williams, W. Lloyd (1957), *History Trails in Melbourne*, Sydney: Angus and Robertson.

Willingham, Alan (1996), 'A permanent and extensive exhibition building', in D. Dunstan (ed.), *Victorian Icon: The Royal Exhibition Building Melbourne*, Melbourne: Exhibition Trustees in Association with Australian Scholarly Publishing, pp. 51–66.

Willis, Elizabeth (2004), *The Royal Exhibition Building, Melbourne: A Guide*, Melbourne: Museum Victoria.

Wilson, Ben (2016), *Heyday: Britain and the Birth of the Modern World*, London: Weidenfeld and Nicolson.

Wilson, Roland and Budd, Dale (2014), *The Melbourne Tram Book*, 3rd ed., Sydney: University of New South Wales Press.

Winkler, Tim (1996), 'New park on Yarra bank', *The Age*, 5 September, p. 3.

Woodhouse, Clarence (1888), *Melbourne in 1838 from the Yarra Yarra*, Melbourne: Hutchinson, http://nla.gov.au/nla.obj-140378613/view. Accessed 1 May 2015.

Yarnasan, Sanay (1974), 'The development of the Port of Melbourne', MA thesis, Melbourne: University of Melbourne.

Index